Building Leaders

Jay A. Conger
Beth Benjamin

Building Leaders

How Successful Companies
Develop the Next Generation

Jossey-Bass Publishers
San Francisco

Jossey-Bass books and products are available through most bookstores. To contact Jossey-Bass directly, call (888) 378–2537, fax to (800) 605–2665, or visit our website at www.josseybass.com.

Substantial discounts on bulk quantities of Jossey-Bass books are available to corporations, professional associations, and other organizations. For details and discount information, contact the special sales department at Jossey-Bass.

Manufactured in the United States of America on Lyons Falls Turin Book. This paper is acid-free and 100 percent totally chlorine-free.

Library of Congress Cataloging-in-Publication Data

Conger, Jay Alden.
    Building leaders: how successful companies develop the next
generation / Jay A. Conger and Beth Benjamin. — 1st ed.
        p. cm. — (The Jossey-Bass business & management series)
    Includes bibliographical references and index.
    ISBN 0-7879-4469-6 (acid-free paper)
    1. Leadership—Study and teaching. 2. Executives—Training of. I.
Benjamin, Beth, 1962-II. Title. III. Series.
    HD57.7 .C658 1999
    658.4'07124—dc21
                                                                98-58113

FIRST EDITION
HB Printing   10 9 8 7 6 5 4 3 2 1

The Jossey-Bass
Business & Management Series

Contents

Part Two: The Future Is Now: Building Twenty-First Century Leaders

Preface

In our work with companies in many industries, it is clear that leadership talent is scarce. But in the face of intense competition and a global economic scene that is far from stable, the need for leadership has never been greater. As a result, businesses have turned their attention to leadership development in a big way.

Many companies know they do not have the depth of leadership talent needed to excel in an increasingly competitive and global economy. This has spurred them into action—so much so that the leadership development field today is a billion-dollar business. But are they taking the *right* action? For example, by now most corporations have sponsored leadership programs for their managers, have had guest speakers on the subject, or have sent executives off to university courses on the subject. Even internal measures such as performance appraisals and 360-degree assessment tools now incorporate leadership in their feedback to managers. Books and videos on leadership can be found on the shelves of most executives, but do they make a difference? Do they produce more and better leaders? Despite the attention and money spent, surprisingly few attempts have been made to answer these important questions. It appears that most companies simply assume that such investments produce results. Yet one has to wonder whether a week-long educational program is enough to produce new mind-sets among a company's managers. Or whether a one-time, two-hour feedback session with a manager on his or her leadership competences is enough to induce changed behavior. The skeptic might ask whether the investment is like a night out at a fine restaurant: pleasurable, but most nights we still eat at home.

For this book, we decided to look further. We take a hard look at whether the corporate world's attempts to develop leadership talent through educational initiatives are paying off. The book comes at an important time for the field of leadership education and development. We say this not because of the phenomenal sums invested in them, but because those investments seem to parallel the remarkable improvements in educational interventions for leadership development. Only a decade ago, for example, leadership training for managers often consisted of a one- to four-week program at a university or training organization. Joining with participants from other companies, an individual would receive lectures on decision making, participation, setting goals, and so forth. There would be general case studies and simple experiential exercises to ground course concepts and theories. In sharp contrast, today's programs are far more customized to a company's immediate needs and the issues it faces. Just as important, education is no longer focused only on the individual learner but increasingly on shaping the worldviews and behaviors of cohorts of managers and, in the process, transforming even entire organizations. Learning methods are more dynamic; they allow learners to address and learn from real challenges and help them resolve real issues. Given a decade of transformation in leadership education, we thought it time to explore the impact of this new generation of interventions—interventions that promise greater impact on both individuals and the organization.

For our research, we sought out companies that innovate and experiment. Most have made significant investments in developing leadership talent. We also looked at failed experiments; not surprisingly, they taught us as much as did the successful ones. We have learned from our multiple-year study and have distilled our research into the findings and guidelines described in this book. In essence, *Building Leaders* has two primary objectives. The first is to provide an in-depth assessment of the current state of leadership development in corporate America. We focus solely on what firms are doing in-company to strengthen and expand their leadership capabilities. Also, we aim to provide a blueprint of how organizations can more effectively build leadership talent using a broad array of approaches. Based on research we conducted at more than a dozen organizations, we identify practices that can improve a firm's success in developing leadership talent at all levels. We also identify common pitfalls to guard against. Detailed case studies accompany our prescriptions and illustrate the mechanics of the better-designed programs.

Finally, we look at the future of leadership to determine what new behaviors and perspectives will be needed to lead in the upcoming century. One of our concerns is that many organizations teach and develop leadership skills that may be outdated by the time younger generations reach the senior ranks. It seems wasteful to train yesterday's skills to tomorrow's leaders. We hope our insights into future leadership competencies will get people thinking more about new directions and about shifting their focus to developing these skills today.

We are also concerned that most organizations treat leadership development casually—in contrast to organizations that truly understand the complexity of building leadership talent, such as the military. Beyond a few educational programs and value statements proclaiming the importance of leadership, we see only a handful of companies attempting deeper, more concerted efforts. Our hope is that this book will not only provide models of what is possible but, more importantly, remind us all that leadership is developed daily through job opportunities, bosses, educational experiences, company cultures, and rewards. As such, to truly develop leaders, many organizations require a change of mind that in the end produces company cultures that value and reward leadership rather than simply "minding the store."

Overview of the Contents

We start in Chapter One by exploring how our paradigms of leadership have undergone radical changes over the last three decades. In essence, our notions have moved from relatively simplistic concepts of leadership to richer theories about how leaders orchestrate change within their organizations. At the same time, the world of executive and management education has been undergoing an equally radical shift in learning approaches and program designs. As a result, educational interventions for leadership development have themselves become far more sophisticated and therefore influential. In contrast, just a decade ago it was assumed that managers best learned leadership on the job. Today we believe this to be only partially true. Depending on how we design our interventions, educational initiatives can play a far greater role in leadership development than imagined before.

With this optimistic backdrop, we begin our excursion into the numerous initiatives we examined. In essence, we found in our research that there are three principal approaches to leadership education: individual skill development, socialization of corporate leadership values and visions, and strategic interventions that promote dialogue and the implementation of a new collective vision. Each approach is explored in the chapters that follow, with an emphasis on best practices as well as common problems that we found across the programs in each category.

In Chapter Two and in the case study presented in Chapter Three, we turn our attention to the most popular of the three approaches to date: individual preparation and skill development. Their objective is to assist individual managers in learning essential ideas about leadership, exploring new skills, and receiving feedback on their own capabilities. Throughout the chapter, we examine important design and process issues such as the value of 360-degree feedback and competency models, how participants should be selected, the strengths and weaknesses of popular learning methods, and the importance of after-program support systems. In our research, we found a number of important shortcomings common to many of these approaches, and we describe for readers common problems that could derail even the best of programs.

Chapter Four and the case studies in Chapter Five focus on educational initiatives that seek to socialize the vision, values, and mission of an organization into its management ranks. Leadership involves learning that leaders must embody and role-model certain values and behaviors and actively translate the overall corporate vision into local visions for their own units. Again, we looked across successful company programs to identify the shared design elements that make these programs more effective than most. For example, we found that better programs perform an organizational needs assessment beforehand, use practicing leaders to provide instruction, design formats around participant exchange, and put in place support systems throughout the organization. Still, we found a number of problems confronting these programs. For example, many face hidden challenges in using company leaders as instructors. Some reinforce interpersonal values but overlook crucial strategic or marketplace competencies that leaders must develop that, in turn, may lead the company to suffer strategic mistakes. In several cases, operating units feel they have little ownership of programs and as a result fail to support them in meaningful ways. We explore these challenges in depth and describe how organizations can overcome them.

Chapter Six and the case study in Chapter Seven examine the use of leadership programs designed to facilitate strategic interventions. Given an increasingly more competitive and rapidly changing world, these have steadily grown in popularity. Typical designs employ action learning, task forces, and facilitated group discussions to identify organizational initiatives that can accelerate major strategic changes within the firm. In essence, company managers work together to understand a common vision and, through challenging assignments, learn to lead the implementation of that vision. Such learning activities, in turn, advance the organization's new strategic imperatives. Using executive learning cohorts, cascading initiatives, active feedback mechanisms, and collective dialogue forums for these are among the more powerful practices we discovered. But they are also complicated and

demanding, so we identify common problems that can easily undermine their long-term impact and suggest how to minimize them.

In Chapter Eight, we turn our attention to a popular educational
format called action learning. It falls outside of our typology of the
three approaches because it is a learning *method* rather than a design
outcome such as socializing a company vision into the ranks of junior
leaders. Today, entire leadership programs may be built around action
learning. As such, any of the three approaches described in Chapters
Two through Seven may use action learning. We single this method
out because of its widespread use in today's leadership development
efforts. In spite of its popularity—or perhaps because of it—action
learning programs have failed to receive sufficient scrutiny. Given
the zeal with which these programs have been adopted, we felt it was
important to examine this learning method's objectives and discuss
not only its pluses but also its minuses. Athough they have great
potential for developing leadership skills, common design problems
can significantly lessen their impact. We explore why many action
learning programs do not deliver on their promise of substantial and
sustainable learning and suggest ways to improve them.

In our closing chapter, we turn our attention to the future. We
want to give readers a sense of where we think the future of leadership is headed. In this case, we direct our discussion not so much in
terms of education but toward the characteristics that will be
demanded in the next generation of leaders. It is our strong belief
that tomorrow's attributes are what we must begin to train and
develop today. Our observation, however, is that too many companies teach yesterday's leadership skills to tomorrow's leaders. We
hope this book will convince them to teach tomorrow's skills today.

Acknowledgments

Several individuals played an important role in the research behind
this book. We would particularly like to thank Evan Bouffides for
his help. Evan was Jay Conger's research assistant for a portion of
this project. He conducted the interview research on the National

Australia Bank and did a superb job of assessing National's program efforts for us. As well, Chris Farkas conducted a computer-based analysis of that data for us. Chris coded and analyzed innumerable transcripts and provided us with his thoughts on key findings. We are grateful to both of these individuals. Jay Conger has also been fortunate to work with a faculty colleague at the University of Southern California, Katherine Xin, and one of his doctoral students, Kimberly Jaussi, on several projects exploring the world of executive education. Their work shaped some of the ideas and insights in this book. A former colleague of Beth's at RAND, Matthew Lewis, has long written on the training applications of technology. Matt lent us his expertise on computer assisted instruction, management flight simulators, and microworlds to help us envision how technology will likely play a greater role in future leadership development efforts. We also thank the inspiring men and women who participated in the 1997 Future Leader Development of Army Noncommissioned Officers Workshop. For the Noncommissioned Officers' Corps, leadership development is more than an initiative or program; it is a way of life. We thank the Corps for the honor and integrity it brings to the field and for its ongoing commitment to self-reflection, critical evaluation, and improvement. Beth would like to thank her colleagues at both RAND and Booz·Allen & Hamilton for allowing her time to write the book. Jay's wife Nadege deserves a special thanks. She has always been available for comments on the text and, most importantly, for support in the face of the trials and tribulations of writing a book. Beth would also like to thank her parents, Judy and Glenn, who have been an unwavering source of strength and perspective and instrumental to her own development.

Los Angeles, California
April 1999

BETH BENJAMIN
JAY A. CONGER

The Authors

BETH A. BENJAMIN is an associate with Booz·Allen & Hamilton's Strategic Leadership Practice, which focuses on serving senior management in the areas of organization, leadership, transformation, and corporate renewal. As a member of the SLP, Benjamin specializes in the implementation of large-scale change, organizational structure and redesign, strategic human resource management, and leadership development. Prior to joining Booz·Allen, she held joint appointments at the University of Southern California's Leadership Institute and RAND. During that time, she performed a wide variety of work on implementing change in traditionally bureaucratic institutions in the military, federal court system, health care industry, and large private-sector firms. She holds a Ph.D. in business (organizational behavior) from the Stanford Graduate School of Business, an M.A. in industrial organizational psychology from the University of Maryland, and a B.A. from Cornell University.

JAY A. CONGER is executive director of the Leadership Institute and professor of management at the University of Southern California. One of the world's experts on leadership, he was chosen by *Business Week* as the pick of American professors to teach leadership to executives. Author of over sixty articles and eight books, he researches leadership, boards of directors, the management of organizational change, and the training and development of leaders and managers.

His articles have appeared in the *Harvard Business Review, Boards & Directors, Organizational Dynamics, Business & Strategy, Leadership Quarterly, Academy of Management Review,* and *Journal of Organizational Behavior.* He is currently associate editor of *Leadership Quarterly.* One of his books, *Learning to Lead* (Jossey-Bass, 1992), has been described by *Fortune* magazine as "the source" for understanding leadership training. His other books include *Winning 'Em Over* (Simon & Schuster, 1998), *The Leader's Change Handbook* (Jossey-Bass, 1998), *Charismatic Leadership in Organizations* (Sage, 1998), *Spirit at Work* (Jossey-Bass, 1994), *The Charismatic Leader* (Jossey-Bass, 1989), and *Charismatic Leadership* (Jossey-Bass, 1988).

In recognition of his work on leadership education, Conger was invited four years ago to join the Harvard Business School as a visiting professor to assist in redesign of the school's organizational behavior course around leadership issues. In addition, he has been involved in executive education at INSEAD, a European business school located in France. While a professor at McGill University in Montreal, he received on two occasions McGill's Distinguished Teaching Award. His insights have been featured in *Business Week, The Economist, Fortune, The New York Times, Training,* and *The Wall Street Journal.*

He received his B.A. from Dartmouth College, his M.B.A. from the University of Virginia, and his D.B.A. from the Harvard Business School. Prior to his academic career, he worked in government and as an international marketing manager for a high-technology company.

Building Leaders

The New Imperative
Building Effective Leaders Throughout the Company

Since the mid-1980s, interest in leadership has skyrocketed throughout the corporate world. Today strong leadership is often viewed as one of the most important keys to organizational growth, change, and renewal. Unfortunately, however, leadership is also viewed as a resource in short supply. This shortage, many argue, is a major reason why so many organizations are having difficulty adapting to a world of intense global competition. Faced with the need for more and better leaders, corporations are investing an unprecedented amount of time and money in leadership development. Researchers at the Harvard Business School, for example, calculated that corporations increased their expenditures for management training from $10 billion in the mid-1980s to $45 billion by 1995. Of this amount, *Business Week* estimated that approximately $12 billion was devoted to executive education—just one of many forms of leadership development (Vicere and Fulmer, 1997).

At the same time, our very notions of leadership have undergone a remarkable transformation since formal academic theories first appeared in the 1950s and 1960s. In those days, we essentially understood good leadership to consist of three principal activities: structuring the tasks and roles of subordinates well, treating them well, and involving them in decision making. These insights were based on early studies that examined managers doing relatively simple tasks—for example, how they directed small groups such as supervisors running operations on the factory floor or airplane pilots directing their cabin crews.

As more researchers began to investigate the fundamental tenets of effective leadership, our understanding of leadership became more complex by the mid-1960s and 1970s. Leaders not only structured activities and demonstrated concern for their subordinates, they also put in place appropriate goals and incentives. Leadership, it was argued, could be viewed as a transaction or exchange between a leader and his or her subordinates. Good leaders managed their transactions well. They identified the personal goals of the people that worked for them, set clear expectations, defined roles, established incentives that made rewards contingent on performance, and helped people achieve their goals. Most important, leaders assessed their situations and adapted their leadership tactics to match them. When the situation was ambiguous, effective leaders knew how to provide clarity and leverage rewards. When the situation was more straightforward, they refrained from being overly directive and relied more on incentives to provide the appropriate direction (House, 1995).

During this era, leaders were most interested in getting their subordinates to follow well-defined mandates. The times were still relatively stable and objectives were fairly clear, so the major challenges facing a leader were those associated with inducing the behavior they wanted. Individual motivation and control were the primary concerns. Mirroring the interests of the business world, researchers at that time showed relatively little interest in studying leaders who were trying to effect major change. Considering today's demands this lack of interest may seem somewhat paradoxical, but it is important to remember the context of the times. Following the Second World War, the United States played a major role in the world economy and its industries dominated those of most other countries. Competition was fairly limited, and corporate America focused more on growth within existing markets than on reinvention. Manufacturing drove the strength of the American economy

and leaders were concerned with efficiency and maximizing productivity rather than building new markets or dramatic change. As
a result of these and other forces, academics turned their attention
to front-line managers—trying to determine how effective managers
lead their subordinates to achieve well-defined goals. Looking back
in light of current leadership theories, today we might say that the
"leadership" studied in those earlier years was in reality not leadership at all; rather, it was effective management.

These simple, early paradigms of leadership would soon be challenged as we entered the 1980s. The accelerated pace of foreign
competition and changing markets was like a powerful fist punch-
ing the underbelly of corporate America. Faced with deregulation,
globalizing markets, and rapidly changing technology, corporate
leaders established initiatives aimed at customer connectedness,
product quality, reengineering, and teamwork as they struggled to
reinvent their organizations. But these programs produced only
mixed results. Corporate officials began to realize that programmatic
approaches in and of themselves were not enough to reinvent organizations. Change had to be more fundamental and more systematic. Moreover, it had to produce results that satisfied not only top
management but also the expectations of increasingly sophisticated
and demanding shareholders. To regain a competitive edge, firms
would have to do a lot more than improve efficiency and tighten
control, they would have to fundamentally change the way they
viewed the world and conducted business. This would mean transforming systems that had been in place for years, changing firmly
established cultures, and modifying behavior that had long been
rewarded with success.

But who would be the catalysts for such enormous change? After
all, these were not incremental changes aimed simply at doing
things better and faster; these were radical transformations. Only a
handful of managers and executives appeared to possess the leadership competencies needed to carry out such major transitions.
Indeed, most managers remained too steeped in company traditions,

power structures, and bureaucracies to advocate anything other than incremental—and therefore largely ineffective—change. Most, but not all. Leaders like General Electric's Jack Welch, Mitsubishi's Minoru Makihara, and Asea Brown Boveri's Percy Barnevik represented significant departures from the norm. Though different from one another in style and demeanor, each of these leaders demonstrated a keen ability to lead their organizations through turbulent times.

Noting the distinctive capabilities of these individuals (and others like them) and recognizing the demands of the times, researchers in business schools and consulting firms turned their attention to understanding the capabilities of these visionary change agents. Their findings challenged earlier, more simplistic notions of leadership that focused on structuring tasks, goals, and incentives. In light of the strategic complexities that leaders in the 1980s and 1990s faced, it became evident to many researchers that establishing clear goals and structuring incentives was only a small part of the overall leadership challenge. Understanding the organization's competitive environment, identifying the capabilities needed to compete, and taking appropriate actions to transform the organization's environment in favorable ways is what leadership was now about. Moreover, no longer would leadership capabilities be required solely at the top—leadership would now be needed throughout the organization. Only with a strong cadre of leaders—strategically adept and interpersonally skilled—would change of the scope and magnitude needed to transform a major corporation be possible. Over the course of a decade, the capability to orchestrate complex transformational change had become the new centerpiece of many leadership theories.

As the need for change-agent leaders grew, many companies began to realize that they had failed to develop a sufficient depth of leadership talent throughout their ranks. For example, a 1988 Harvard Business School study conducted by John Kotter found that the majority of executives surveyed in a dozen successful U.S. corporations felt there was a significant lack of leadership skills within their firms (Kotter, 1990). Asked to rate all the individuals throughout their management cadres, almost two-thirds of the executives reported they had "too many" individuals who were strong managers but weak leaders. Virtually all reported "too few" individuals who were both strong managers and strong leaders. Kotter concluded that leaders capable of effecting large-scale change were clearly in short supply.

Because of these forces, leadership development today has become a high priority for many companies. The significance of this trend is nicely illustrated by the American Society for Training and Development (ASTD)'s decision to devote its entire 1994 annual survey of human resource practices to the issue of leadership development (American Society for Training and Development, 1994). Asking "To what extent is leadership development a priority for management in your company?", the survey found that 60 percent of surveyed companies reported that leadership development was a high to very high priority. Only 12 percent said it was either not a priority or else a low one. More surprising was the finding that three-fourths of the surveyed companies offered some form of leadership development for their employees either through training or on-the-job experience. Most companies focused their development efforts on middle and senior management and offered a wide variety of development options at each level. When the ASTD repeated the survey in 1996, the number of companies making leadership training a high or very high priority remained strong. Moreover, of the 80 percent that reported currently offering leadership development to their employees, 66 percent responded that these offerings were becoming increasingly important.

Other studies have also found greater emphasis being placed on leadership development. In a 1991 study of management development training, researchers at West Virginia University surveyed six hundred U.S. companies to determine the extent to which their management development programs focused on nine content areas

(Lane, Blakely, Gerald, and Martinec, 1992). Of the nine areas examined, "human relations and leadership" training consistently ranked highest across all levels. Firms focused more of their management development efforts on "human relations problems of leadership" than on areas such as "general management," "problem solving and decision making," or "entrepreneurial skills." In another survey conducted for the International Consortium of Executive Development Research, leadership again emerged as the number one content area for future executive education (Conger and Xin, 1997). Focusing this time on the development efforts of large global corporations—such as British Airways, Daimler Benz, Motorola, and Samsung—this study found that between 50 and 80 percent of the executives in these firms were slated to receive formal education on leadership during the next three years. Moreover, the percentage of companies reporting that the purpose of their executive education programs was "to enhance the overall *leadership* and change management effectiveness of their executives" grew from an already astonishing 72 percent in 1995–96 to 84 percent in 1997–98 for the same pool of organizations.

These surveys suggest that leadership development has become a significant concern for most organizations and that formal training is the primary vehicle for accelerating the development of leadership talent. This brings us to the focus of this book: If training has become the primary means by which companies are trying to develop their future leaders, how effective is it? Can it truly meet corporate expectations and build leadership capabilities throughout an organization? If training can in fact enhance leadership development, which types of programs or designs are most effective? And how must these programs be supported to fully achieve their goals? These are the questions we tackle in the pages that follow.

This book makes a timely contribution to our understanding of leadership development not only because corporations are paying more attention to and investing more money in leadership training today than ever before, but also because so little is known about the effectiveness of the various approaches being used. Fred Fiedler (1996), one of the leadership field's preeminent scholars, recently lamented: "While the number of available training programs is considerable and continues to grow at an increasing pace, the scarcity of sound research on training has been one of the most glaring shortcomings in the leadership area. Most of the training programs are untested and, at best, of uncertain value . . ." (p. 243). One of our objectives in writing this volume is to provide a broad comparison of the development models being used across a wide variety of organizations. In doing so, we hope to significantly enhance our understanding of the roles that leadership development can play in organizations and we hope to improve our insight into the strengths and weaknesses of the various approaches currently in use. Equally important, we also identify and discuss a number of other factors that must be in place to ensure that development efforts are more than just an empty exercise—noted and appreciated but then forgotten. Decades of research on organizational training have warned of the barriers to knowledge transfer—the capacity to take what is learned during the development experience and apply it successfully to one's job. Efforts to articulate these barriers, however, have typically been too vague or abstract to be of much use to the practitioner. We attempt to remedy this void by highlighting potential pitfalls and identifying specific organizational issues that must be addressed if leadership development is to have a meaningful impact on organizational practice.

The research behind this book builds on and complements earlier work that one of us undertook in 1990–92. That research looked at well-known leadership programs offered by independent training organizations. Used primarily by large corporations that send managers and executives to enhance their leadership capabilities, these programs have grown increasingly popular in recent years. To understand their impact, the earlier research focused on the methods used by these outside providers to teach leadership and the types of learning that program participants experienced. The results, published in *Learning to Lead* (Conger, 1992), revealed that training could and did play an influential role in helping managers become more effective leaders. At the same time, the research showed that numerous forces reduced the application of learning and thus its potential for both the individual and the organization.

In this book we turn our focus from specific training providers and techniques to what companies themselves are actually doing in-house to strengthen and expand the leadership capabilities of employees throughout the ranks. We document and evaluate a wide range of development approaches used by companies that have devoted considerable attention to building their leadership talent throughout the entire organization. In the process of conducting our research, we examined a number of companies and their undertakings. Many of the designs we observed were quite innovative and appear to hold promise. Other programs, however, were far less successful. But these programs taught us as much as—if not more than—our success stories. They demonstrated the importance of critical support systems and ongoing reinforcement by showing problems that occurred in their absence.

Not surprisingly, we found that company programs have become increasingly sophisticated in recent years. The notion of "one-size-fits-all" training (off-the-shelf courses that can be applied universally) appears to be on the decline. Today, leadership training tends to be far more tailored to the needs of the individual, to specific management levels, and, most notably, to the strategic demands facing the organization. Yet despite the significant investment that companies are making in their development efforts, we also observed many companies undermining these investments through poor designs, inappropriate support systems, and a lack of follow-through and commitment. Often the very companies that claimed the greatest need for leadership development did the least to support it. They failed to recognize that leadership development itself requires systematic changes throughout the organization.

Leadership Development in the Workplace

If you ask managers where they learned their leadership abilities, they will often tell you that their job experiences and bosses have contributed the most. Rarely will formal training be mentioned, despite the number of programs being designed and implemented. For example, in a poll of 1,450 managers from twelve global corporations, respondents cited experience as the best teacher for leadership—not the classroom (Ready, 1994). Job assignments, special projects, and task forces were ranked either first or second as the most effective means for learning leadership competencies. Feedback on performance also rated high in shaping leadership ability. Managers ranked classroom education high only in helping them to articulate a tangible vision, values, and strategy. Moreover, they reported that university-based training played little role in the leadership learning process. In short, many managers appear to view formal education as having only a limited impact on how they learn to lead.

From these findings, we might conclude that formal training and education are of limited or little value when it comes to real leadership development. But there are reasons to be far more optimistic. As we will argue throughout this book, leadership education can play a number of roles. It can heighten an individual's appreciation for leadership and strengthen one's motivation to develop leadership capabilities. It can facilitate the development of skills (communication skills, for example) needed to build these capabilities. It can promote a common understanding of an organization's vision or intended culture and clarify the roles and responsibilities needed to advance them. It can also foster continuity by indoctrinating new or up-and-coming leaders to the organization's history and values. And it can strengthen the organization's long-term viability by integrating training with relevant, well-timed job experiences that increase leadership depth throughout the firm. In the chapters that follow, we explore these roles and a number of programs that companies have created to fulfill them.

First, however, we set our stage by providing a brief overview of the many factors thought to influence leadership development and of the important trends in management and adult education that have influenced how corporations work to build leadership skills. We conclude this chapter by describing how today's corporate training programs differ from the leadership development approaches of the past. At the risk of spoiling our punch line, leadership training has become more strategic in focus and better integrated with the ongoing objectives of the firm. It makes greater use of a wide array of media, and it utilizes more tailored, experience-based learning methods than ever before.

Development Experiences

Many factors are thought to shape the extent to which an individual develops as a leader (Conger, 1992). These factors range from innate genetic predisposition to early family environments to later life job experiences to formal and informal training. For example, language skills, basic confidence, achievement drive, interpersonal skills, and many interests are shaped by family environments. At work, poor bosses teach the need to be proactive, to share responsibility, and to develop a capacity for self-reflection. Good bosses teach about empowerment, the importance of networks and relationships, constructive values, and strategic thinking. Certain job assignments promote team-building skills, an appreciation for priorities, entrepreneurial attitude, and the value of a broader perspective and vision. Coursework and training help one to understand conceptually what leadership is about and can teach certain skills such as effective problem solving or communication techniques. No one factor can claim full responsibility for the quality we call leadership—despite the claims of those who believe that leaders are either born (genes and families) or made (workplace experiences).

Theories asserting that leadership abilities develop early in a person's life rest on a central premise that the "right" environments (in this case, family environments) are rare. This scarcity, they argue, explains why we see so few leaders. These theories often maintain that leaders develop when there is an intense positive bond between the mother and the future leader. This bond leads the child to develop a high positive self-regard, which in turn gives him or her greater confidence in actions as well as greater comfort with risk taking and the breaking of conventions—certain trademarks of leadership. But there are many reasons to question this premise. Most obvious is the fact that leaders come from many different childhood environments (Conger, 1992). Thus the right environments may actually be quite plentiful. Also, we know from a large body of research that successful performance in many work endeavors can be attributed to effort and persistence, not just inborn talent or early-life experiences (Ericsson and Charness, 1994). For example, interesting parallels can be drawn with studies on the development of musical talent in children and the performance of young prodigies. Young children lacking signs of musical talent have been found to develop performance levels comparable to the prodigies of earlier times when exposed to training using techniques such as the Suzuki method. The great music teacher Suzuki argued that the failure of young performers to attain high levels of performance was due largely to incorrect training methods and to an inability to induce motivation and enthusiasm. Indeed, the great majority of outstanding adult performers were never child prodigies. Instead their expertise typically derives from early and sustained instruction and substantial and consistent training and practice (Ericsson and Charness, 1994). Without continual practice, prodigies themselves rarely if ever attain exceptional performance as adults. Similarly, when asked about the forces that have influenced their development, many business leaders point to experiences taking place much later in life, often during periods of intense challenge, hardship, or "derailment" (McCall, Lombardo, and Morrison, 1988). In light of diverse childhood experiences, some extensive research, and leaders' own reports, we suggest that intense learning experiences often later in life play a significant role in developing leadership talent and in unlocking leadership potential.

This raises an interesting question: Because we often see leadership capabilities emerge as people mature, what explains why some people develop strong capabilities and others do not? Can leadership potential go unrealized and eventually diminish over time? We believe that it can and offer several reasons why leadership potential often diminishes in later years. First, and of most relevance to educators, organizations themselves are often to blame. They fail to cultivate leadership talent in their junior managers. They pay little attention to structuring job experiences, do little to furnish appropriate role models, and rarely provide ongoing reinforcement and support for the skills and competencies espoused in training. Instead, repetitive job assignments and rigid compensation systems encourage managers to increase functional depth at the expense of stretching and broadening their skill sets. Training programs raise awareness and new ideas, but rarely couple new insight with relevant opportunities to apply them. And because managers often receive training at different times and apart from those with whom they work, they may receive little encouragement, reinforcement, or feedback when experimenting with new concepts and behaviors. As a result, individuals who truly want to develop and change the organization may ultimately leave in frustration.

Of course, not all the blame can be laid at the doorstep of the organization. Certain individuals may possess leadership ability but simply choose not to exercise it (Boyatzis, 1990). Some may prefer less demanding responsibilities and may wish to avoid the hardships that accompany leadership roles. Others may feel uncomfortable challenging the status quo and prefer to conform and be accepted rather than take risks and push limits (Loevinger, 1980). In short, some people simply do not want to assume the responsibilities or engage in the behaviors typically associated with leadership.

Individual preferences, however, should not be viewed as minimizing the impact of organizations. To the contrary, they actually increase the role that organizations can play through proper selection and job assignment. By providing a range of job assignments early in a manager's career, carefully tracking the development of particular skills and sensibilities, and channeling potential leaders through appropriate developmental experiences, organizations can leverage individual differences to their best advantage.

Indeed, we suggest that organizations control a large number of forces that can enhance the development of leadership skills. Though the research on management development is surprisingly limited, there is empirical evidence suggesting that organizations can, in fact, do a number of things to cultivate leadership skills in willing individuals. One of the most insightful studies was conducted at the Center for Creative Leadership (CCL) in the mid-1980s. This study examined the experiences of several hundred executives to determine which factors executives felt contributed most to their own development (McCall, Lombardo, and Morrison, 1988). Although the study examined management development in general, leadership was a central component. The study confirmed that job assignments, bosses, and hardships did indeed play the most pivotal roles in executive development and therefore presumably in leadership development. For example, assignments helped people to learn about building teams, taught them how to be more strategic in their thinking, and helped them to develop leadership and persuasion skills. Bosses taught either directly or through their actions about the importance of leadership and human values, about politics, and about models of success. Bad and flawed bosses could be just as instructive as good ones. In addition, difficult situations and hardships taught lessons about handling problematic relationships, one's personal limits, and how to confront and act on people problems.

Though training and coursework were seldom mentioned as particularly influential, positive comments about training and coursework led the research team to a surprising discovery: they improved developing leaders' self-confidence. This took several forms:

1. Confidence from realizing that one already knows more about an area of knowledge than he or she previously thought (for example, a manager who learns about marketing on the job and then discovered she already knows much of the course material)

2. Confidence from learning that one is as talented as managers from other firms or divisions also attending a particular course

3. Confidence in one's career progress as a result of being selected for a high-prestige or exclusive course

Some executives also reported that coursework involving self-examination and candid feedback had prompted them to reexamine personal characteristics or habits that could have become derailing flaws. These included arrogance or being insensitive to others. In addition, training served to refresh one's perspective on the balance between work and life. This, in turn, helped executives better manage their own responsibilities and made them more sensitive to the demands and stressors facing their subordinates.

Finally, the study also discovered that the impact of any development effort critically depends on its timing. Learning has to have a direct bearing on what an executive wants to accomplish. In the case of training, the lessons taught in a formal program or development experience had to have relevance to the challenges the executive was facing back on the job.

Given that the CCL's research was conducted in the mid-1980s, and that leadership development has since grown more sophisticated and pervasive, we now believe that its findings actually underestimated the potential impact of educational initiatives—especially as they are conducted today. In contrast to the leadership training approaches practiced a decade ago, today's educational programs have become more advanced in their learning methodologies and in their understanding of organizational dynamics. These changes in many ways reflect changes that have occurred in the more encompassing field of management development and, to a limited extent, in the field of adult education. Understanding major trends in these "parent disciplines" may provide greater insight into the evolving shape and contour of programs described throughout this book. As such, we briefly explore some of these trends next. Their influence will be seen repeatedly in the chapters that follow.

Leadership Development Within the World of Management Education

The world of management education has influenced leadership training significantly. As an analogy, we can think of the general field of management education as the European Economic Union. Leadership training is analogous to Germany—one of training's most important areas. Although its influence is strong, larger forces within the field of management education have shaped its character—specifically, its delivery.

If we think back about twenty years, education for mid- to senior-level managers consisted largely of university-based programs and seminars offered by specialized training organizations. Individual managers from different organizations jetted off to a campus or training center where they spent anywhere from a week to a couple of months studying various topics. Learning was teacher centered, using off-the-shelf case studies and exercises as instructional vehicles. Participants learned about the latest theory and techniques for effective management largely by studying what other companies had done and listening to lectures. In some instances a case or two might involve an industry or company in which a participant worked, but in most cases the context or industry dynamics were of little relevance.

The content of training was usually decided by university faculty who taught from a given area of expertise. Functional skills—such as finance or brand management—were typically of greatest concern in this classroom-based training, and education was generally seen as both a reward and as preparation for a manager's promotion to a higher level. It was prestigious to attend an Ivy League advanced-management course for three months and to return with a broader general management perspective. Moreover, the chance to mingle with managers from other companies was considered an important networking opportunity.

Also popular during this time was a more radical form of education called sensitivity training, usually in the form of encounter groups or T-groups. Whereas university programs focused their attention on conceptual learning, sensitivity training targeted the manager's emotions and interpersonal behavior. In small groups at retreat centers, managers engaged in group dialogue under the supervision of trainers. There was no set agenda other than self-discovery. Participants learned about themselves as they dealt with group members through whatever dialogue emerged. They learned directly from experiencing and reflecting on the needs, attitudes, and interpersonal behaviors that participants demonstrated within the group setting. In contrast to university programs, this was highly learner centered and relied principally on intuitive learning; formal procedures and techniques were rare.

In those days, sensitivity groups were a particularly important way to learn about leadership. Remember that conceptions of leadership of the 1950s and 1960s were based entirely on small-group behavior and how well managers structured tasks and involved subordinates in decision making. Given these dimensions, it was presumed that an individual could learn about his or her leadership style by interacting in a T-group setting. Because opportunities for learning about organizational change and strategy formulation were largely absent, training remained focused on interpersonal dimensions of leadership and a leader's influence on his/her immediate followers.

In addition to sensitivity group experiences, leadership training also came in the form of short courses offered by training companies. The best examples were programs such as that of Paul Hersey and Kenneth Blanchard. Hersey and Blanchard provided their program in small-group seminar settings using a diagnostic question-naire to orient and assess participants. The questionnaire, called the Leadership Effectiveness and Adaptability Description (LEAD), described twelve situations and four possible leadership actions for each situation. Trainees were asked to choose the action they felt most accurately represented their leadership style. This self-diag-nosis served as the starting point for helping participants expand their repertoire of leadership behaviors by heightening their ability to see their own strengths and weaknesses. Role-playing and skill-building exercises exposed participants to the "ideal" responses in each situation and provided opportunities for course members to improve on their weaknesses. Built around a contingency theory of leadership effectiveness, participants learned that successful lead-ership entails tailoring one's style to the situation at hand. For example, in certain situations, leaders need to be more task ori-ented; in other situations, they need to be more people oriented. Like most management education approaches of the time, training was centered on helping the individual acquire specific behavioral skills. In contrast to today's programs, relatively little emphasis was placed on the larger organizational and strategic concerns of the developing leader's company.

Beginning in the 1980s, however, management education began to change. Exhibit 1.1 lists some of the more important shifts that began to take place around this time. As discussed earlier, these shifts were due in large part to the new competitive demands that organizations were beginning to face. Intensifying competition at a global level drove companies to search for educational experiences that would simultaneously enhance management capabilities and speed solutions to the organization's strategic problems. Under these conditions, sending one or two managers off to a university program to study cases written about other industries seemed to be a poor solution. It took managers away from the organization and did lit-tle to generate specific solutions or momentum. Moreover, the open enrollment of university-based programs meant that coursework and materials could not be tailored to a single company or industry.

Exhibit 1.1. Historical Changes in Management Education

1960s–1980s		1990s–Future
Functional knowledge	⟶	Leadership/organizational change/ highly relevant specialized knowledge
University based	⟶	In-company
Case studies	⟶	Action learning projects
Multi-industry focus	⟶	Single industry focus
Theoretical/analytical techniques	⟶	Highly applied learnings addressing organizational challenges
A few executives/managers	⟶	Executive teams/managerial cohorts
Restricted to one or two levels/functions	⟶	Cascades down multiple levels and across functions

Economics also played a role. As corporate cost cutting became increasingly common, budgets for education received far greater scrutiny. There was greater pressure to see more immediate payback and to achieve more visible outcomes. The economics of custom, in-house programs became increasingly attractive. After all, bringing five university professors to design and teach an in-company program to fifty managers was significantly less expensive than sending each of the fifty to executive development programs at universities.

These forces combined to promote the use of customized, in-house management education programs delivered either by a university's executive education arm or by a corporate human resources department. Indeed, the growth has been so strong that over 75 percent of all executive education dollars are now spent on customized programs (Fulmer and Vicere, 1995). In addition to economic advantages, other benefits made company-specific programs attractive. For example, materials and subjects could be tailored to each company's immediate needs. As a result, program designers began to append an additional objective to the education agenda: strategic change. Recognizing a growing need to fundamentally transform their organizations, CEOs realized that educational forums could be an important tool for furthering their strategic agendas. These forums could serve as vehicles for rapidly communicating a firm's strategic direction. They could build unity throughout a company by providing a context for dialogue and building shared vision. And, by combining theory, relevant learning, hands-on experience, and corporate-wide commitment, they could create a cadre of change agents.

The focus on effecting change helped to promote another management education trend—the use of "action learning" formats. Though action learning has come to refer to a whole range of educational approaches that involve "learning by doing," the original definition of the approach is more precise. Developed by Reg Revans, a Cambridge physicist, in the 1940s, action learning can be formally defined as a continuous process of learning and reflection, supported by colleagues, with a focus on getting things done (Revans, 1980). In the management development world, the action learning approach typically involves a group of managers who work together on a project encompassing issues of strategic importance to the organization. The idea is that managers who work together on a challenging yet unfamiliar task will bring their individual experiences to bear, share, reflect, and learn. The approach is perhaps best exemplified by designs used at General Electric's management development facility at Crotonville, New York. A typical GE program places developing managers in team-based experiential exercises aimed at solving real-life problems with immediate relevance to the company (Noel and Charan, 1988). So, for example, a company division might be contemplating new markets in Malaysia. Action learning teams would conduct market research on these new markets. They would test ideas and implementation issues and present recommendations for action on proposed programs. In essence, they would learn by doing.

Action learning programs also reflect another, more general trend in management development: the shift from individual to team-based training. With the exception of T-groups, management development has for the most part been an individual experience. By this we mean that learning is typically geared toward a single individual rather than a work unit or managerial cohort. But as the field has become more sensitive to transfer issues and organizational dynamics, there has been greater emphasis placed on groups of managers—that is, conducting training in cohorts of peers, bosses, and subordinates. The motivation for this trend is twofold. First, when managers attend training by themselves they often find themselves returning to their offices as the sole individual committed to or familiar with new ideas. As a result, there is typically little support for or understanding of what the returning manager has learned. Whatever momentum a course provides for the individual manager generally dies when he or she returns to the job, either due to a lack of adequate coaching or because organizational systems have not been aligned to reinforce and support the manager's new knowledge. Second, when managers attend training individually they may each develop a slightly different interpretation of the same lesson or message. There may be no opportunity to have a dialog with others with whom they work, thereby ensuring that everyone is on the same page. By crafting development efforts around groups of managers who must work together through the course of the learning experience, there are greater opportunities to reinforce learning and to ensure that managers share a common understanding of roles, responsibilities, and the organization's larger vision.

Finally, management development today utilizes defined competencies to describe in behavioral terms what is meant by vague concepts such as leadership or problem solving. These competencies serve as a common thread or link that ties together an organization's development, formal evaluation, and succession systems. Competencies allow organizations to define what leadership or other skills mean in their particular organizational context. Moreover, by including competencies in performance evaluations, organizations can provide greater incentives for leaders to apply lessons learned during formal training to ongoing responsibilities at work.

Taken together, these management development trends—greater industry and company focus, in-company customized programs, action learning formats, team-based training, and the use of defined competencies—have had a strong and direct impact on organizational efforts to develop leadership skills. We close our first chapter by describing three forms of leadership development that have evolved in light of these trends. Each plays a distinct role for both the organization and the individual leader.

The Three Roles of Leadership Development

The role and scope of leadership education has increased dramatically in recent years. For example, leadership initiatives today are far more pervasive and less elitist. They are increasingly designed around an understanding that leadership development is a continuous, lifelong process rather than a single discrete event. Reflecting the action learning movement, they are also more ingrained in the actual doing of work and more integrated with organizational support systems such as performance feedback. As such, our study of leadership education and development detected three major roles for the educational process: individual skill development, the socialization of corporate leadership values and vision, and strategic intervention that promotes dialogue and effects change throughout an organization (see Exhibit 1.2). Historically the most popular approach has been *individual preparation and skill development*. With an individual management approach, managers learn essential ideas and skills about leadership and receive feedback on specific capabilities. As such, programs focus almost exclusively on the manager participant, rather than any one work group or the organization as a whole. External programs, then, such as those provided by universities, typically offer little or no program content specific to a participant's own organization and its mission, goals, and values.

The second role of leadership education is to *socialize the vision, values, and mission* of an organization throughout its management

Exhibit 1.2. Leadership Education by Objective

Individual preparation	Personal leadership effectiveness
↓	Career transition to more senior levels
Socialization	
↓	Vehicle for instilling vision/values
Strategic intervention	Implementation of strategic imperatives

ranks. This is rapidly becoming a primary objective of many leadership training programs. Typically this type of education occurs as preparation for a manager's promotion to more senior management levels or as a means to drive cultural change into the management ranks. Leadership, in this case, involves learning that company managers or "leaders" need to embody and role model certain values and to actively translate the corporate vision into local visions for their own units. Given their focus on a given organization's needs, these programs tend to be conducted in-house.

Finally, there is a growing use of leadership programs for *strategic intervention*. For instance, educational formats center on action learning, task forces, and facilitated group discussions to identify organizational initiatives that can facilitate and accelerate a major strategic change. Leadership, in this case, translates into participants taking ownership for "leading" initiatives at their own levels that help to implement the new strategic imperatives and build important leadership capabilities in the process.

In recent years, we have witnessed the migration of leadership programs in the direction of the latter two objectives—socializing visions and values and driving strategic change. Individual preparation is diminishing as the primary objective of many leadership development programs, though individual 360-degree feedback programs have begun to play a much larger role in building specific competencies. This feedback activity also fulfills a socialization objective since many of the feedback competencies are behaviors and attitudes that have in essence become values of the company.

These shifts have enhanced the importance and impact of leadership development in organizations and in turn heightened interest in ways to improve current methods. They reflect the fact that leadership development has become more broadly defined. No longer does it apply only to an individual manager's ability to lead but also to the development of a "leadership mind-set" for the entire organization. As a result, programs today involve significant numbers of managers and action-oriented learning. The models for these interventions have come from visible, large-scale initiatives designed and conducted at companies such as Ford, Levi Strauss, and Philips. They, in turn, have shaped the new objectives for leadership education:

- Creating dialogue, common vision, and shared commitments to facilitate effective organizational change

- Orientation toward the bottom line

- Imparting relevant knowledge that can be applied immediately

- Building teams of leaders and leaders of teams

- Disseminating leadership throughout the organization

- Providing mechanisms and opportunities for self-development

- Aligning management and support systems to promote and reinforce ongoing leadership development

In the chapters that follow, we explore the ways that companies are trying to achieve these outcomes.

Part I

Out of the Classroom, Into the Trenches

Evaluating Approaches to Corporate Leadership Development

2

Developing the Individual Leader

Leadership is first and foremost an individual capability and leadership development is first and foremost an individual experience. Whether a training program hopes to enhance a leader's skills, familiarize the leader with new roles and expectations, or effect change throughout an entire organization, the individual must be influenced first.

It is not surprising then that leadership development has historically been concerned with advancing the individual's nascent leadership talents. The objective has been to teach developing leaders about the essential dimensions of leadership, have them reflect on their own leadership capabilities, and in turn stimulate their desire to seek out developmental experiences.

There are a number of reasons why organizations design so many programs aimed solely at developing the individual. The first and most obvious is to improve leader effectiveness. To the extent that budding leaders become more proficient, they presumably will be more effective in their jobs and provide greater benefit to the organization. Another reason, however, is to personalize the development experience to the leader's individual capabilities. Adult learning theory tells us that adults learn best when topics are relevant to what they need and want to know and thus fit their learning style. Programs aimed at individual development can facilitate the learning process by highlighting the relevance of particular concepts and by tailoring a program's pace and content to specific needs. Finally, as leadership experts James Kouzes and Barry Posner (1987) point out, leadership development is very much about "finding your own voice." Because credibility and authenticity lie at the heart of leadership, determining and defining one's own guiding beliefs and assumptions lie at the heart of becoming a good leader. By focusing on the individual, providing structured feedback, and prompting reflection, individual development programs can stimulate an important self-discovery process.

The best programs accomplish these objectives using a number of strategies. Most offer a mix of learning experiences, including lectures, case studies, experiential exercises, simulations, and other practices. Lectures, for example, convey models and theories that provide frameworks for thinking about leadership and the actions and behaviors that go into it. Case studies illustrate these concepts by describing applications within actual corporate settings. Simulations and exercises allow participants to experiment with typical leadership challenges, which in turn may help them to develop a feel for leadership behavior and hone particular skills. Perhaps most important, feedback from course members, trainers, and coworkers can provide opportunities for developing leaders to assess and reflect on their own leadership style.

Individual development programs tend to be relatively short. The learning experience typically ranges from a few days to a few weeks and is usually a one-time event with little or no follow-up. The goal, quite simply, is to impart knowledge that individuals can use to enhance their own leadership performance.

Leadership programs emphasizing individual development create a number of benefits. For the individual, they provide knowledge, awareness, and greater insight into one's own leadership abilities. Because most organizations continue to leave leadership development largely to chance, few if any opportunities exist on the job to learn concepts and frameworks that may guide a manager in becoming a better leader. Formal programs can accelerate and improve learning by structuring and guiding a manager's experience in ways that facilitate the interpretation of complex relationships. Programs aimed at the individual can also increase awareness. They can provide exposure to a range of experiences that a leader has yet to encounter. Moreover, case studies of successful—as well as not-so-successful—leadership illustrate how leaders good and bad can influence an organization and its outcomes. This gives managers a greater appreciation of the importance of leader behavior and may motivate some individuals to actively seek out opportunities to improve their capabilities. Finally, formal programs can provide one of the few windows that managers can use to look objectively at their own leadership style. Well-designed programs afford opportunities for detailed feedback from facilitators and other participants, giving leaders a chance to reflect on their strengths and weaknesses. Interestingly, studies have shown that development programs can actually change self-perceptions even with very little feedback. It appears that participation alone can encourage self-evaluation and insight (Schmitt, Ford, and Stults, 1986)—factors that in turn may lead to improved performance.

Programs aimed at individual development can also provide benefits to the organization. First, these programs can identify strengths and development areas that can subsequently be used to formulate development plans or training programs. Development plans may be tailored to the needs of a particular individual or, to the extent that similar issues emerge across a number of individuals, programs may be developed as formal offerings to all managers at a certain level or facing certain challenges. Second, individual development programs can help in the early identification of managerial talent. Identifying high-potential individuals allows the organization to channel these developing leaders into positions where their talents can best be utilized. It also allows the organization to conduct effective succession planning that subsequently improves the long-term strength of the firm, as well as its ability to retain talent. Third, training at the individual level can, in fact, improve group-level processes. Research has shown that training managers to improve their problem-solving skills actually helps teams solve problems more effectively. Last, individually oriented programs benefit the organization by allowing greater visibility into the workforce as a whole. Valid information about the leadership capabilities of managers at different levels throughout the organization can help guide the allocation of limited development dollars and other resources, and may even affect strategic business decisions. For all of these reasons, leadership development programs tailored to the individual will continue to enjoy great popularity.

Given the continued importance of these programs, our purpose in this chapter is to explore individual development programs in depth. We look at some typical program designs and provide a set of best practices to guide those hoping to build even better programs in the future. We discuss common pitfalls and offer suggestions to overcome design shortcomings. We follow up in Chapter Three with a case study of the National Australia Bank to illustrate one well-designed program.

A Typical Design

To illustrate a program focused on individual development, we use the example of a leadership course designed for a manufacturing company. The company had a long history of promoting leadership development and had recently become concerned about building a cadre of "change-agent" leaders capable of coping with the accelerating pace of innovation in the industry. Two professors from a leading business school, experts in leadership, were called in to design a program around the leadership competencies required to effect organizational change. Together the professors and company sponsors produced and delivered a four-day learning experience structured around three distinct modules: the leader's role in change, skills for implementing change, and motivational and empowerment practices.

At the start of day one, participants received survey feedback from a dozen of their workplace colleagues (superiors, peers, and subordinates). This feedback was structured so that the competency categories that were reported corresponded with each of the course's three themes. This ensured that participants could personally gauge their strengths and weaknesses against the competencies described in the modules about to be taught. It was assumed that feedback early in the course would stimulate the participants' desire to learn.

Following this feedback and a personal review session with an on-site coach, the program began with a module on leadership vision and change. Using a series of case studies from companies such as General Electric, Microsoft, and the Virgin Group, participants learned lessons about core leadership concepts such as strategic vision, unconventional market perspectives, and environmental scanning for opportunities. During course discussions, the professors encouraged participants to share their own experiences. This created dialogue that allowed the core concepts to be applied to the individuals' own leadership challenges and personal work situations.

A second module was presented in days two and three that emphasized skills required for implementing change. Another series of case studies illustrated how effective leaders at several companies had successfully orchestrated large-scale organizational change. For example, participants explored the successful turnaround of the international advertising agency Ogilvy & Mather by its senior leader Charlotte Beers. This case study taught lessons about the process of developing a strategic vision and ways to implement the vision once it was defined. Experiential exercises were used to teach communications and influence skills. A portion of day three and all of day four explored the remaining themes of motivation and empowerment—again using experiential exercises and case discussions as the principal vehicles for conveying lessons and insight. Participants learned about the personal philosophies that leaders often draw on in their efforts to empower others, and about the importance of leaders demonstrating their values and beliefs in day-to-day actions. Throughout the program, participants were continually required to reflect on their own actions. They were encouraged to think about the extent to which they embody the skills and worldviews they were being taught and they were asked to discuss their own personal challenges. There were also opportunities to practice some of the skills and to receive performance feedback.

Such is the design of a fairly typical in-company program aimed at developing individual leadership capabilities. A carefully tailored assessment tool gathers feedback from colleagues prior to the course and provides detailed input on the developing leader's effectiveness along course dimensions. This gives the individual a good sense of specific strengths and weaknesses and motivates the need to learn. Case studies, practice sessions, and reflective exercises convey and teach essential ideas, frameworks, and techniques. In the end, participants learn about the characteristics of effective leaders and learn what these leaders actually do. Individuals are compelled to contemplate these leadership characteristics in light of the beliefs and behavior they demonstrate in their own jobs. With this knowledge, it is presumed that participants will return to their workplaces and implement the skills and worldviews they have learned.

Though the course meets a larger organizational need around change leadership, the experience is geared toward the individual learner. There may be limited attempts to address some of the leadership challenges facing the organization itself, but the emphasis remains on the individual. Moreover, participants may or may not attend the development program with colleagues they work with on a regular basis (in this example, they did not). In programs where participants attend individually from different parts of the organization, they are likely to have greater difficulty applying their learning back on the job due to a lack of common understanding and support among their work group. As a result, learning often stays an individual experience built around the one-time learning event. This is particularly true with open-enrollment university programs where participants may be the sole representative from their company.

Best Practices for Effective Programs in Individual Development

Based on our research, a number of design features can heighten the impact of programs aimed at individual development. These "best practices" can significantly enhance an individual's learning experience and hold great potential for improving the effectiveness of leader behavior back on the job. Because of their overall importance, we describe each in some detail. In the ideal world, optimal learning environments would incorporate as many of the following design elements as possible.

1. Build Around a Single Well-Delineated Leadership Model

In order to improve one's leadership ability, it is important first to have a clear understanding of what leadership is and what effective leaders do. One of the biggest problems that many development programs must overcome is a vague concept of what they are trying to accomplish. In many cases, a lack of consensus about what leadership entails results in program designers incorporating as many leadership dimensions as they can into the learning plan. This tends to overwhelm participants, and it diminishes the emphasis placed on those skills and characteristics most relevant to the individuals and organization at hand.

It is clear from our research that a single well-defined model or framework of leadership improves participants' learning. In contrast, multiple models increase the probability that participants will forget essential components or find themselves confused about differing frameworks. Having a well-defined model allows more opportunities to explore in depth the various dimensions of a given framework— an important consideration when one considers how short most programs are. In programs where we saw multiple leadership models being emphasized, participants typically received only a brief, singular exposure to an individual dimension of each model. This caused participants to have problems discerning which dimensions were most important and resulted in them forgetting many of the dimensions that had been presented.

Having a single model of leadership, however, does not mean that the same aspects of leadership are taught across all levels of the organization. On the contrary, many of the best organizations we observed emphasized different facets of leadership for individuals at different levels of development or in different functions or domains. Federal Express, for example, provides leadership development at three distinct levels of management through three separate but mandatory core courses. Similarly, the U.S. Army also believes in differentiating development experiences by level even while adhering to a common leadership framework throughout. "There are some aspects of leadership that apply to everyone, regardless of rank. . . . On the other hand, leadership in some ways is not the same for the sergeant as it is for the colonel. . . . [There are] unique aspects of leadership that exist at the specific levels of leadership" (Army Leadership, 1997, p. iii). Because leaders at each level differ in the types of tasks they are responsible for, the spans of control they oversee, their level of operations, planning horizons, and the like, the Army tailors its development programs to the responsibilities required at each successive level. Although the Army adheres to a single leadership framework across its entire military workforce, it recognizes that leadership progresses along a continuum of roles and responsibilities and requires different skills and abilities as the leader advances.

In recent years, most programs have moved toward the use of a single model or framework. These are often built around a set of competencies—that is, bundle of desirable skills. Competencies, in turn, form the skill categories that participants learn in exercises and on which they receive personalized feedback. Later in this chapter we discuss the distinct advantages and disadvantages of these competency-based programs.

2. Use a Participant Selection Process with Clear Criteria

Who is selected to attend a development program depends primarily on what the program is intended to accomplish in the first place. As a result, criteria for selection can range widely from firm to firm and from program to program. Some programs, for example, are designed to provide accelerated development experiences for individuals who are essentially candidates for the company's next generation of senior leaders. These "high-potential" individuals may be selected through a formal succession system or may be nominated by senior management. Other programs are designed to provide skills that may be needed when assuming a new position. Selection for these programs may be based on promotion to a certain level— maybe the person's first management role—or else on a sizable jump in scale and scope from prior responsibilities. Other programs are designed to build leadership strength in a particular functional area or division. These programs may be intended to improve leadership capabilities in a unit that is performing below par, or they may be designed to strengthen capabilities in an area that is extremely important to the firm from a strategic standpoint. Selection into these programs would obviously be based on belonging to the particular unit. Finally, some programs are designed to enhance the leadership strength of an organization overall. Selection into these programs is usually based on an individual's performance. In some cases, programs may be designed to reward and improve the skills of those who have done particularly well. In other cases, programs may be more remedial, aimed at improving interpersonal skills, teaming, or other factors that hamper an individual's ability to lead effectively.

It is nice to think that selection into a development program will be based on the program's defined purpose, but the reality is usually quite different. In many cases, selection criteria are either undefined or poorly enforced. It is clear from many of the programs we observed that organizations have difficulty maintaining consistent selection processes over time. In most instances, selection becomes muddied as programs begin to develop a reputation. People watch who attends a program, what opportunities they are allowed, and what transpires when they return to the workplace. Often, attendance is viewed as a form of recognition and becomes associated with advancement and success. Other times, misleading rumors arise that distort a program's intended purpose and potentially taint it in the eyes of future participants. Programs may be viewed as the fad of the week, a waste of time, or the only way to get ahead in the organization. To minimize misleading rumors, it is important to be clear and up-front about selection criteria, to publicize requirements, and to push for adherence. When these steps are overlooked, selection can easily become politicized, thereby undermining the program's credibility. Maintaining a focused selection process means that those responsible for nominating and selecting participants must clearly understand the selection criteria and the rationale behind them. They must also be able to apply these criteria reliably when making judgments about potential candidates.

In one program we encountered, designers had decided that participants should represent a mix of levels, business units, functions, and geography in order to ensure that information from the program flowed throughout the organization. Beyond this mix, the program's designers had also established another set of criteria. Because the program sought to focus on the company's future leaders, participants were also to be selected according to their demonstration of leadership. The selection criteria, along with a description of the program and its purpose, were sent to the senior executives of each of the company's operating groups. These executives were then responsible for nominating a list of candidates that would be sent to the human resources group for the final selection cut. It is important to note that nominations were based solely on the judgment of the executives. However, the extent to which these senior officials had the expertise and motivation to select appropriate candidates was at times in question. Many of the executives were, in fact, part of the "old guard" and represented the type of leadership that the firm wanted to move away from. To the extent that these executives selected (consciously or otherwise) nominees in their own image, the nomination process fell into question.

Maintaining a valid selection process also means ensuring that selection criteria are adhered to as the program matures and develops a reputation. This can be particularly difficult because, in many ways, the program begins to take on a life of its own and may become politicized. In the first year of the program just described, very little was known about its merit or the implications of participating. In the intervening years, however, the program garnered greater and greater prestige. The program's status was in part fueled by the support that it received from the organization's senior management. As a result, inclusion in the program is now well regarded, and exclusion from the program is often viewed as a signal that an individual does not belong to the "new world order." This, in turn, has created a strong feeling with many in the organization that the program is the pathway to promotion and success at the firm. As a result, strong political pressures have arisen to extend nominations that are not necessarily based on the designers' original set of leadership criteria but rather on the personal ambitions of the participants.

3. Conduct Precourse Preparation

Based on our interviews with program participants, precourse preparation can be very helpful in getting individuals to carefully contemplate their own leadership style and the potential applications of course knowledge back in the workplace. By sending out exercises and materials that encourage participants to reflect on their styles and those of others in their organization, precourse preparation can heighten an appreciation for the upcoming learning experience and its importance. It may also allow participants to see potential links between their own daily challenges and the training program that lies ahead. This may further increase their motivation for learning.

The Army relies heavily on precourse preparation. In light of military downsizing and budget cuts, the Army's Training and Doctrine Command increasingly seeks ways to squeeze more out of its training dollar. As many programs have become shorter, it is paramount that the Army takes every available step to increase each program's impact on the individual. By sending program participants materials several weeks before a program commences, instructors and participants are able to hit the ground running. Participants enter the program with a common understanding of some of the themes of the course and have already begun to grapple with difficult topics.

Our case example in the next chapter, the National Australia Bank, is another excellent example of using prework to jump-start the learning process and stimulate motivation. About three to four weeks before the program begins, participants receive a package of materials: articles on the leadership and teamwork topics to be presented at the seminar, video overviews on the concept of leadership, and questions to reflect on. The questions in particular are designed to encourage participants to think about their own leadership and teaming styles. Course lessons build directly on the issues raised by these questions and the other prework material.

4. Use Personalized 360-Degree Feedback to Reinforce Learnings

Extensive research on learning and education has shown that feedback is a critical part of any learning process. Feedback is particularly important in the leadership development process because as leaders progress in the organization they have fewer opportunities to get direct and objective input on how they are perceived by others. Rewards may depend more on the performance of one's unit or division and less on one's method or style for achieving results.

Moreover, as one moves up in the hierarchy, others may be less likely to offer constructive criticism or provide other feedback that may facilitate a superior's development.

From research on training, we know that feedback facilitates the development of leadership skills (Conger, 1992; McCauley, Moxley, and Van Velsor, 1998; Wexley and Thornton, 1972). Better-designed programs tend to employ more comprehensive forms of feedback such as structured 360-degree assessments based on input provided by colleagues. They utilize these assessment tools in a manner that tightly aligns feedback to course material, focusing on the very dimensions of leadership that participants will soon be taught.

Feedback in the form of 360-degree surveys is increasingly a standard component of many leadership training programs. In certain ways, this comprehensive feedback is a surrogate for the sensitivity or T-group experience of the 1960s where relative strangers in one's group provided their observations of an individual's style. Today feedback comes in a more packaged form along a set of specific dimensions and directly from one's coworkers.

Given its growing use over the last several years, it is important that we discuss what we know about the use and effectiveness of 360-degree feedback. We draw heavily upon the conclusions of Hollenbeck and McCall (1999), who have summarized current thinking. As they point out, few human resources tools have achieved as much popularity as quickly as the 360-degree evaluation method. Essentially, 360-degree assessment involves enlisting multiple raters, often including a self-rating, in assessing an individual along a series of dimensions that are behaviorally specific and related to valued performance measures. Typically, in educational initiatives the feedback is derived from the competencies associated with the course's leadership model. In the ideal situation, this model reflects a set of competencies for the future of the firm and usually describes actions and behaviors that support change and strategic vision within the organization.

Assessments are usually gathered from a minimum of three to as many as twenty or more colleagues of the individual. These colleagues typically include subordinates, peers, and bosses—and in some cases customers—who fill out an assessment in the form of a questionnaire with a rating scale. In addition, there may be open-ended questions where respondents can write further comments about the individual. Once completed by raters, the questionnaires are returned to a central location where summaries are compiled for presentation to the assessee. Normally the identity of raters is not revealed. It is assumed that confidentiality for the assessor increases the chances of greater candor. When used in conjunction with leadership development programs, the intention of 360-degree feedback is typically developmental rather than evaluative (in the sense of a performance appraisal). As such, there are no direct rewards or punishments, and feedback is entirely for the participants' benefit.

As Conger (1992) discovered in his examination of feedback-based training programs, the impact of these types of formal surveys varies dramatically. Some individuals are prepared to use them as a source of real learning and insight; others react more defensively. It basically depends on the person. However, to have impact potential, as Dalton and Hollenbeck (1996) point out, feedback in any form must meet certain criteria. First, the sources of feedback need to be perceived as credible and competent. In other words, the individual must believe that his or her evaluators—subordinates, peers, and bosses—are in a position to make realistic and objective assessments. Second, the information must be seen as meaningful and in a form that makes sense. Measured dimensions must be useful. They should be easily translated into tangible behaviors and actions, and they should be presented in a manner that makes interpretation straightforward and reliable. Third, the confidentiality of evaluators must be maintained. Feedback should not be attributed to any individual or group of individuals to ensure that evaluations remain as candid as possible. Finally, feedback should be timely, reflecting recent assessments. If not, those being evaluated may feel that the information is dated and therefore does not accurately depict their current situation—in which case they may simply choose to ignore it.

Despite the popularity of 360-degree feedback, there have been criticisms of the approach (Waldman, Atwater, and Antonioni, 1998). First of all, it can be very time-consuming. A boss might have to fill out one or two dozen forms for her peers and subordinates. Technology can alleviate some of this burden by placing assessment forms on a company intranet or other platform; however, even technology does little to reduce the burden of evaluating numerous colleagues who may be at different levels and performing different jobs.

Given that behavior is driven by what gets measured and rewarded, organizations must be very clear about the behaviors they are seeking to reinforce—as well as discourage—and how these relate to company goals. Raters themselves may not see a link between an individual's behavior and problems facing the organization. For example, at one organization we examined, the company was experiencing a significant downturn in market share due to its failure to understand changing customer needs. At the same time, 360-degree feedback surveys of the company's managers showed high ratings across the organization on dimensions pertaining to managers' understanding of and sensitivity to customer needs. Clearly, there was a critical and misleading disconnect between reality and the results of the survey instrument. Other potential shortcomings with these assessments include poor follow-up and coaching, feedback that is too vague or imprecise to motivate change, and the use of a "one-size-fits-all" approach that uses a universal set of dimensions for all levels and all jobs.

We also know from research (Waldman, Atwater, and Antonioni, 1998) that raters themselves may commit a host of common rating errors. They may rate too harshly or too leniently or simply play it safe by using mid-point scores. So it is important that raters receive some form of guidance beforehand to avoid such errors. In addition, certain organizational cultures that are highly autocratic or conflict-averse may inhibit respondent candor and thereby produce feedback that is, on average, more positive than it should be.

In answering the all-important question of whether 360-degree is truly an effective feedback mechanism, there has been a surprising absence of sound research. We believe, however, that its selective use is appropriate on the grounds that research in other contexts has shown that feedback in itself can be of developmental value when it is detailed and behaviorally specific (Boehm, 1985). Moreover, to the extent that 360-degree assessment highlights expected performance dimensions and places all employees in the role of potential evaluator, it increases the attention paid to desired competencies and produces subtle peer pressure to perform accordingly. As a result, participants may gauge the extent to which they need to focus their energies on developing weaker competencies or at a minimum be more aware of their shortcomings and find ways to compensate. In the end, however, the potential for 360-degree assessment as a developmental tool depends on how tightly linked its performance dimensions are to the themes emphasized in development programs. The better aligned they are, the more they will enhance the individual's overall learning experience.

5. Use Multiple Learning Methods

Multiple learning methods are essential to a well-designed leadership program (Conger, 1992). Adult learning theory suggests that individuals differ in their learning styles. Some people learn best from lectures, others from structured exercises, and still others from direct experience. There are numerous ways by which we learn. Multiple instructional techniques increase the likelihood that at least one, if not several, methods will be compatible with an individual participant's style. Also, learning occurs at several levels. For example, it helps to have an intellectual or conceptual understanding of the basic roles and activities of leadership as it contrasts to management. At the same time, there are behavioral skills that the learner can acquire through actual practice and experimentation. As we noted in the prior section, personalized feedback is useful to target the learner's attention and awareness. Learning that taps into the psychological and emotional needs of the learner may also be necessary to stimulate interest in seeking out developmental opportunities after classroom experiences. The more a learning environment can touch upon these multiple dimensions, the higher its probability of success.

We can categorize most training approaches to leadership into four fundamental pedagogies (Conger, 1992), each with distinct assumptions about how leadership is learned as well as distinct instructional methods. These four approaches are conceptual awareness, feedback, skill building, and personal growth. A training program may contain elements of all four, but there is a tendency for one approach to dominate at the expense of the others. In other words, each program has a dominant paradigm or methodology. This occurs largely because of differences in the backgrounds of program designers. Their orientations can produce sharp differences in actual designs. In Exhibits 2.1, 2.2, and 2.3 we illustrate some of the differences between the approaches in terms of key learning assumptions, principal methods, and backgrounds of the designers.

The first of the approaches—conceptual awareness—is built around the notion that individuals need to understand leadership from a conceptual or cognitive vantage point. In other words, participants require mental models and frameworks that will help them grasp the many dimensions of leadership. With this awareness in

Exhibit 2.1. Designer Backgrounds of the Four Approaches

Training Approach	Designer Backgrounds
Conceptual awareness	Academics
Feedback	Psychologists
Skill building	Training organizations
Personal growth	Outward Bound, "new age" trainers, and psychotherapists

Source: Conger, J. A. "Education for Leaders: Current Practices, New Directions." *Journal of Management Systems,* 1998.

Exhibit 2.2. Assumptions About Learning Process

Training Approaches	Learning Assumptions
Conceptual awareness	Adults learn through mental models and conceptual frameworks. Often built around contrasts—e.g., managing versus leading.
Feedback	Survey and personal feedback allow learners to identify their strengths and weaknesses along a set of competencies. This positively reinforces strengths and encourages learners to later seek developmental experiences that address weaknesses or to find a means to compensate for them.
Skill building	From behavioral modeling, personal experimentation, and feedback, learners can develop leadership competencies. The process employs structured exercises that allow participants to practice skills, receive feedback on their implementation, and further experiment and refine them.
Personal growth	Emotional and physical challenges force reflective learning about the individual's behavior, world-views, and personal aspirations in work and life.

Source: Conger, J. A. "Education for Leaders: Current Practices, New Directions," *Journal of Management Systems*, 1998.

place, they can seek out developmental experiences after the course has ended. Not so surprisingly, this approach has been influenced primarily by the work of academic researchers (such as Bass, 1985; Bennis and Nanus, 1985; Conger, 1989; Kotter, 1990; Tichy and Devanna, 1986) whose models become the centerpiece of instructional designs. As a result, we find that this more analytical approach to training leadership has long been the domain of business school executive education and MBA programs. Theory oriented by nature, business schools use the traditional tools of conceptual learning—case studies, lectures, films, and discussions—to convey knowledge to participants. They often rely on contrasting ideas to build conceptual understanding—for example, contrasting leadership with management to distinguish their unique qualities, activities, and

Exhibit 2.3. Learning Methods of the Four Approaches

Training Approaches	Principal Learning Methods
Conceptual awareness	Written and video case studies, lectures on conceptual models, discussion groups
Feedback	Observed exercises; "fishbowls" with feedback; survey and verbal feedback from trained observers, fellow participants, and workplace colleagues
Skill building	Practice exercises; simulations; lecturettes; modeling by trainers or video case studies on behavioral competencies
Personal growth	Outdoor adventure or indoor psychological exercises with an emphasis on reflective learning, risk taking, teamwork, and personal life goals

Source: Conger, J. A. "Education for Leaders: Current Practices, New Directions," *Journal of Management Systems,* 1998.

characteristics. Participants might, for example, learn that leaders rely on strategic visions to set direction for their organizations, whereas managers direct through formal planning systems and a focus on shorter-term operating targets. Written and video case studies illustrating these differences are typically employed along with discussions and lectures to teach fundamental ideas.

The principal advantage of this more cognitive approach to learning about leadership is that it helps participants understand intellectually the important differences in the behaviors and worldviews of leaders versus managers. In addition, if programs are of limited duration, it is an efficient approach. It is far more realistic for an individual to develop a mental model of leadership in two days than to successfully acquire new behaviors in the same period. The hope of such programs, of course, is that after exposure to essential ideas about leadership the learners will be motivated to seek out opportunities to develop their leadership capabilities.

The most serious limitation of this approach, however, is that concepts about leadership are insufficient in themselves to develop

an individual's leadership ability in behavioral terms. Understanding something intellectually often has little to do with our ability
to implement the behavior ourselves. If it did, we would certainly
see many more young Jack Welches (chairman of General Electric)
given that most managers and MBA students today read case studies and watch videos on his leadership style. As such, it is important to see conceptual learning as only a first step in the process of
learning about leadership. It is a critical one, however, because we
require mental models to orient ourselves in understanding any phenomenon. They also sensitize us to where our own developmental
needs may lie and the skills one needs to acquire.

The second approach—feedback—is based on the premise that
learners need behavioral feedback in order to attend to deficiencies
as well as to build self-confidence in their areas of strength. This
approach assumes correctly that most of us cannot completely see
our behavioral selves. Due to psychological defenses and biases, we
have only a partial picture of what we do and how we are perceived.
Therefore we require a mirror of some form to discern more fully
our strengths and weaknesses as leaders. The mirror in the feedback
approaches comes in the form of outside observers. In addition to
360-degree assessment tools, feedback designs employ in-class simulations and fishbowl exercises where participants conduct tasks
under the watchful eyes of trained observers and fellow participants.
After completion of an exercise, the numerous observers provide
survey or direct feedback concerning each other's behavior in the
exercise. More comprehensive programs such as those run at the
Center for Creative Leadership also provide interviews with staff
psychologists so that participants are able to develop an integrated
understanding of the many sources of feedback they have received.

As we noted in the previous section, there are several advantages
to feedback approaches. For one, feedback is essential in any learning
process especially as it applies to the acquisition and improvement
of behavioral skills. They help learners clearly identify important
strengths and weaknesses in skill areas and help them gauge progress.

For motivated learners, they serve to focus their efforts on specific developmental areas. For younger managers, positive feedback can boost confidence, which in turn enhances their leadership back on the job (Conger, 1992).

Beyond these advantages, however, are several drawbacks. Programs built largely around feedback have a tendency to overwhelm participants with information. Individuals might receive data on two or three hundred different dimensions of their behavior—their coaching style, conflict approaches, orientation to innovation, decision making, communications, and so on. As a result, information overload and selective recall may occur. To compensate, participants tend to actively remember and focus on only two or three areas as developmental goals (Conger, 1992). On occasion, some of these might include behavioral changes that involve a fundamental shift in the individual's psychological makeup. But such outcomes are rare. Because the training environment is limited in its ability to help participants make profound adjustments, participants tend instead to gravitate to changes that are more superficial in terms of dispositional traits (Conger, 1992). Yet these dimensions may be the ones that are the least significant for developing the individual's leadership potential.

The greatest shortcoming of these programs, however, is the limited opportunity to experiment with new behaviors that may remedy competency deficiencies or reduce dysfunctional behavior. For example, a participant might discover from a simulation that his interpersonal influence skills or ability to communicate compelling goals are in need of greater development. In theory, this should be followed up immediately with opportunities to improve these skills through practice and experimentation. In many programs, however, participants simply move on to the next feedback exercise, with limited time for skill development. In addition, given the number of participants in a given program and the time demands on instructors, there are few windows of sufficient time for personalized coaching. Therefore, although feedback should be an essential element of any program, it needs to be modified and complemented extensively by other approaches.

This brings us to the third approach—skill building. This approach focuses on visible, behavioral skill development. It is the "tennis clinic" of leadership development, where participants go and literally practice certain basic competencies associated with effective leadership. For example, program designers might construct a learning module around inspirational speaking skills. Participants would be introduced to a list of behaviors associated with inspirational communications. An exercise would follow where each participant devises a five-minute presentation employing these inspirational behaviors. In small groups, they deliver their presentations and then are rated by teammates and instructors on their effective use of the new behaviors.

The principal advantage of this approach is that it attempts to turn leadership into a set of teachable behavioral skills. As such, participants are given opportunities to learn from behavioral models and to experiment with the behaviors themselves. Generally, immediate feedback on the participant's demonstration of the skill is provided after each exercise. In many ways, this approach is similar to how recreational sports such as tennis or golf are taught. The instructor explains and demonstrates the skill. Then the participant practices the skill as demonstrated and afterward receives feedback on her performance from the instructor and others. In more effective programs, there are further opportunities to practice.

To a great extent, the success of skill-building approaches depends on how teachable a particular leadership competency is. For example, by following a series of practice exercises an individual might indeed improve certain communication skills. But complex competencies such as strategic vision may not be easily taught. We know from research on visionary leaders (Conger, 1989; Westley, 1992) that such competencies often have a long gestation period and involve a multiplicity of skills. Moreover, timing and luck play a role. Given the complexity of forces behind vision, it is unlikely that an individual could be taught to be more "visionary" in three days. However, an appreciation for the importance of vision could be taught in a three-day workshop. Similarly, receiving advice on the work experiences that might facilitate one's future vision is also feasible.

Skill-building programs face a second dilemma concerning time. To truly develop expertise in a skill, an individual needs multiple and varied experiences—studying the basic characteristics of the skill, experimenting with it, getting coached, and then making improvements and refinements (Ericsson and Smith, 1991). Yet many programs attempt to cover a wide range of leadership skills within just a few days. A half-day might be spent on motivation, an afternoon on inspirational speaking skills, and a morning on empowerment. In the course of three days, as many as ten or fifteen skill categories might be covered. By analogy, this experience would be similar to an individual attempting to learn golf, basketball, tennis, and racketball in a three-day program. As a result, participants often receive only a single opportunity to practice a particular skill and receive feedback. With so little exposure, the experience simply builds awareness rather than true understanding and skill development.

Finally, the exercises employed by the skill-building approaches may be flawed. They often attempt to simulate work environments, but may be far from actual workplace realities. For example, to simulate task demands on the job participants might be asked to lead a team of counterparts in assembling toy trucks. But unlike one's real workplace, there are no career consequences, no political issues, no investment risks, and no post-task implications involved. Yet all these profoundly shape behavior at work. Their absence in the simulation renders it a make-believe exercise with few of the consequences that would be encountered at work.

The final of our four training approaches is personal growth. This approach has its origins in outdoor adventure programs such as Outward Bound and in personal development seminars from the 1970s such as EST or "new age" psychotherapies such as Gestalt.

Adopting their interventions to the business world, trainers and psychotherapists from these programs developed management education programs in the 1980s, bringing with them their humanistic orientations to leadership development. Personal growth approaches typically employ emotional and physical challenges that provoke reflection on one's behavior and life choices. These experiences are intended to help trainees ascertain their natural tendencies around risk and teamwork, their career ambitions in contrast to their current career status, and their choice of priorities between work and personal life. In the end, most of these programs attempt to create experiences whereby participants take greater responsibility for the destiny of their lives through clear personal goals and behavioral changes.

Underlying these programs—particularly the psychologically based ones—is a singular premise that effective leaders are in touch with their personal dreams and are confident enough in themselves to realize them. In addition, we often find a second premise: leaders are balanced human beings in terms of their work and personal lives. These programs argue that most participants are some distance from these two states of being. Instead, they have chosen to ignore their inner callings and personal priorities. To direct participants' attention to these contradictions, the personal growth approach relies on "upending" emotional experiences—adventures that become metaphors for the issues they wish participants to learn from. So, for example, a rafting trip down a difficult-to-navigate river might teach participants about the necessity of teamwork and the pleasures of risk taking.

There are several advantages to personal growth approaches. They do offer opportunities to experience risk taking, emotional expressiveness, highly cooperative teamwork, and empowerment. As well, we know from research in adult education that the more levels a learning experience engages, the more powerful the learning will be. The personal growth approach engages a wide variety—emotional, imaginative, cognitive, and behavioral. Learning can also be magnified by experiences that are perceived as risky and that challenge us to act in new ways or to see the world vividly with a new set of eyes (Conger, 1992).

In terms of drawbacks, personal growth programs fall short on several dimensions. Like skill building exercises, the actual character of an exercise may not truly reflect workplace realities. For example, one might jump from a cliff wearing a harness tethered to a safety line. This experience is used to teach risk taking. Yet how comparable is this to a manager making a multimillion-dollar product investment at work? Both entail risk. But the cliff-jump exercise offers the participant no real guidelines for taking thoughtful risks back at the office. Instead, much like a pep talk from a motivational speaker, the cliff-jumping participant leaves emotionally excited about taking risks but with no gauge for measuring them back at work. When the participant faces the product investment decision at the office, there are other dynamics at play. First, the risk is shared by the management team. Second, it depends on a rigorous analytical process. Third, there are potentially important career consequences with few figurative "safety harnesses."

A second problem with personal growth approaches is a higher probability of learner disappointment or letdown upon return to the workplace. These programs create an emotional high that generally cannot be sustained as risk-averse bosses and bureaucratic inertia undermine the trainee's newfound zeal to exhibit leadership.

The underlying premise of personal growth approaches—that within each of us lie important passions and values that will help us lead—may also be faulty. Younger managers, for example, may be lacking in sufficient experience to ascertain their potential talents, interests, and passions. Moreover, a few days of training cannot substitute for the insights and opportunities that multiple work experiences can provide. As well, getting in touch with one's talents and interests is no guarantee of leadership. For example, a manager may discover that her real interests lie in acting or photography. Quite simply, many passions have little to do with leadership.

With their emphasis on work-life balance, these programs tend to improve participants' personal lives far more than their work lives (Conger, 1992). In various exercises, trainees might confront the personal trade-offs they have made with their families. With a strong emphasis on our emotional dynamics, it is not surprising that we turn to our private lives. The family allows us to live out our deeper emotional needs that the workplace cannot hope to fulfill. Unfortunately, the premise itself that leaders are well balanced is not borne out by actual biographical evidence on leaders. Instead, many leaders have devoted their lives largely to their work.

6. Conduct Extended Learning Periods and Multiple Sessions

We know from research on the transfer of learning from training that information learned under distributed periods of training is generally retained longer than in a one-time program (Briggs and Naylor, 1962; Naylor and Briggs, 1963). As well, feedback-oriented programs that span multiple periods appear to move participants from awareness to an enhanced probability of effecting change in their behaviors and perspectives (Young and Dixon, 1996). Our case study of the National Australia Bank exemplifies this idea of spreading learning out over an extended time. Consisting of several stages, it provided multiple opportunities to reflect on and revisit key learnings.

The research that perhaps sheds the greatest light on why extended and multiple periods of learning are required for learning leadership comes from a growing body of knowledge on expertise—on how individuals become experts. The topic has been explored extensively in a great variety of domains, including art, chess, medicine, music, physics, and sports. Although each domain shapes how expertise is acquired, it is possible to draw generalizations that are fundamental to the acquisition of expertise across many fields, including leadership.

First, becoming an expert takes time. In studies of experts who attain international levels of performance across diverse fields, ten years of preparation appears to be the norm and often the period is substantially longer. For example, in a review of the existing research, Ericsson, Krampe, and Tesch-Romer (1993) found that this ten-year rule was remarkably accurate.

During this extended time, a second developmental experience must take place: deliberate, focused, and repeated practice (Ericsson and Charness, 1994). Practice during this period results in the acquisition of tacit knowledge. Tacit knowledge—knowledge that is not formally transferable or describable—is a key part of expertise and is therefore difficult to train per se. It must be learned through multiple and varied exposures to the area in which one wishes to become an expert. Finally, training and coaching play a key role during this period of practice. It is clear that to reach exceptional levels of performance individuals must undergo a very extended period of active learning, where they continually refine and improve their skills under the supervision of a teacher, coach, or mentor (Ericsson and Charness, 1994).

This literature makes an important distinction between exposure and deliberate practice (Ericsson and Smith, 1991). Simple exposure to an area does not suffice; rather the efforts put forth toward learning must be deliberate, focused, and repeated. Deliberate practice is defined as an activity involving effort that is motivated by the goal of improving performance (Ericsson and Charness, 1994). This insight applies to both executive training and on-the-job learning. Training built around a few days of practice is clearly insufficient; it takes a longer-term orientation with multiple, focused sessions, ultimately over several years. Similarly, on-the-job experiences would need to deepen learning in a particular domain through deliberate practice accompanied by immediate and specific feedback. At the same time, on-the-job learning may not necessarily occur if it is not focused and continual feedback is largely absent. This is especially the case for complex skills such as leadership. The expertise literature would argue that leadership, like any form of expertise, requires intensive, focused learning over extended periods of time to be developed.

7. Put Organizational Support Systems in Place

One of the core dilemmas facing individuals who return from these programs is a lack of reinforcement for the leadership behaviors they have learned. For example, it is rare that an organization's performance appraisals and rewards have been altered to reflect incentives for leadership behavior. In addition, the participants' superiors may not have attended the program and so are in no position to coach their subordinates on the new skills they have learned. Even the newly acquired program vocabularies may sound foreign to a participant's superior. Yet research (Huczynski and Lewis, 1980) shows that the attitudes and management styles of trainees' bosses are the most important factors in the transfer of management training back to the job. In fact, studies that specifically examine the factors that either inhibit or facilitate learning discovered that a trainee's application of new learnings on the job was largely dependent on his or her superior's support. In significant part, this is due to the boss being the principal source of a subordinate's rewards. Through praise, promotions, pay, and challenging assignments, the supervisor can reinforce the use of new skills or similarly discourage them. Simple encouragement itself can have a significant influence. In one recent study (Facteau and others, 1995), it was discovered that managers who perceive a greater measure of support from their immediate bosses report a higher degree of motivation to both attend and learn from training. Similarly, a boss may choose to ignore or even punish the leadership initiatives of their subordinates, which in turn will stunt their development.

The supervisorial behavior required to support a subordinate's development following training can take many forms (Baldwin and Ford, 1988): encouragement, goal-setting activities, modeling, and reinforcement. For example, supervisors can encourage subordinates to attend a leadership development program in the first place. (They discourage attendance by showing disinterest or by not providing time off for education.)

To further motivate learning, bosses can discuss program learnings and benefits both beforehand and afterward and set action goals for the individual to learn and implement specific behaviors or actions. The boss's own role modeling also influences subordinate behavior (Sims and Manz, 1982). For example, staff will imitate their supervisors in order to obtain rewards. In the ideal case, supervisors would model behavior that is congruent with the training objectives and what is being taught. Finally, supervisors can support new behaviors through rewards and by providing opportunities to practice new skills. For example, they may place subordinates on special projects or provide them with new responsibilities that require leadership to succeed. The greater the number of opportunities that trainees have to practice and experiment with their new skills, the higher the probability that the skills will be developed and behavior change will occur (Noe, 1986). As such, work assignments following training experiences can reinforce and deepen learnings. Yet rarely is such a connection made.

Common Shortcomings of Individual Development Programs

If an organization seriously wishes to expand its cadre of leaders, these programs are a relatively slow path to achieving such an outcome. If they rely on external programs, opportunities are usually more limited in terms of linking learning directly back to one's organization. In addition, there may be few or no opportunities in external programs for an organization to capitalize on the educational experience as a window to socialize its own values and visions of the future. Similarly, skills-based programs may focus so much on one's personal development that they overlook opportunities to instill company philosophies or to tie leadership to new company strategies or implementation challenges. These are but a few of the common shortcomings we discovered in programs focused on individual development. Following are the most typical pitfalls we discovered.

1. Failure to Build a Critical Mass

One of the principal drawbacks of individual development programs is that they are not always geared to cohorts of individuals from a single workplace—especially programs offered on the outside such as at universities. As a result, participants may be among a handful of individuals from their own organizations who attend the leadership program. Upon their return to the office, they discover that their learnings and new vocabulary are little appreciated or understood by others. This creates an enormous hurdle for the application of learnings. The dilemma is tied to the fact that work is essentially a collaborative experience. As Brown and Duguid (1991) have shown, an individual's learnings at work are inseparable from the collective learning of their work group. Learners, in essence, apply and construct their understandings not only from formal educational experiences but from the world in which they work and from their relationships with others at work. What gives new learnings the potential for taking hold is that one's workgroup also endorses, promotes, and reinforces them. Without that social support and pressure, new ideas and behaviors may receive neither sufficient reinforcement nor rewards to survive for long.

Moreover, an integral part of a workplace learning community is a shared language and a set of stories about what is valued (Brown and Duguid, 1991). This is influenced by the fact that one of the principal means we have to convey learnings is through our words and stories about experiences and approaches. Similarly, a central aim of educational programs on leadership is to sensitize participants to a set of behaviors and values that are also conveyed through a special vocabulary and through stories. Here, however, we find a dilemma. If only a single individual or a handful of individuals attend a program, there may not be a sufficient critical mass returning to the workplace to propagate learnings. With no experience with course lessons, coworkers have little comprehension nor appreciation for the knowledge and language that program participants might share with them. As a result, the normally powerful influence of the workplace community is negated in its role to both spread and reinforce an individual's learnings.

2. Shortcomings of Competency-Based Leadership Models

Competency models have become enormously popular in leadership training. Most training programs today employ these models, and increasingly these attributes show up in performance appraisals. The term "competency" itself gained popularity after the publication of Richard Boyatzis's 1982 book *The Competent Manager*. In it, Boyatzis defined a competency as "an underlying characteristic of a person—a motive, trait, skill, aspect of one's self-image or social role, or a body of knowledge which he or she uses." Within the leadership field, however, competencies typically refer to behavioral dimensions of leaders. Competency models as such provide a catalogue of the leadership traits desired by the organization in its managers. These traits in turn become key attributes to be acquired.

As Hollenbeck and McCall (1999) point out, what constitutes a "leadership competency" has evolved tremendously over the last two decades. Drawing on assessment research on managers at AT&T, they cite a prominent reference, *Formative Years in Business* (1974). It identified only one leadership competency, human relations skills—"How effectively can this man lead a group to accomplish a task without arousing hostility?" (Hollenbeck and McCall, 1999, p. 16). By 1982, the assessment definition for leadership had become "To what extent can this individual get people to perform a task effectively?" (p. 476). By the 1990s, leadership competencies at AT&T numbered eight (Schaffer, 1994): (1) learns continuously, (2) thinks strategically, (3) inspires a shared purpose, (4) creates a climate for success, (5) seizes opportunities, (6) transforms strategies into results, (7) builds partnerships, and (8) leverages disagreements. By 1997, these would expand to the eleven shown in Exhibit 2.4. AT&T would also begin to recognize that competencies varied to a degree by level of management—higher levels requiring more than junior levels.

Exhibit 2.4. AT&T Leadership Competencies

Competencies	Individual/Team Contributor	Manager/Team Leader	Executive
Establishes direction			x
Thinks strategically			x
Empowers others		x	x
Builds alignment		x	x
Enables individual/ team effectiveness	x	x	x
Communicates openly	x	x	x
Plans proactively	x	x	x
Implements with excellence	x	x	x
Self-awareness	x	x	x
Openness to learning	x	x	x
Technical/ functional skills	x	x	x

Reprinted with permission.

This increasing sophistication about competencies is most likely the by-product of several trends occurring in the 1980s and 1990s. As noted in Chapter One, leadership theory itself has evolved in its complexity over the last decade. Today we think of leadership as encompassing far more behavioral dimensions than twenty years ago when leadership models often consisted of two roles—a task and a people-oriented role—or a set of decision-making steps ranging from autocratic to participative styles. Leadership models have also moved toward reframing the leader's principal role to that of change agent. So a greater number of today's competencies are concerned with implementing organizational change; the manager who has these competencies "has a vision of the future," "builds alignment," "thinks strategically," "plans proactively," and "implements with excellence." This latter trend reflects that competition has intensified globally and that corporations have become increasingly concerned about their need to adapt and reinvent themselves. In other words, the ability of their managers to lead change is today a competency of paramount importance.

Our own reactions to the rise of competency models in training and development are mixed. On the one hand, they bring certain advantages. First, they are often constructed around tangible dimensions—behaviors, outcomes, or activities—that can be visibly measured. Second, they send a clear message to an organization about the specific attributes considered valuable at this moment. If they are linked to rewards and performance measures, they can establish clear expectations. Third, they provide a framework or checklist for both individual managers and their organizations to benchmark themselves—in other words, to see which competencies are strong or weak within the individual and within the management ranks of the organization.

On the other hand, however, there are important drawbacks to competencies. First, there is a strong tendency to use them as universal criteria that all must somehow possess, such that a manager must be strategic, empowering, self-reflective, a fast learner, a developer of subordinates, an expert on marketplace trends, and the list goes on. We forget that many of these competencies are derived from ideal types of leadership—what the best-in-class leader would look like if this were a perfect world. It is doubtful that many real managers can possess in depth all or most ideal qualities. In essence, these models reinforce the notion of the perfect leader, and such people do not exist in reality. The average and even outstanding manager cannot help but fall short.

Second, when employing "universal" and "ideal" criteria, competency models often fail to recognize that leadership requirements vary by level and by situation. The leadership skills demanded at senior executive levels are vastly different from those at front-line levels. Different functions and operating units may demand different leadership styles given their unique requirements. For example, a more directive style may be necessary in an operating unit that has minute-to-minute delivery demands than in a strategic plan-ning unit where a consultative approach is often the norm. Yet many models do not provide for this level of differentiation.

Part of the problem may be related to where and how these models are actually sourced. Many are derived from academic mod-els that tend toward very general competencies such as possessing strategic vision or communicating goals clearly. They are a by-prod-uct of the type of research typically conducted across many differ-ent organizations through surveys. As such, these models rarely produce customized dimensions. Some consulting firms devise tai-lored lists for their clients, but the level of actual customization can vary widely depending on the provider. Similar competency lists now appear across many providers, raising doubt as to the true level of customization. For this very reason, companies would be well advised to carefully select among consulting firms.

There are other problems. Competency models tend to stabilize in the sense that, like a paradigm, they become well established. Many of the leadership competencies we see today have been in cir-culation for nearly a decade. Often competency models themselves are derived from research comparing high and low performers within an organization—the high performers being the benchmarks. Although today's high performers may tell us about today's essential skills, they may or may not tell us about what is needed in the future. In a rapidly changing business environment, these models may sim-ply reinforce behaviors that are soon to be outdated (Woodruffe, 1993b). Therefore organizations need to ask themselves whether their competency lists are still appropriate given changes in com-pany marketplaces and in the organization.

Finally, there are the issues of integration and ownership. Many organizations use these models in their training programs but in isolation from the actual reward and performance measurement systems of the firm. So while the competencies draw attention to behaviors such as "empowering others," a manager may in reality be rewarded solely on her performance outcomes, not on her actual behavior. For example, quarterly results rather than the level of team participation a manager has fostered may determine pay and bonuses. As long as the individual meets his or her budget or revenue goals, there may be no real penalty for demonstrating inappropriate authoritarian behavior. This dilemma is partly a problem of who owns and promotes the competency models. Typically, human resources departments are the sources or sponsors for the leadership competency models of a firm. Given their mandate for employment development, these human resources-generated competencies tend to reflect an underlying concern for the humane treatment of employees ("he/she is an empowering manager"; "he/she cultivates participative decision making") and for more reflective behavior on the part of a manager ("he/she is self-aware"). These are the advantages of human resources ownership. The trade-off, however, is that the development of the competencies resides outside the very functions that are being served.

From our own perspective, we feel there is a role for competencies in sensitizing an organization and its managers to behaviors that are critically important for its present and future. Competencies are also a simple format for sending a clear message about what is valued in a firm at the moment. Our concerns about competencies arise largely because they can be taken too seriously. Their most effective role is as a heuristic, a framework. We return to our earlier point: few if any managers can approach the ideal of perfect leadership. Moreover, most competency models fly in the face of another reality: they rarely acknowledge that competencies vary by level and function. These are important shortcomings. Finally, we believe that the most essential competencies must be embedded in an organization's reward and performance measurement systems if they are to have any long-term impact. The challenge then becomes one of recognizing their limitations and updating both the competencies and corresponding organizational measures as leadership needs shift.

3. Insufficient Time Spent on Developing Individual Skill Areas

One dilemma facing programs is that they attempt to cover too many dimensions of leadership and in turn do justice to only a few. In one of the companies we examined, an educational program focused on two areas of leadership competencies, interpersonal skills and strategic thinking. But, first of all, the majority of learning time focused on leadership. Only 25 percent of the workshop was devoted to learning about strategic thinking. Second, the rhetoric employed by the program designers emphasized the interpersonal aspect over the strategy aspect. For example, strategic exercises were labeled "leadership projects." Third, numerous participants already employed strategic thinking in their work environments and considered the information they received from the program to be old news. Fourth, for those participants whose actual job responsibilities did not require a great deal of strategic thinking, there was no substantive follow-up from the program; they had no opportunities to practice what they had learned. Finally, the approach employed to teach strategy-making skills was simply to bundle information about the strategic environment within which the company operated and to share that with participants. As one participant summarized, the outcome was therefore limited: "I certainly feel that the program assisted in developing strategic capability in terms of saying, 'Hey, these are what the issues are. . . . This is where we're going in terms of some of the change paradigms that we need to move forward in the future.' But I don't know whether or not it necessarily taught you how to think strategically." In other words, the program built *awareness* of strategic issues but did not require actual *application* of strategic thinking based on this awareness.

A preferable option would have been to run a separate program that addressed the "how-to" side of strategic thinking. We chose this example because one would assume that a week-long program focusing on essentially two dimensions of leadership would provide ample opportunities for learning. Yet like so many dimensions of leadership, these two are complex and require intensive learning experiences. Ultimately, it would have been best to design separate programs for each skill area.

4. Limited or No Program Follow-Up

One of the most common dilemmas facing programs of leadership development for individuals is a lack of follow-up. When the program ends, there are no additional experiences to reinforce learnings nor are there ongoing programs of feedback to allow participants to gauge their development efforts around specific leadership competencies.

Our case example, the National Australia Bank, experimented with a number of follow-up initiatives. Some had an impact, others did not. One of the principal outcomes of the program was the formation of an alumni network. The notion was that each year's alumni would have specific initiatives they would champion. For example, alumni of the 1995 program developed initiatives that supported participants to continue their own leadership development and that contributed to the long-term success of the National Bank. One, called "The Big 5 Issues," required project teams to meet every six months to develop a list of five major issues they saw as critical to the bank. These in turn were presented to the company's strategy group and to senior management. Another initiative involved establishing a committee of program graduates who reviewed the potential impact and acceptability of leadership projects prepared by course participants. A "Buddy System" was also developed in which graduates of the program volunteered to guide or mentor one or several incoming program participants. Finally, an annual meeting was proposed where graduates would be linked via a worldwide video conference.

According to the designers of the program, some of these initiatives—the Transformers Buddy System, Major Project Involvement, and the Annual Meeting—have been successfully implemented. A number of the team projects have led to initiatives within the company. The Strategic Project Assessment is still in the works. The Big 5 Issues has not come to fruition. Interviews with participants paint a slightly different picture. There is a range of responses in terms of individuals' involvement with these initiatives. For example, some people have been asked to work on significant company projects (such as through National's Change Center); others have not undertaken additional strategic projects outside their normal day-to-day activities. Similarly, the extent to which the Buddy System is working is highly dependent on the individuals involved; some take the role quite seriously, whereas others' interactions with their buddies appear to be less meaningful. It may be too early to gauge the success of these initiatives, but it appears that the enthusiasm and commitment for postprogram activities ranges widely among participants. Certainly, it can be argued that for any program of this kind there is often a tendency to drift away from follow-up because of the demands of participants' lives and jobs.

As a general rule, follow-up initiatives must be handled with care for several reasons. Often they represent the first set of tangible outcomes that emerge from a program and so have symbolic importance to the rest of the organization. For better or worse, they are the visible manifestations of the program's outcomes. This is especially true in the case of follow-up presentations to company executives for whom this may be their only direct experience of the program. Also, poor follow-through on initiatives may be interpreted by company management as a lack of commitment by participants, which in turn may portend trouble for the future of the program. Key decision makers might be disinclined to support a program if the initial group of participants shows apathy so early in the game. Furthermore, if the participants themselves perform poorly on follow-up initiatives, others in the organization may reach the conclusion that these people are poor leaders and that the training they received was wholly inadequate.

Many of the problems related to follow-up initiatives can be traced back to the issues of ownership, time, and rewards. For example, who claims responsibility for learning after a program is over? Who makes sure that learnings get extended throughout the organization? Often the burden of ownership falls on either the program designers or the participants. But in many cases these groups may not control needed resources or have the political clout necessary to make changes in the structures and systems of the organization. For these reasons, ownership often must reside with influential individuals at the senior operating levels—people who can provide the clout and resources. In addition, follow-up assignments are commonly done in one's spare time, beyond normal working hours. As a result, they rarely receive the time and dedication needed to succeed. Far better to build initiatives into the job requirements of individuals. Rewards may be limited or nonexistent for one's efforts related to a follow-up initiative. Ideally, formal rewards would be tied to initiatives to ensure that performance is not only recognized but, more importantly, that a motivational impetus is provided to get the task done and done well.

Organizations themselves need to accept greater responsibility for postprogram activities. In practical terms, this means establishing a set of expectations for the participants upon completion of the program as well as a system of tangible rewards. It means providing a method of monitoring participants' progress toward meeting prescribed goals. Currently these types of appraisals rarely occur. An unwillingness by certain participants to accept ownership for initiatives suggests that organizations need to more tightly control their selection process in the first place.

One increasingly popular solution to the follow-up dilemma is executive coaching. Though its use has been historically restricted to senior organizational ranks due to cost, we are seeing companies experiment with the idea of coaches "on call" for other levels of management. Today, it is most often employed as a follow-on to a 360-degree feedback experience (Hollenbeck and McCall, 1999).

In essence, coaches interpret the results of the feedback and then work with the executive or manager to create a personal developmental plan. Ideally, the coach offers a supportive relationship in which the manager can explore new behaviors and attitudes while working through their resistance to personal change (Kilburg, 1996). Coaches also provide a structured means of reflection for the manager on his or her own behavior and performance.

Two applications of how coaching is commonly used can be found at Avery Dennison and Texas Commerce Bank. At Avery Dennison, eight external coaches were offered to senior executives to provide twelve hours of coaching based on 360-degree feedback evaluations (Hall and Otazo, 1995). The first session was devoted to exploring simply the feedback itself. Follow-up meetings then focused on planning and implementing developmental actions based on the feedback. After the twelve hours of coaching, executives could continue at their discretion and from their own budgets. At Texas Commerce Bank (Hollenbeck and McCall, 1999), each of the company's top twenty-five executives was assigned one of five external coaches for six individual sessions over a six-month period.

Coaching is not for everyone. Moreover, there is a matchmaking process involving the personal chemistry between coach and client that can profoundly shape the effectiveness of interventions. For this reason, it is often advisable that managers have some measure of freedom to choose a coach with whom they feel they can work effectively.

We have little research on coaching effectiveness to go on. Two studies suggest favorable results on the whole. Specifically, Edelstein and Armstrong (1993) surveyed participants in a coaching-based executive program and found that participants rated the experience valuable (3.95 out of 5) and described making consistent changes (4.7 out of 5). Similarly, Hall and Otazo (1995) in a survey of executives reported that the most frequent response was 4 (Very Satisfactory) on a 5-point scale.

But coaching is not always the ideal solution. For example, research (Mohr, 1995) suggests that clients with any of the following characteristics are not likely to experience successful outcomes from coaching: major character or severe interpersonal problems, a lack of motivation, unrealistic expectations of the coach or coaching process, or a lack of follow-through on homework and suggestions. Similarly, problems can arise with coaches themselves. For example, the following characteristics in coaches can create problems: insufficient empathy for the client, lack of expertise in the client's problems, major or prolonged disagreements with the client about the process, or a failure to accurately estimate the severity of the client's problems.

Given the costs of executive coaching, formal mentoring programs may be a more cost-effective option for many organizations, especially when coaching programs target middle- and junior-level managers. The effectiveness of formal mentoring programs has a mixed history, but some recent innovations hold potential. As proposed by Kaye and Jacobson (1996), one of the more interesting mentoring approaches is the "learning group." Specifically, a formal mentor is paired with a group of four to six high-performing managers, and members learn from the mentor as well as from one another. A learning group typically meets with its mentor once a month for several hours. The agenda is open-ended with a general focus on leadership challenges. The group continually links its dialogues to the members' experiments and learnings on the job concerning leadership. In addition, group members take on specific developmental projects or assignments that help them learn more about leadership at work and report on their progress.

To work effectively, the mentors themselves must be carefully selected for their orientation toward individual development. In Kaye and Jacobson's model, this individual is ideally a senior manager who has shown a history of personal learning, an interest in others' learning, and an orientation toward the future of the organization. The mentor's experience base should be broad and deep, encompassing not only a range of different assignments but also different areas of the company. Kaye and Jacobson (1996) also feel that to be effective mentors must possess the following:

- Success in their field

- A wide network of relationships

- Substantial position power

- A history of developing subordinates

- Control over substantial resources

- Broad organizational knowledge

- Success in managing teams

In addition to these background characteristics, the authors also identified several important style dimensions. These include a facility for storytelling, emotional openness, an incisive mind, an ability to help a group discern the essence of any issue, and a Socratic teaching approach.

5. Few or No Links to Job Assignments

Work on the job is essentially the best ongoing laboratory for managers to learn about leadership. As McCall (1998) has argued, the principal classroom for leadership for managers is "on-line experience." Despite this, little or no links are made between educational experiences for managers and their work assignments. There are a few exceptions. General Electric positions its training programs around key developmental transitions in a manager's career. The company has identified transition points where there are changes in two dimensions of a manager's responsibilities as a leader: scale and complexity. Scale has to do with the number of individuals they must lead, as when the salesperson becomes sales manager and must now lead several individuals. Similarly, a senior manager who runs a plant of eight hundred experiences a scale change when she is promoted to division manager in charge of ten thousand. Complexity has to do with the job itself. Managing the inventory requirements of a manufacturing plant is a less complex task than managing all plant operations. As managers are promoted, they face leaps both in scale and complexity. At General Electric, therefore, leadership training is targeted at these transition points so that managers can synthesize and learn from experiences at the previous level and simultaneously learn about upcoming leadership demands at the new level.

But the General Electric approach is relatively rare in the corporate world. More commonly, there are no links at all. It is ironic, because we know a fair amount about the impact of specific job experiences on leadership development (McCall, Lombardo, and Morrison, 1988; McCauley, 1986) and, in theory, could tailor assignments to take advantage of education. For example, we know that job experiences containing significant challenges, often adverse ones, are fertile ground for leadership development. As McCall points out, those with the greatest impact have at their core certain potent characteristics such as "managing difficult relationships with superiors or key staff members, playing for high stakes, facing extremely harsh business situations, struggling with complexity of scope and scale, having the wrong background or lacking a needed skill or credential, and having to make a sudden, stark transition" (1998, p. 64). In analyzing more precisely the types of workplace experiences conducive to development, McCall identified a number of specific situations: start-ups, turnarounds, jobs with significant changes in scope of responsibility, special projects and task-force assignments, staff positions, international assignments, and placement with both effective and flawed bosses. In essence, all of these situations demand new learnings and often the demonstration of leadership ability.

These situations generally stimulate individuals to perform well (McCauley, 1986), and they demand high amounts of learning. In addition, challenging jobs often center around important issues facing an organization, so by their nature these jobs have high visibility. Success in such situations can then easily lead to more challenging assignments that perpetuate learning opportunities.

Despite knowledge about the importance of job assignments in shaping leadership ability, the majority of organizations still fail to capitalize on it (Hollenbeck and McCall, 1999). There are several deep-rooted reasons. A principal one is the conflict between maximum development and maximum performance (Yukl, 1994). The manager who has mastered the skills necessary for a particular assignment is most likely to get that particular assignment. As well, there are other organizational criteria such as grade levels, succession plans, and compensation that determine who is assigned to a position. But if maximum development were to guide selection, a manager who had limited experience and needed to acquire new learnings would be chosen instead.

As Hollenbeck and McCall note, even organizations that consciously place their high potentials into challenging assignments may fail to take full advantage of on-the-job learning. For example, to increase the probability of real learning there should be reflection opportunities for managers to assess what they have learned and then support by follow-on coaching and continual performance feedback. Instead the premium is too often placed on results rather than the acquisition of leadership ability. As a result, an individual can have success on the job but may not fully comprehend what contributed to his success—he failed to learn deeply.

In the ideal case, training programs would be used in conjunction with on-the-job experiences as transition and preparation devices or as reflective learning windows. For example, immediately following a program participants would be given assignments that build on course learnings by requiring the demonstration of leadership ability. Similarly, courses could be designed for individuals who are in the midst of a challenging leadership assignment. In that case, the program becomes a formal means of reflecting on learnings to date and an opportunity for assessment of one's leadership approach over the upcoming months. Sadly, most organizations fail to take advantage of such opportunities and create few or no links between a program and one's work assignments. This translates into fewer opportunities for a manager to apply course learnings and a greater probability that learnings will be lost.

In conclusion, we see that leadership development programs geared toward the individual hold the promise of helping participants learn more about their leadership abilities as well as fostering an understanding of the essential basics of effective leadership. In the best of cases, these experiences also provide a motivational stimulus for managers to seek out developmental opportunities that will deepen their skill set. They may also encourage a greater reflective capacity—helping managers to be more alert to their strengths and weaknesses as leaders and the implications of these. But individualized approaches have important shortcomings, particularly if an organization is trying to grow its cadre of leaders internally, promulgate new visions, or socialize important cultural values and mind-sets. In Chapter Four, we look at how these shortcomings can be tackled by other program designs.

3

How National Australia Bank Develops Leaders

National Australia Bank, like so many companies in the 1990s, underwent significant changes in its external and internal environments. This led the bank to feel that the depth of its leadership capabilities was limited. The bank's CEO Donald Argus, in conjunction with its human resources department, decided that leadership development should receive high priority. In 1994 a process was initiated to develop an educational program.

The program design took shape during a retreat involving twenty high-potential managers from across the company who met with the human resources manager charged with the program's development, Peter McKinnon. It was decided that the program should focus principally on three key dimensions of leadership: contact, clarity, and impact. Contact refers to competencies that involve a leader's ability to be in touch with themselves, their businesses, and their team. Clarity has to do with the idea that leaders must be pathfinders who set new directions for their organizations and teams; they need to provide clarity about future goals and directions for their organization. Impact refers to whether the actions and ideas of the leader influence others. Under these three categories came ten core leadership behaviors and characteristics (see Exhibit 3.1). The program's principal aim was to build an awareness of these competencies and to help participants develop them. The emphasis, then, was primarily on helping individuals develop themselves as leaders.

Exhibit 3.1. National Australia Bank Leadership Competencies

1. *Impact*
   Flexible and adaptable
   Committed to making a difference
   Communicates with impact
   A clear service orientation

2. *Clarity*
   Intellectually robust
   Constantly extends business knowledge
   Recognizes the imperative for change
   and creates new directions

3. *Contact*
   Strong self-regard
   Acts with integrity
   Brings out the best in people

Reprinted with permission.

Working with Merrin Butler, also from human resources, McKinnon began to craft the mechanics of the program. The program would serve certain organizational ends, but it was decided that the principal focus should be on the individual. As such, a great deal of program time was devoted to individual reflection and experiential learning on a personal level. Learning would be built around six modules: (1) a series of three self-directed learning exercises, (2) a one-day introductory seminar, (3) a six-day residential workshop, (4) a team-based learning project focused on understanding competitive issues facing the bank, (5) a concluding seminar, and (6) several follow-up initiatives in the form of an alumni network, executive feedback on the projects, and participant self-evaluations on behavior shifts over time.

Three to four weeks before the program began, participants received an assignment to be conducted on their own. This was the first self-directed learning module. As background material, they were given an overview of the program, readings on leadership, a video on leadership, and the bank's global strategic agenda. After reviewing these, they were asked to respond to a series of written questions about leadership as well as to identify inconsistencies between the ideas put forth by the material and the reality of their work environments. Typical questions had them reflect on their leadership style, their personal developmental challenges, and the leadership challenges presented by the bank's global strategic agenda. Participants also had to prepare a statement describing their notions of leadership.

This prework served several purposes. First, the designers wanted to challenge participants' conceptions of a learning environment; most thought of learning as occurring in a classroom. This experience would be different, drawing instead on the learner's reflections outside of class. Second, they wanted participants to begin challenging their assumptions about the concept of leadership before they arrived. As Butler explained, "We knew that most people here think of leadership as a 'storm-the-hill' activity—led from the front. We wanted them to think much more about it as a relationship between people and why leadership is so important to the National at this point in time." So questions were crafted to stimulate thinking in these areas.

Following this prework experience came a one-day introductory seminar by teleconference. Like the prework, the introduction was purposely decoupled from the workshop. Explained Butler, "The idea was to give people time to process their ideas about leadership and to start becoming more conscious of it within their workplace, so that by the time they arrived at the workshop they would have formed some initial ideas. They would also have more time to reflect on their own leadership style and the challenges they personally faced. It created a time to absorb and begin to apply what they saw around themselves." The seminar included sessions on the objectives of the program, overviews of the various modules, a learning styles exercise, and a team-building exercise. The objective was to get the participants thinking more deeply about leadership and themselves. At the end of this day-long session, participants were given a 360-degree leadership style feedback survey (based on the ten leadership competencies in Exhibit 3.1) for distribution back at their offices. Between the one-day session and the upcoming workshop, participants were to conduct a self-evaluation in addition to having their boss, two subordinates, and two peers fill out evaluations of their leadership style. This information would be fed back during the upcoming six-day workshop. In addition, participants were also given a team questionnaire that highlighted the team roles individuals preferred to play. This was a self-assessment questionnaire chosen by the course designers because a portion of the workshop would focus on learning about team dynamics.

Sometime shortly after the one-day orientation seminar, participants received a second self-directed learning exercise. This contained articles and questionnaires on teamwork. Participants were asked to consider the success factors for high-performing teams. Shortly afterward, they joined the six-day residential workshop.

The workshop was built around four learning goals: strategic issues facing the bank, leadership competencies, interpersonal relations, and teamwork. Of these, the participants' leadership styles and teamwork received the greatest attention. In this regard, the bank's program most closely resembles programs geared toward individual development, despite certain elements related to socializing certain values and worldviews and action components related to the organization's future challenges. The focus was more on helping the individual manager become a better leader. In terms of pedagogy, classroom lectures were blended with experiential exercises. Learning journals were also employed to create a vehicle for disciplined reflection on workshop learnings.

The first day and a half of the six-day workshop focused on the bank's external environment—competitive and marketplace issues. Organizational change, the bank's global strategy, competition, and specific industry shifts caused by electronic banking were all covered. During this module, participants were also introduced to a transnational team project that would involve an analysis of competitive issues facing the bank and a presentation to senior management after the residential program.

On the second day, the program shifted to the participants' personal leadership styles. They received the results of the 360-degree feedback on their leadership style and of the bank's surveys on employee opinions and company culture. In addition, they were provided an overview of the basic dimensions of effective leadership behavior, the core idea being that effective leaders create quantum change through their "circle of influence." On the third day, they were introduced to the interpersonal dynamics of leadership through an emotionally challenging set of ideas about the hidden assumptions and values that shape an individual's behavior toward leading others. The emphasis was on uncovering sources of ineffective command-and-control behaviors.

Days four and five moved the emphasis to teamwork and collaboration. Participants learned the basics of team dynamics. This was followed by education on the challenges facing team behavior in a transnational setting. A set of experiential exercises was introduced to answer certain fundamental questions: How does my behavior shape how I influence others in teams? What patterns of my behavior come out under pressure? Are these valuable or a hindrance?

The final day was devoted to the teams reporting on their competitive analysis projects. This was followed by an exercise where individuals brainstormed a list of actions they would begin to take upon return to their offices to apply the leadership lessons they had learned. The highlight of this closing day was an experiential exercise called "traffic jam" that illustrated the power of teamwork in solving problems quickly.

Following the workshop, a one-day concluding seminar was hosted in several locations around the world. During the day, a two-hour video conference was held between all locations so that all one hundred participants could be in touch with one another. The CEO was present to show his support. The seminar served two purposes. First, it was a chance for teams to reflect and share their experiences working together transnationally. Second, it offered a forum to identify future steps for everyone now that the formal program was ending.

National Australia Bank exemplifies a well-designed individual development program. First of all, it employs a single model of leadership. Program content is reinforced with structured 360-degree feedback to participants on the exact competencies associated with the leadership model of the course. Along with the structured feedback are prework, journals, and reflective exercises that encourage individuals to more deeply reflect on themselves as leaders in both workplace and seminar settings. A blend of teaching methods are employed in the design so that there is variety as well as the heightened probability that differences in learning styles will be tapped. Certain of the learning experiences themselves mirror the very dimensions that are being taught. For example, teamwork and cross-cultural dynamics are learned not only through lectures but through the transnational team-based projects and the participant mix. In addition, the learning experience is staggered over several periods rather than a single workshop. This gives participants more time to reflect and incorporate learnings back on the job. Finally, there is an attempt to incorporate follow-up mechanisms and initiatives after the program ends, though this proved to be, at times, challenging to implement successfully.

4

Socializing Company Vision and Values

One of the most important functions of a leader is defining the key assumptions and values that will guide the decisions and actions of organizational members. Leaders inculcate these assumptions by building a shared understanding of what the organization is about and how it should operate. We often refer to this understanding as the organization's culture. Leaders are able to play this special role in building and maintaining the culture of an organization because people pay particular attention to what their bosses say and do. Indeed, leaders not only determine what it takes to get ahead in an organization but also represent what is valued and expected. As a result, most people follow the example of their leaders—adopting their values and imitating their management styles. Doing so increases the probability that they too will be effective and successful.

Because of a leader's influence over an organization's culture and because leaders must send consistent messages to move their organizations in a unified direction, it is important that the next generation of leaders accurately understand and embody the vision and values they are expected to perpetuate. Recognizing this, many leadership development programs today are focusing on socializing these crucial cultural elements. They do so with two broad objectives in mind: to indoctrinate new leaders to the company's core vision and the values formed throughout its history, and to facilitate career transitions by involving new leaders in a dialogue about their upcoming roles and responsibilities. Programs of this type aim to build a shared interpretation of the organization's key objectives and a commitment to the values and assumptions that underlie its culture. As such, they focus less on developing individual skills and talents and more on imparting a collective ethos and leadership philosophy that is acted upon as much as it is acknowledged.

One corporate leader who has made extensive use of education as a vehicle to socialize his company's vision is Jack Welch, CEO of General Electric. In his reinvention of that company, Welch relied heavily on the GE corporate university called Crotonville (named after its location at Croton-on-Hudson, New York) to disseminate key values and worldviews. As Noel Tichy, a University of Michigan business professor and former director of Crotonville, explains:

> Above all, he [Welch] wanted Crotonville to provide a wide-open channel of communication between GE's top management and the more junior employees taking courses. . . . Welch also expected Crotonville to indoctrinate managers in GE's new values, from constructive conflict to integrity to "ownership." So Crotonville had to become deliberately evangelical, its every graduate capable of spreading the word to the larger organization. . . . [Welch said,] "I want Crotonville to be part of the glue that holds GE together." [Tichy and Sherman, 1993, pp. 130–131]

For Welch, Crotonville was the ideal vehicle at the corporate level; it could pull individuals from the many diverse operating units and provide them with a common experience.

Leadership development programs can facilitate and expedite this socialization process in a number of ways. First, they bring attention to the importance of corporate values. They also make those values explicit. Next, they provide conceptual models that guide decision making consistent with those values. The very act of structuring a leadership development program to teach a set of guiding principles not only underscores the importance of key principles but also forces existing leaders to define and articulate those principles more clearly. In addition, the better programs address the issue of *competing* values. They acknowledge apparent contradictions in values, strategies, and objectives and resolve them by specifying priorities. Last, and most important, effective programs structure interaction among new and existing leaders. They encourage collective dialogues about what the stated values mean, and they also educate incoming leaders about their new roles and expectations around performance. By creating an occasion for discussion and an opportunity to reflect and grapple collectively, socialization programs facilitate a shared understanding of where the organization is going and the role that each leader must play in getting it there.

In this chapter we illustrate how these programs socialize the important values and behaviors connected with leadership on multiple levels. As an example we use the United States Army. We then explore in greater depth why development programs that focus on socialization are so important and how they can enhance an organization's overall leadership capabilities. We describe the mechanics by which these programs impart a common understanding of corporate values and a collective responsibility for safeguarding those values in ongoing operations. From there, we move to a discussion of when and where socialization programs can provide the most benefit and identify a variety of program designs. Because programs are typically structured to enhance the socialization of leaders at key transition points, we examine programs intended for leaders at multiple levels. At the close of this chapter, we explore two programs in depth: one for front-line managers at Federal Express and the other for senior managers at PepsiCo.

One Model: The United States Army

If someone were asked to list five organizations best known for their leadership development capabilities as defined by their ability to develop high-caliber leaders consistently over time, the U.S. Army would probably be mentioned. Though exact estimates of its investment in leadership training are difficult to come by, the U.S. military unquestionably devotes more resources and research to instilling a leadership ethos than any other organization in the world. In 1996 the Army invested $309.7 million in professional development education alone (U.S. Department of Defense, 1996).

Considering only formal training programs that offer leadership development to middle- and senior-level managers through intermediate and senior service schools and enlisted leadership training courses, the Army conducted 1,253 student years of training in 1996. Even this figure underestimates the Army's actual investment in leadership development because it excludes on-the-job or unit-provided training (U.S. Department of Defense, 1996).

One notable feature of the Army's leader development process is the extent to which it embeds leadership ethos and development within the Army culture. How many organizations have a formal leadership doctrine that defines and describes the corporate leadership process and all that it entails? The Army does, and it also has a Center for Army Leadership that conducts ongoing research on leadership issues and an Army Leader Development Support System that monitors and accommodates changes in Army leader development needs. In addition, a Leader Development Office develops, evaluates, and coordinates leadership training programs across all Army career tracks, and a Leader Development Decision Network comprised of senior ranking officials ensures that the Army's approaches to leadership change in sync with larger social, political, and technical environments (U.S. Department of the Army, 1994).

Even more important than the breadth of the Army's leadership structure is the depth with which it penetrates individual thinking and action. The Army strongly emphasizes its leadership ethos in almost every development program and operational assignment that leaders take part in. Yet more important than its formal doctrine, offices, and networks are the informal mentoring, role modeling, and on-the-job training experiences that instill the leadership ethos in the culture and daily activities of Army life. Through an extensive socialization process, developing leaders learn and internalize the Army's leadership creed through years of direct interaction with more experienced leaders. This interaction not only demonstrates consistency in values across levels of hierarchy and occupational specialties but also demonstrates a shared commitment to teaching and developing subordinates. Indeed, the training and professional development of officers is considered one of the most important responsibilities of all Army leaders (U.S. Army, 1997, nondraft version).

Through an integrated process of formal classroom instruction, on-the-job training, informal mentoring, role modeling, and self-development, the Army's leadership development system clarifies and reinforces the Army's vision and values along with the duties and expectations associated with carrying them out at each level of management. The Army maintains that through this integrated system it builds a common understanding of the character, attributes, and skills that its leaders are expected to possess and a shared dedication to the values and ethics that drive its culture and operations.

The Importance of Socializing the Next Generation of Leaders

Socializing any workforce—let alone one of the largest in the world such as the Army's—is a significant challenge. But it is a challenge all organizations must meet if they hope to unleash their potential in full pursuit of corporate objectives. A shared understanding of what the organization is about and where it is going is especially important in a world marked by rapid change and rising competition. Companies such as Intel, Nordstrom, Federal Express, and others have discovered that effective socialization establishes a base of attitudes, habits, and values that foster the cooperation, integrity, and communication necessary for rapid innovation and adaptation (Pascale, 1985). These companies have learned that socialization to a culture that emphasizes trust, self-discipline, and support can facilitate the commitment, collaborative work ethic, and initiative that lies at the heart of organizational learning and renewal (Bartlett and Ghoshal, 1995).

Because socialization processes are so important, there has been a great deal of research on the topic. Some of the best work has been done by John VanMaanen and Edgar Schein (1979) at MIT. They argue that socialization processes are critical to an organization's very survival. In the socialization process, leaders play a dual role. On one hand they influence the socialization of all those below them, but on the other hand they too must be socialized to the organization's vision and to their role in bringing the vision to fruition. For several reasons, leaders, like other organizational participants, require socialization. First and foremost, it facilitates the transmission of information and values that leaders need to operate within the organization's culture: long-standing rules of thumb; special language; unwritten norms; standards of relevance about what is important in accomplishing the firm's work; customs and expectations about how to interact with colleagues, superiors, subordinates, and outsiders; and general knowledge about what is rewarded by the firm. Most of these come from long experience that teaches how organizations and their members can succeed.

Leaders need to share a common understanding of this information, not only to collaborate effectively with their colleagues and subordinates but also to ensure that those with different interests and backgrounds interpret the firm's vision in the same way. As almost anyone who has studied or participated in efforts to execute a strategic vision can attest, subtle differences in interpretation can slow things down or mix things up considerably. Indeed, these differences often become apparent only after the fact—after significant time and resources have been spent developing what ultimately turn out to be competing implementation schemes. In the process, resources are wasted, political battles ensue, and inconsistent messages are sent throughout the corporation. As a result, strategies and support systems appear misaligned and the firm's vision becomes increasingly murky or poorly implemented. In this and the following chapter we discuss how effective leadership programs seek to indoctrinate their leaders against interpretive quagmires by structuring occasions for them to clearly spell out their visions and values and, in turn, to air and resolve interpretive differences before problems arise.

Another and related reason that socialization processes are so important is that they ensure that newly appointed leaders do not disrupt ongoing strategies or upset existing social relations. The challenge is that new leaders have different backgrounds, varying preconceptions about what they are expected to do, and, sometimes, values at odds with those of existing leadership. To avoid rehashing past debates, new leaders must be educated about the history and rationale behind the organization's current values and strategies. According to VanMaanen and Schein (1979, p. 211), "Put bluntly, new members must be taught to see the organizational world as do their more experienced colleagues if the traditions of the organization are to survive."

In many cases, leaders promoted from within have already formed a good understanding of many of these unwritten traditions. However, in many organizations—especially large and diversified conglomerates—cultures vary considerably from business unit to business unit and from function to function. As a result, newly appointed corporate leaders must be socialized to the broader needs of the organization and to the cultural expectations of senior management. They must learn the assumptions and expectations underlying their new roles and responsibilities. They must adopt a higher-level, more corporate-wide perspective on organizational issues and a better understanding of the broad organizational vision held by existing corporate leaders.

This presumes, of course, that the vision and strategies held by current leaders adequately address the demands of the organization's external world. But an ever-present concern is that socialization processes can lead to corporate inbreeding—a myopic perpetuation of the status quo that some leadership experts call the "General Motors syndrome." This is especially true if company insiders are the principal instructors. Because the careers of many executives were part of an earlier period in the company's history, they may teach outdated worldviews. An example is IBM in the late 1980s. The careers of the senior team members had been built around an era of mainframe computers; as a result, they failed to fully comprehend the growing importance of personal computers and software.

Firms with effective socialization processes, however, socialize leaders not only to the firm's vision and internal values but to the importance of external focus and adaptation. In a recent autobiography, Andy Grove, chairman of Intel, opens his book with this very value (1996, pp. 3–4):

> I believe in the value of paranoia. Business success contains the seeds of its own destruction. The more successful you are, the more people want a chunk of your business and then another chunk and then another until there is nothing left. . . . I worry about products getting screwed up. . . . I worry about factories not performing well. . . . I worry about hiring the right people. . . . But these worries pale in comparison to how I feel about what I call strategic inflection points. . . . For now, let me just say that a strategic inflection point is a time in the life of a business when its fundamentals are about to change. . . . They are full scale changes in the way business is conducted, so that simply adopting new technology or fighting the competition the way you used to may be insufficient. . . . A strategic inflection can be deadly when unattended to.

What firms like Intel and others have learned is that leaders must share a strong commitment to monitoring changes in the outside environment and to questioning and challenging internal strategies in light of those changes. These values become part of the socialization process, and they ensure continual learning.

In addition, socialization processes benefit the organization by reducing some of the anxiety and confusion that new leaders experience as they move into greater roles of responsibility. When entering any unfamiliar situation, individuals assuming a new role—particularly one that entails more responsibility and accountability—are likely to experience anxiety. Socialization processes provide structure and guidance to a seemingly new and sometimes overwhelming world. By bringing perspective and ways to order and make sense of the world, socialization processes can help incoming leaders fit more naturally into the existing leadership structure and to act in accordance with others' expectations.

Finally, socialization programs provide opportunities for the organization to assess its talent pool. This is especially true when programs involve smaller groups of high-level managers who interact with executive-level instructors. For example, in PepsiCo's "Building the Business" program, CEO Roger Enrico has taught over one hundred senior managers. They, plus senior managers to whom he has been exposed, have provided a special pool of talent for his change efforts at the company. In essence, the course provided him with an opportunity to know in detail the talent levels of individual managers. As a result, Enrico knew who to put in his top positions.

Formalizing the Socialization Process Through Leadership Development

In general, leaders work to achieve two basic objectives: to come up with the strategies or solutions needed to overcome organizational challenges and to implement those solutions efficiently and effectively. Socialization processes represent a powerful mechanism for advancing both of these objectives.

By facilitating common interpretations and expectations around goals, they enable organizational leaders to communicate and collaborate better, examine organizational problems from a broader perspective and with more information, and therefore formulate more informed solutions. To improve implementation efforts, organizational leaders can systematically pay attention to important initiatives, measure and control outcomes associated with desired strategies, provide rewards and recognition to those who accomplish strategic goals, and role-model behavior consistent with chosen solutions. Each of these tactics represents an informal socialization mechanism that communicates the corporate vision throughout the organization and reinforces actions consistent with it. Moreover, each provides information about what is valued and expected in the organization and what is not.

Indeed, most leaders already use a variety of informal socialization tactics to communicate their vision and values as well as reinforce desired behavior. For example, they may state certain values in meetings and highlight them in company memos and e-mails. Their choice of daily activities such as spending time with customers may reflect the values they wish others to endorse. These informal processes, however, tend to be imperfect mechanisms for socializing leaders—especially in times of change. They tend to be slow and inefficient. They often lag changes in strategic direction and provide leaders with few opportunities to ensure that their vision and strategies have been interpreted correctly. Moreover, informal tactics can do little to improve strategies that are vague or inadequate to begin with. If leaders have varying interpretations of the corporate vision, or organizational structures and support systems fail to align with the firm's stated direction, informal tactics will simply reinforce the existing confusion. As a result, many organizations have begun to formalize their socialization efforts using their leadership development programs. By structuring collective dialogues and facilitating communication among corporate leaders, these programs improve both individual transitions and organizational change. They help individual leaders adapt to new role demands, and they help the organization as a whole to shift and adapt to new strategic challenges. In our examination of the more exemplary leadership development programs, we discovered that programs taking a socialization approach tend to possess a number of common design elements. In the following section, we discuss features of some of the more effective programs and explain how these features socialize new leaders to their new roles, remind current leaders of existing commitments, and strengthen the ties and alignment of all leaders to the firm's values and strategic vision.

Design Features of Effective Programs

In our research, we found that certain design features enhance the overall effectiveness of socialization programs. Here we describe these features and their contribution to the socialization process in detail.

1. Careful Selection of Program Participants

We introduced the importance of selection in the previous chapter, but leadership programs aimed at socialization must pay particular attention to their selection of program participants. Many programs seek to provide leadership training only to those individuals who have demonstrated significant leadership potential through their past performance and their embodiment of values and styles consistent with the existing leadership ethos. There are several reasons why firms are highly selective in choosing candidates for leadership development. First, high standards and rigorous selection processes increase the likelihood that program participants will be similar in important ways. Selectivity increases the probability that participants will hold values similar to the stated values of the corporation, to the values of the existing leadership, and to the values of other participants. Such consistency serves to strengthen communication and inquiry both within the learning environment and later when the candidate returns to the job. Thus it facilitates the transfer of important cultural information and strengthens cohesion in pursuing corporate goals.

Second, selecting only those individuals who consistently demonstrate certain traits and values symbolizes that such characteristics are important to the organization, and that they will be rewarded. This encourages others to develop similar capabilities, thereby embedding these desired values and behavior more deeply in the culture. Third, by making selection criteria clear the organization provides important information to potential leaders about the type of work they will perform should they be selected. Realistic job previews improve the screening process by enabling individuals who might not like the responsibilities of leadership to self-select out of the development program before resources are invested. This leads us to the fourth benefit of careful selection: the efficient investment of limited training dollars. Leadership development is an expensive endeavor. Recent estimates suggest that the cost of developing a one-week in-company program ranges from $75,000 to $242,000 and that its delivery costs between $20,000 and $100,000 (Fulmer and Vicere, 1997). One executive we interviewed, who had recently completed an in-house leadership development program, commented, "for what we spent in travel expenses alone, you could have bought each of us an MBA at Harvard." An MBA at Harvard would have done little to strengthen this executive's understanding of his firm's vision and values, but the point remains that development dollars must be invested wisely. Firms that apply rigorous selection criteria increase the chances that they will realize a positive return to their training investment.

Of the firms we studied that recognized the importance of a strong vision and guiding philosophy, almost all recognized that leadership would be a dominant force in driving and sustaining their corporate visions through the rest of the organization. Because of the critical role that leaders would play in this process, these firms were extremely selective about the individuals they enlisted in their development efforts. In essence, participants were expected to be missionaries. Their organizations use formal development programs to socialize the next generation of leaders to a highly centralized culture critical to the corporation's vision and ongoing operations. These organizations also rely on extensive evaluation and rigorous selection criteria. PepsiCo, for example, selects only nine senior managers at a time to participate in its "Building the Business" course taught by CEO and Chairman Roger Enrico. Participants are chosen through careful review of the corporation's strategic needs and the talent available to meet those needs. Similarly, many of the Army's leadership development programs are also highly selective, especially at the senior levels. For example, a Department of Army Selection Board determines who will attend senior officer training at the U.S. Command and General Staff College. The board evaluates an officer's assignment history—the scope and variety of tasks as well as their performance—the level of responsibility the officer has supervised, and the Officer Military Personnel File that chronicles all performance evaluations recorded during the course of an officer's career (U.S. Department of the Army, 1990).

Among the most extensive selection processes we examined was Federal Express's Leadership Evaluation and Awareness Process (LEAP). At Federal Express, leaders are expected to cultivate a "people-first" environment. The firm's guiding philosophy is that "when people are placed first, they will provide the highest possible service, and profits will follow" (American Management Association, 1994, p. 10). To maintain a culture consistent with these beliefs, only individuals who have demonstrated excellence along nine specific leadership dimensions are given an opportunity to apply for managerial positions. Once in a management role, they have the opportunity and responsibility to participate in the required and elective courses offered by the Leadership Institute. As shown in Exhibit 4.1, each leadership dimension pertains to individuals' ability to interact effectively with others and to provide them with the guidance, inspiration, and resources they require to deliver high-quality service. LEAP

Exhibit 4.1. FedEx's Leadership Dimensions (LEAP)

1. *Charismatic Leadership*

   Charisma derives from the ability to see what is really important and to transmit a sense of mission to others. It is not exclusively the province of world-class leaders or a few generals or admirals. It is found in people throughout business organizations and is one of the elements that separates an ordinary manager from a true leader.

   Individuals who are charismatic leaders serve as symbols of success and accomplishment to others. They make others enthusiastic about assignments, command respect, and have a sense of purpose. Subordinates have faith in charismatic leaders and are proud to be associated with a leader whom they trust to overcome any obstacle. A charismatic leader instills pride, faith, and respect among subordinates.

2. *Individual Consideration*

   Managers who practice the individualized consideration concept of transformational leadership treat each subordinate as an individual and serve as coaches and teachers through delegation and learning opportunities. They avoid treating subordinates alike. They discover what motivates each person individually and act on this discovery. These leaders have a "developmental" orientation toward followers and consciously or unconsciously serve as role models. They also show appreciation and give special attention to newcomers and those who appear neglected.

3. *Intellectual Stimulation*

   The importance of a leader's technical expertise and intellectual power is frequently overlooked, particularly in high-performing organizations, because of the emphasis placed on interpersonal skills. However, intellectual stimulation is a vital part of leadership that:

   • Arouses an awareness in subordinates of problems and of different methods by which to solve them.

   • Provides compelling and convincing reasoning and evidence.

   • Stirs imaginations.

   • Promotes thought and insight prior to actions rather than immediate, emotionally stimulated reactions.

4. *Courage*

   Leaders stand up for unpopular ideas: they do not avoid confrontations by giving in to pressure. They are willing to give negative feedback to subordinates and superiors. A leader has confidence in his or her own capability, desires to act independently, and does the right thing for the company or subordinates in spite of personal hardships or sacrifice.

Exhibit 4.1. FedEx's Leadership Dimensions (LEAP), cont'd

5. *Dependability*

Leaders follow through and keep commitments, meeting deadlines, taking responsibility for actions, and admitting mistakes to superiors. Leaders work effectively with little or no contact with supervisors, but keep supervisors informed of progress.

6. *Flexibility*

Leaders function effectively in a changing environment, provide stability, and remain objective when confronted with many responsibilities at once. Leaders handle several problems simultaneously, focusing on critical items. A leader changes course when required.

7. *Integrity*

Leaders adhere to a code of business ethics and moral values, behaving consistently with the corporate climate and professional responsibility. A leader does not abuse management privilege, but gains trust/respect. A leader serves as a role model in support of corporate policies, professional ethics, and corporate culture.

8. *Judgment*

A leader uses logical and intellectual discernment to reach sound and objective evaluations of alternative actions. Decisions are based on logical, factual information and consideration of human factors. A leader knows his or her own authority and is careful not to exceed it, and uses past experience and information to gain perspective on present choices.

9. *Respect for Others*

A leader honors rather than belittles the opinions or work of others, regardless of their status or position in the organization. A leader demonstrates a belief in each individual's value regardless of background, culture, or other similar factors.

Source: Federal Express Corporation. Reprinted with permission.

is a thorough evaluation process that involves multiple steps and requires participants to be evaluated by their supervisors, peers, and a formal assessment panel. Specifically, the evaluation process (American Management Association, 1994) entails the following:

- *Attendance at an introductory one-day course entitled "Is management for me?"* This program describes the managerial responsibilities of a front-line supervisor and presents employees with a realistic picture of both the challenges and dilemmas that supervisors encounter. The program is normally held on a weekend—on the employees' own time—in order to send a symbolic message that as managers they can expect to put in extra time without additional remuneration. In recent years, this preview of the job resulted in 63 percent of course participants deciding not to pursue a management position, which in turn has reduced the actual turnover in supervisors. Presumably, such a preview improves the likelihood that those who do pursue managerial openings will be more prepared for and better aligned with corporate expectations.

- *Compilation of an employee's leadership profile.* The employee must document in a written statement the successful demonstration of all nine leadership dimensions based on past work experiences that they feel illustrate their leadership potential.

- *Formal assessment by the superior (the Manager's Focused Recommendation).* A formal assessment of the individual's leadership ability is submitted by the employee's manager, typically after a three- to six-month development and evaluation period. During this period, the manager evaluates and coaches the candidate according to the nine leadership dimensions. The manager then makes a written evaluation supporting or opposing the candidate's ability to lead.

- *Formal assessment by peers.* An evaluation is conducted by at least three of the candidate's peers selected by his or her manager. Coworkers use this peer assessment to confidentially assess whether the candidate has shown promise as a leader.

- *Formal evaluation by the LEAP Panel.* A panel of mid-level managers especially trained to conduct LEAP evaluations assesses candidates on the answers they provide to specific leadership scenarios. This panel interviews candidates about their written responses to the scenarios and then reaches a consensus about the adequacy of their answers. The panel compares this assessment with the results of the manager's focused recommendation, peer assessment, and employee's leadership profile. The panel uses these components collectively to determine whether it will endorse the candidate for front-line management opportunities. If endorsed by the panel, a candidate may apply for a management position. They are not, however, guaranteed a position. If they are not endorsed, the candidate must wait six months before reapplying to another LEAP panel. In the interim, candidates typically use this time to reevaluate their interests and improve on attributes and skills deemed lacking.

Federal Express's remarkably selective evaluation and nomination process ensures that managers not only demonstrate traits and values consistent with the firm's philosophy, but that they are also deeply knowledgeable about the philosophy and motivated to live it. Like the other firms in our study, FedEx recognizes that leaders play a critical role in the firm's socialization process. And like the other firms, FedEx realizes that socialization to the firm's core vision is too important to be left to chance.

FedEx is currently developing a selection process that will be more predictive of management success. Some of the steps will be similar to what has worked in LEAP for ten years. The new process will continue to look at leadership abilities. It will also look at interests, experiences, and preferences, as well as the individual's ability to solve problems, reasoning, data interpretation, and so on. This is additional evidence that FedEx strives to continuously improve systems and processes, even when existing ones appear to be effective today.

2. Organizational Needs Assessment, Tailored Content and Design

In order for a firm to establish a base of attitudes and values consistent with its core philosophy and vision, it must first assess whether there is broad consensus around the vision to begin with. Our investigation revealed that effective leadership development programs spent considerable time assessing their organizations' leadership needs up front. These findings are consistent with a wealth of training research that has strongly established the importance of conducting formal needs assessment prior to determining program design and content (Goldstein, 1986). Indeed, many programs have been doomed to failure from the outset because trainers were more interested in delivering a leadership program than in assessing the needs of their organization.

Thorough assessment of a firm's leadership development needs consists of analysis on three levels—the organization, the task, and the person (Goldstein, 1986). Organizational analysis involves the assessment of the firm's short- and long-term strategic goals, as well as the trends expected to affect those goals. So, for example, in the case of the National Australia Bank, the primary emphasis was on individual development but a strategic theme of transnational cooperation and integration was threaded throughout the program.

In a similar fashion, task analysis involves a careful assessment of what leaders will be expected to accomplish upon completion of the development program. Often these analyses require that senior-level managers reflect on where and how the firm's current leadership is lacking. For example, prior to designing executive development programs at PepsiCo, Paul Russell spends considerable time talking with senior leaders about areas that have been identified as strategically essential to PepsiCo's business. Leaders are asked to reflect on the firm's strategic challenges and the leadership competencies needed to overcome them. Russell then uses this information to determine the focus of PepsiCo's leader development programs. He also uses this feedback to identify the executives who are most widely respected by their peers in each identified area and to enlist their involvement as instructors. By involving the firm's leadership in the analysis of critical leadership needs and by utilizing executives known for their particular expertise in the program's delivery, Russell enhances the effectiveness of socialization for more junior leaders. They leave programs with knowledge of the firm's strategic concerns and an understanding of the competencies valued and perceived to be critical by the current leadership.

Our final assessment area—the person or individual analysis—evaluates the extent to which leaders across a firm actually demonstrate values, attributes, and behavior consistent with the corporate vision. In other words, a careful analysis is conducted of how well the organization's existing leaders perform along valued dimensions. In developing Ernst & Young's Leadership 2000 program, Sallie Bryant, director of the Leadership and Organizational Change Group, and Mike Powers, vice chairman for professional and organization development, conducted an "Area Effectiveness Survey" designed to evaluate how well area leaders worked together to implement the corporate vision at the local level. The survey asked partners to evaluate how effectively their area leaders communicated the firm's vision to line partners and staff, involved others in planning and decision-making processes, and worked across organizational boundaries to align systems and eliminate barriers. The results of this survey provided a general assessment of the main issues facing leaders across the firm and a relative assessment of which leadership teams were doing particularly well or poorly. This information not only helped Bryant and Powers design a development program targeted at the firm's most pressing leadership needs, it also identified the areas and functions that lacked a solid grasp of the firm's vision. Moreover, the survey itself signaled to partners and managers throughout the firm the importance of the very values and behaviors that it measured.

In short, careful needs assessment ensures more effective socialization of corporate leaders by requiring existing leaders to articulate their fundamental assumptions about the firm's strategic challenges and the competencies needed to overcome them. Armed with this information, program designers are better equipped to design a program consistent with the corporate vision and the competencies deemed necessary to achieve it.

3. Well-Articulated Vision and Philosophy

On the surface, what we are about to say seems obvious. Yet paradoxically several organizations we studied failed on this dimension of design effectiveness. Programs cannot effectively socialize a corporate vision and philosophy if the organization itself is conflicted about its own vision and values or if these are constantly in flux. Similarly, if the company has poorly articulated its vision and value set it is difficult to socialize them. For example, one organization we studied did not have a clear strategic vision nor were its values well articulated. This lack of strategic direction and corporate philosophy led to a sense of frustration and powerlessness among employees in the organization as well as among program participants. One individual captured the dilemma in these terms: "The organization hasn't clearly articulated its value proposition and strategic intent. It's tough to discuss behaviors, competencies, and skills on the leadership side of the organization if you don't know what face you're trying to present to a target market." Participants in the program had hoped that this frustration would produce upward pressure on the CEO to articulate such a vision and set of values. This, however, is a backward way of approaching the issue, and one that is not likely to produce results. In another case we studied, the CEO wished to socialize a corporate value around high-quality standards using the company's educational programs. At the same time, he cut resources for the customer service department. This mixed signal undermined his attempts to instill new values around quality because managers down the line doubted his sincerity.

It is crucial therefore for the success of any socialization program that the organization possess a vision and value set that are reasonably well articulated and lived out. This, for one, ensures that the skills, mind-sets, and values being taught in programs match up to the strategic and cultural requirements of the organization. Frameworks or competency models within the program can also be aligned to support and reinforce the company's vision and its culture.

In part, the success of FedEx's program can be tied back to having a very clear company vision known as the People-Service-Profit philosophy, or PSP. It is widely disseminated and reinforced through orientations of new employees, personnel manuals, appraisal and performance measurement systems, and through the company Leadership Institute's coursework. It is also stated simply: "Take care of our people; they, in turn, will deliver the impeccable service demanded by our customers, who will reward us with the profitability necessary to secure our future. People-Service-Profit: these three words are the very foundation of Federal Express." In the company's Manager's Guide, practices such as those cited in Exhibit 4.2 are specifically used as examples of how the company can live out the people side of the philosophy. The PSP philosophy also figures annually in the company's top strategic objectives. In addition to linking the philosophy directly to the company's strategic objectives, additional systems work to reinforce the people side of the philosophy such as performance appraisals, company-wide climate surveys, and grievance appeal procedures.

Exhibit 4.2. FedEx's Corporate Philosophy and Actions on the People Dimension

What exactly does being a people-oriented company mean? Among other things, this philosophy is reflected in the following management practices:

- Giving employee considerations a high priority when developing Corporate programs and policies, when acquiring and designing facilities, equipment, and systems, and when scheduling and arranging work.

- Involving each employee as a valuable team member in all Corporate activities. After all, who knows more about how the job should be done than those doing it?

- Being dedicated to promotions from within unless the needed skills cannot be found in existing employee ranks.

- Spending the time and effort necessary to manage the personnel issues—especially training and coaching.

- Maintaining outstanding communications and making available any information requested that is not personal, privileged, or controlled by government regulation.

- Enacting progressive programs such as our Open Door, Survey-Feedback-Action, and Guaranteed Fair Treatment Procedure/EEO Complaint Process policies to ensure that problems are solved and no individual is subjected to unreasonable or capricious treatment.

- Treating every single employee with respect and dignity.

- Saying "Thank you" and "Well done" often.

Source: Adapted from the Federal Express Manager's Guide, 1996.

4. Practicing Leaders Provide Instruction

Because leadership development programs aimed at socialization seek to impart a greater understanding of a firm's guiding philosophy, core values, and particular strategic strengths, many programs increasingly use their own executives as instructors. Though a well-known leadership guru or knowledgeable business school professor can provide insight into the latest theories on leadership or competitive strategy, outside experts typically have less to say about the strategies and practices that have worked well for one's own firm. Moreover, outside experts may only have superficial knowledge of a firm's culture or history and little understanding of the idiosyn-cratic relations that dictate current practice.

Many organizations have long recognized the importance of for-mal mentoring programs for teaching junior leaders "the ropes." Many have also recognized that outstanding leaders can from time to time make outstanding teachers. The Army, for example, strongly encourages its leaders to take on teaching assignments but only allows the most qualified to serve as instructors. For many courses, in fact, the Army would consider outside instructors inappropriate. This is because instilling an understanding of the Army's leadership ethos represents a key component of most of its leadership devel-opment programs. Each leadership course imparts or refines a shared definition and understanding of what leaders in the Army should be, know, and do at each level of responsibility.

The policy of leaders teaching leaders, however, has not gone unquestioned. In the face of recent downsizing and outsourcing trends, the value of using Army leaders as instructors for noncom-missioned officer (NCO) training has been scrutinized. Yet NCOs have fought hard to keep their leadership training in-house. They maintain that only by having NCOs teach NCOs will junior lead-ers come to learn the culture, values, and ethos of Army leadership. Through interaction with more experienced leaders, developing NCOs observe, imitate, practice, and receive immediate feedback about how to handle difficult situations in ways that are consistent with Army values. Because leader-instructors have actually "been there before," they are viewed as more credible and knowledgeable than more academic instructors. As junior leaders interact with these experienced instructors, they develop greater trust and confi-dence in their own understanding of the Army, as well as in their colleagues and the system overall.

Federal Express also recognizes the value of using successful lead-ers as faculty. It has developed an in-house pool of faculty called management preceptors. Drawn from the ranks of senior managers and managing directors who are themselves recognized as company leaders, preceptors are chosen to teach and facilitate in FedEx's Leadership Institute. Because one of the institute's dominant goals is to ensure that all managers understand the corporate philosophy, preceptors are selected who mirror the values and philosophy of the company through their own track records. Preceptors serve a term limited to twenty-four to thirty months at the institute, which allows a continual rotation of new preceptors and introduces new perspectives and ideas into the curricula.

As in the Army, FedEx selects only its best performers to be preceptors in order to guard the reputation of the Leadership Institute and the credibility of what it teaches. Preceptors, in essence, must be role models of leadership. Selection is therefore an important part of the process. Prospective candidates initiate the selection process with an informal phone call or meeting with the Leadership Institute director to discuss available opportunities. The majority of inappropriate candidates are screened out at this point. Candidates who pass the initial screening must then be formally nominated by their direct manager or an officer of the corporation. (If they do not already report to an officer—vice president or senior vice president—the nomination must also have the approval of a company officer in addition to their supervisor.) To be eligible for a nomination, the candidate must already have had three years in a FedEx management position and at least one year managing other managers. After receipt of the candidate's nomination, the candidate then goes on to the next stage of screening. At this point, the institute carefully evaluates the individual's past performance evaluation scores. To pass this review, the candidate must score in the top 20 percent of the company's annual survey assessing the leadership capabilities of its managers. The survey is compiled from individual manager assessments completed by a manager's direct and indirect reports that can include up to several hundred respondents. In addition, the candidate's performance evaluations over the two prior years are also examined.

Candidates who pass this review are then placed in a pool of nominees for openings that appear in the future. Over two and a half years, the Leadership Institute has no more than ten openings for preceptors so the chances of becoming one remain low. Even if a nominee is selected from this pool, there remains one further hurdle: he or she must be evaluated by a formal selection panel consisting of the institute's managing director, the manager of management education, and the institute's resident specialists. The panel evaluation assesses the candidate's communication and facilitation skills and ability to convey the corporate philosophy in a meaningful way. Again, the rationale for such rigorous selection processes is that preceptors serve as critical leadership role models who will not only teach front-line leaders the fundamental principles of leadership, but also demonstrate through their actions acceptable work standards and appropriate conduct.

It is worthwhile to note that former preceptors have done very well upon returning to positions of leadership within the company. Approximately sixty-five senior managers and managing directors have been selected to serve as preceptors; of that number, more than twenty have been promoted at least one management level, including one to the level of senior vice president and many others to vice president.

At PepsiCo, the company's most senior leaders serve as instructors. For example, in a course for executive-level participants entitled "Building the Business," the principle instructor is Roger Enrico, the company's CEO and chairman. In five-day sessions with nine high-potential junior executives, Enrico teaches about his personal philosophy of leading and the importance of building businesses as a core leadership competency. As at FedEx, careful attention goes into selecting the executive teachers. Program designer and vice president for executive development Paul Russell identifies executives who are known to be outstanding in the competency areas that need to be taught. As Russell explains, "I am absolutely convinced that what is missing from most adult learning models is the importance of the person that you put in front of an audience as the leader. They must be respected, and people must want to learn from them. It is these characteristics that I carefully check out before selecting anyone to instruct."

In sum, using practicing leaders as instructors facilitates the socialization of more junior leaders in a number of ways. First, by facilitating interaction with leaders who embody the company's values and live out its philosophy, the corporation provides living role models of the ideology it hopes to embed and perpetuate through successive generations. Second, using practicing leaders ensures that classroom learning remains grounded in the reality of the workplace and the current culture. Existing leaders directly convey their beliefs, experience, and expectations to program participants, thereby facilitating the transmission of cultural knowledge. By creating this opportunity to interact and discuss with existing leaders the firm's philosophy and guiding values, leadership development programs facilitate a shared understanding of what the organization is about and where it is going. Finally, a system of leaders teaching leaders creates a two-way exchange of information and learning. By increasing interaction between new and existing leaders, leadership development programs can improve the probability that new information and insight will be properly integrated within the firm's existing culture. Moreover, through their teaching, leaders themselves are likely to reflect more on the firm's existing vision and may therefore be less likely to simply perpetuate old routines.

5. Crystalize Theories into Explicit Models, Attributes, and Behaviors

In some cases, firms adopt well-established theories of leadership; the Army teaches Fiedler's Contingency Theory and Federal Express employs a transformational model and a servant leadership model. In other cases, company leaders develop their own points of view about the essentials of leadership. For example, at PepsiCo Roger Enrico developed his own model. Working with Paul Russell to flush out his implicit ideas about leadership into a framework, Enrico distilled his leadership experiences into a model built around several major themes. Simple and to the point, five key themes were identified:

1. *Think in different terms.* The central idea is that leaders must constantly be working on big ideas that provide a competitive edge for the organization in its future. Incremental changes are insufficient for long-term success. These continuous improvements are valuable, but thousands are required to drive the business. It is through "big changes to big things" that an organization builds the business. Moreover, effective leaders continually search for the big ideas. Once one growth idea has full backing from the organization, a leader then turns attention to the next one. It is a continuous process.

2. *Develop a point of view.* Leaders must have a clear point of view. They are able to pinpoint and crystallize the opportunities into ideas. These ideas are, however, based on solid evidence and a belief in them is shared by important constituencies throughout the organization.

3. *Take it on the road.* Effective leaders sell their ideas throughout the organization to get buy-in. But before making the grand sell, they test market them on smaller groups of constituents who provide critical feedback and help in developing the initiative. Enrico likes to call this testing phase "going off Broadway before you go to Broadway." This is also a time to test whether the language used to describe the idea evokes interest and passion.

4. *Pull it all together.* Once the idea is crystallized, the leader then must translate it into a clear vision, establish the right measurements, gain commitment from important stakeholders, and effectively anticipate and deal with resistance.

5. *Make it happen.* Finally, leaders must communicate their vision using clear, vivid messages that both motivate and provide direction. This also involves identifying the key constituencies that need to support the initiative, enrolling them, and getting into place the processes and support systems that would give the efforts staying power.

This model then became the framework for Enrico's course.

There are multiple benefits to this approach. For one, it forces company leaders to reflect deeply not only on their own experiences but on the leadership needs of their organizations. They must then clearly articulate the leadership qualities they see as essential into models and well-defined attributes. Unlike theories developed by academics, these frameworks are often more practical and applicable to the business at hand. Second, company executives end up teaching what they know from experience not from theories or models developed by others. From the executive's standpoint, this ensures a certain comfort and confidence in the approaches they are teaching. From the participants' perspective, there are further advantages. As these models reflect the wisdom and experience of the company's most senior leaders, they command more attention and respect as frameworks to follow. After all, they reflect the behaviors and mind-sets that ensured the success of the present-day company leaders. In addition, the frameworks are usually richly illustrated in programs through stories told by the leader. These stories reinforce important values, behaviors, and assumptions in the context of the organization, its markets, and its history. It is learning at its most applied. Finally, opportunities for a collective dialogue with the leader are frequent in these programs. They allow participants to take the leader's ideas and apply them more concretely to their own situations as well as to explore in greater depth aspects of the leader's experience that are most relevant to an individual participant's needs.

6. Program Format Designed Around Participant Exchange and Structured Interaction

Well-designed programs incorporate numerous opportunities for participant exchange. For example, Motorola's program for new corporate vice presidents (the Vice President Institute) involves senior executives in teaching and dialogue with participants about their roles. Through structured interaction, these newly appointed executives learn about the company's expectations for them as leaders at the corporate level. In essence, the message conveyed is that they are now operating across the corporation rather than within their individual organizations and that leadership demands are different. This process of dialogue and joint interpretation clarifies expectations and delineates more clearly the roles and responsibilities associated with the new positions. Similarly, in the PepsiCo program with Enrico, not only are there group dialogues but one-on-one sessions with Enrico. In these, he coaches participants with a leadership initiative they are undertaking as well as discusses their career issues and general leadership challenges. Learnings then are tailored directly to the learner.

At FedEx, CEO Ted Weise spends one and a half to two and a half hours with every supervisory leadership course. In these sessions, he discusses the company's strategic objectives, his definition of leadership, and how important he believes front-line managers are to the success of FedEx and its PSP philosophy.

7. A Systems Approach Emphasizes Integration and Support

To be truly successful, socialization depends on continual, progressive, and sequential development, as we saw in the Army's approach. In addition, existing leaders must be unified in their understanding of the corporate vision and in the values deemed important in achieving that vision.

But it is not enough to focus solely on the educational dimensions and the company leadership around vision and values. Other organizational systems need to be properly aligned to send consistent messages about what is valued and what is not. Consistent structures, work processes, and reward systems must maximize the probability that the values and assumptions instilled during the development program will be reinforced and supported once leaders return to the job.

Few companies do this as consistently as FedEx. The company is a good example of a firm whose culture and organizational systems support and reinforce the leadership ethos promulgated by the firm's formal development programs. For instance, the firm's vision and values are clearly articulated in its People-Service-Profit philosophy. The philosophy and the values that derive from it are reflected in quality initiatives, management guidelines, and compensation or recognition programs throughout the firm. Its culture is open and participative. Managers adhere to the belief that front-line employees possess a great deal of knowledge. Moreover, senior executives serve as role models, demonstrating through their behavior the values and principles emphasized in the firm's formal development efforts. Finally, a number of other company programs reinforce desired leadership behaviors and further instill the firm's core philosophy and fundamental values. Among them are the firm's Survey-Feedback-Action process and Guaranteed Fair Treatment Procedure. We explore the Survey-Feedback-Action process in the next section, but we take a moment here to explain the Guaranteed Fair Treatment Procedure (American Management Association, 1994) because it highlights how the various systems of a company can powerfully reinforce the values it wishes to socialize in future and present leaders.

Given company values surrounding employee treatment, it is imperative that FedEx possess an equitable and thorough grievance procedure. The Guaranteed Fair Treatment Procedure (GFTP) ensures that all company employees have an opportunity to have their grievances heard by progressively higher levels of management and that their complaints will be considered seriously and expeditiously. Initiated in 1981 and modified in 1993 to include discrimination complaints, the process is geared to resolve differences between managers and their direct reports. Events that are typically considered are disputed terminations, disciplinary actions, performance reviews, and job postings where individuals feel that they have been unfairly passed over.

The system works in a straightforward manner. Before initiating GFTP action, employees must first try to resolve the issue with their manager. If they are dissatisfied with the outcome, they then have five calendar days from the occurrence of the eligible issue to file a written complaint. It is first reviewed by a committee drawn up of the employee's manager, senior manager, and managing director, who must examine all the facts and circumstances relating to the incident. The committee can in turn either overturn, modify, or endorse the front-line manager's opinion. This must be done within ten days of the employee's initial petition for consideration. If employees are dissatisfied with the committee's decision, they can appeal in writing within five calendar days to a higher level, the Officer Review— a panel consisting of the vice president of the employee's department and the senior vice president of the employee's division. The panel reviews all the relevant information and offers a decision on the issue. If the employee still feels that the outcome is not satisfactory, a final appeal can be made to the company's senior level—the Executive Review. Composed of five senior executives, this committee reviews employee complaints that have come up through the GFTP one morning a week. The group includes CEO Ted Weise, the executive vice president, the chief personnel officer, one senior vice president, and one vice president. They weigh the appeal. Before the case is submitted to the Executive Review board, however, an individual from the employee relations department spends one week analyzing the file, interviewing witnesses, clarifying the issues, and preparing a summary overview with a preliminary recommendation. At this point, decisions made by the Executive Review are binding. If certain facts or issues still remain in question, a panel can be formed called the Board of Review. This is a five-person jury composed of three members (from a list of six names submitted by the employee) selected by the board chair who must be at the director level or above and two members (from a list of four names submitted by the board chair) selected by the employee with the grievance. They hear oral arguments from the employee and his or her manager. Within twenty-four hours of the case presentation, the board issues a majority opinion that is the final disposition of the case.

Through systems such as these, certain leadership values of an organization can not only be measured but propagated and protected. They are essential requirements if socialization approaches are to be successful in the long run.

8. Evaluation and Accountability for Results

Effective socialization programs assess the extent to which leaders appear to be living the firm's vision and values after their experiences in a development program. Federal Express provides a good example of a program that holds managers accountable for their efforts to perpetuate the corporate philosophy.

In 1979, FedEx developed an annual employee satisfaction survey that continues to this day in the form of the Survey-Feedback-Action system (SFA). This is a voluntary and anonymous process where all employees are given an opportunity to express their levels of satisfaction with their managers and with the company. A remarkable 98 percent participate in April of every year. It specifically queries employees about their manager's leadership ability, the company's reward systems, job conditions, work group cooperation, and the employee's identification with Federal Express itself.

It plays a role in leadership development at the company in several ways. For one, certain dimensions actually assess management's ability to be effective leaders (survey questions 1–10 create the Leadership Average; several of these are shown in Exhibit 4.3). These provide an annual subordinate review of direct supervisors and overall senior management. They are also averaged for the entire company, and the average is publicly released for all to see. Second, because they are built around the people dimension of the company's PSP model, they serve to further reinforce that set of values.

Reports of work group results are available to company managers within a day of the closing of the on-line survey system. These reports in turn provide the basis for discussion in required feedback sessions between each work group and its manager that are held after the survey. For work groups with fewer than three members, group

Exhibit 4.3. FedEx Survey: Feedback-Action Sample Questions

- My manager lets me know what's expected of me.
- Favoritism is not a problem in my workgroup.
- My manager is willing to listen to my concerns.
- My manager lets me know when I have done a good job.
- My manager treats me with respect and dignity.
- My manager provides leadership and support to the Quality Improvement Process.
- My manager's boss gives us the support we need.
- Upper management pays attention to ideas and suggestions from people at my level.
- I am proud to work for Federal Express.
- Working for Federal Express will probably lead to the kind of future I want.
- Rules and procedures do not interfere with how well I am able to do my job.
- I have the freedom to do my job well.
- The concerns identified by my work group during last year's SFA feedback session have been satisfactorily addressed.

These items are related on a 6-point scale: Strongly Agree, Agree, Sometimes Agree/Disagree, Disagree, Strongly Disagree, Undecided/Don't Know.

Source: American Management Association, Blueprints for Service Quality, 1994, pp. 34–35. Reprinted with permission.

results are not provided because they cannot provide anonymity. The feedback meetings are used to identify problem areas and to develop formal action plans for addressing problems. The action plans must include identification of the problem, time lines for resolution, who will be responsible, and what resources and methods will be needed. In numerous cases, the group will meet again in a follow-up session to ascertain whether problems have been satisfactorily resolved. To ensure that this is the case, the SFA contains a question assessing resolution: "The concerns identified by my work group during last year's SFA feedback session have been satisfactorily addressed."

In addition to using SFA locally to help managers become more effective, it is also used to assess the state of the organization as a whole and problem areas across the company. One example of the survey's usefulness in identifying company-wide problems occurred in the early 1990s. SFA scores revealed that despite FedEx's commitment to communicating corporate goals, employees clearly felt it was not doing so. In response, CEO Weise now appears on the company's in-house satellite television network to field questions from employees and discuss the state of the company. SFA scores can also isolate problem units, or "critical groups," by targeting the work groups where employee responses to survey items fall two standard deviations or more below the company average. These groups are then required to have frequent resolution meetings, and a second survey is conducted in six months.

The original assessment questionnaire used in 1979 was developed by a university and contained two hundred items. That proved too cumbersome, and the next year a shortened version of twenty questions was provided by an outside consulting firm. In 1984, the company decided this version was too generic and so developed its own twenty-six-item survey, later enlarged to thirty-two items with seven optional items that individual operating units could add to assess their own situation. (The seven local questions do not go into the company or location averages.)

The only identifiable downside to the SFA system is that some managers attempt to manage to the survey. In other words, they may not as frequently confront employees when needed, or they may hold difficult personnel decisions until after administration of the SFA. In addition, a limited number of groups may have poor SFA results not due to the manager but because of other local factors. There can be, for example, certain work groups that have a long history of dysfunctional behavior that can undermine the efforts of even effective managers.

Problems and Pitfalls

Socialization programs hold the promise of embedding a company's vision and values, but they are difficult to implement successfully and require a long-term commitment from senior executives. They can also be expensive, as they are often supported by an in-house corporate university or an educational center such as General Electric's Crotonville and FedEx's Leadership Institute. Both have permanent staff dedicated solely to the initiative and in GE's case a physical plant equivalent to a small college campus. Here we list additional problems and challenges facing these types of programs.

1. Reinforcing Values While Ignoring Markets

One of the biggest pitfalls that organizations experience in their efforts to socialize leaders is that in the process they may lose sight of their markets and the competition. This is often the case with highly successful organizations whose traditions reinforce worldviews built around past success factors rather than newly emerging ones. In addition, some organizations choose to focus on narrow conceptions of leadership. For example, many programs emphasize the interpersonal competencies of leadership while overlooking its strategic dimensions. One company we studied had developed a week-long socialization program for its managers. Within two years, some two thousand managers had attended the program. Over the next few years, a shortened version of the program was delivered to thousands of line workers within the company. During this time, the company's market share slid from 49 percent in 1990 to 25 percent by 1997 due to marketplace trends that were radically altering the competitive landscape. Not so surprisingly, the content of the company's leadership development program did not focus on these marketplace shifts. Instead, leadership was defined and taught entirely around behaviors such as ethical management practices, empowerment, clear communications, appreciation for diversity, and personal accountability. These, as the company discovered, were skills for leading subordinates, not customers. The organization had failed to include a crucial focus on the importance of strategic vision and, along with it, an acute sensitivity to marketplace trends.

2. Hidden Challenges in Using Company Leaders as Teachers

It would be a mistake to assume that company leaders do indeed make the best instructors or that their use is not without special challenges. As we learned from our research at PepsiCo, several important dilemmas must be addressed with executive instructors. First and foremost, the executive chosen to instruct must be seen as a role model. As Paul Russell at PepsiCo argues, they need to be "world-class people that everyone looks to as the leader or the expert." As such, the choice of a particular individual must have nearly unanimous support from the target group of learners. Russell even argues that they should have "icon status" within the organization. If they do not, it is preferable to turn to outside sources such as university faculty to cover important leadership topics. This is confirmed in our own research where we have seen instances of senior executive instructors who were indeed poor role models. These situations simply generated great cynicism among program participants and in turn undermined the impact of programs.

Another potential risk with company insiders is that organizational worldviews or paradigms will simply be reinforced. If the external environment is changing rapidly and moving away from the company's paradigm, this can only make matters worse. One tactic, however, is to choose iconoclastic leaders and those who have had an innovative track record.

There are also issues of tact and diplomacy to be considered. For instance, how will the company president react to a junior executive (who is the more effective leader) being selected over him? Political issues are important to address in the selection process.

In general, the executive should not be the driving factor behind educational experiences. Rather the internal and external needs of the organization should be the primary drivers. For example, Russell does not begin by first selecting the potential teacher and then creating a course around their expertise; his program ideas are derived from areas that have been identified as strategically essential to the business. For example, one company-sponsored study revealed that three clusters of competencies distinguished successful leaders at PepsiCo. These included setting an effective agenda or direction, taking others with you (in other words, executing the agenda through others), and doing it "the right way" (recognizing that how one gets results can be as important as the results themselves). Russell then identified Pepsi executives who were widely known to be outstanding in each skill area, and programs were developed around a specific competency category. He identified his instructors through a network of contacts throughout the company. In trips to different divisions, he would meet with senior executives and ask them directly: "If you could have anyone teach the skills of taking others along with you (aligning the organization to a new direction and motivating them to succeed), who would that be?"

There are additional caveats. Generally, the executive-as-teacher works best in companies where the culture itself encourages leaders to take responsibility for developing others. A company history of mentoring especially by senior levels of the organization often promotes executive leaders who think and act more like teachers. Next, a strong and visible commitment from the organization's most senior levels is vital. As well, there must be relatively uniform opinion among the key constituents on the areas where they wish the program to focus and on the executives from whom they would most like to learn.

In working to develop a course with an executive, it is essential that the designer remember that it is the executive who really owns the course. As such, it must reflect the executive's view of the world. Course models and frameworks need to be built around their experiences and intuitive understanding of effective leadership. At PepsiCo, for example, Paul Russell's role is to help the executive crystallize his implicit theories into an explicit model.

In working with executives on this process, Russell has found it best to ask broad ranging questions. Have the executive walk through case example after case example while the designer works to identify common approaches and themes. As guiding principles and frameworks are noted, these are continually tested out with the executive. It is also important that the executive identify stories that powerfully illustrate the points they will be making in the classroom. These often prove to be the most vital sources of instruction and learning. Finally, Russell has found that with every executive instructor there is a moment of crisis. This is a time when the course seems to be dangerously close to falling apart. For example, the executive has second thoughts about his or her ability to teach or the subject matter or feels too modest to stand up and be seen as an icon. It is in these moments that Russell must push through with reassurance and coaching in order to turn the tide.

The program designer's role, however, is not simply to assist company leaders in developing applicable frameworks and materials for instruction. An equally important role is to design a learning environment that is most comfortable for the executive instructor. In other words, the seminar format must fit the personal style and comfort level of the executive for maximum effectiveness. In some cases, this calls for a twist of creativity. In one case Russell enlisted PepsiCo's top advertising guru Allan Pottasch, who created the "Pepsi Generation" and Michael Jackson campaigns among many other notable advertising events. He is considered one of the leading advertising figures in the world. Given his icon status, Russell approached him about the possibility of delivering a program on advertising to PepsiCo's marketing executives. Pottasch's first response was, "I'm not a teacher. I have no idea how I do what I do, I just do it." Over a series of lunches, Russell began to realize that Pottasch was not set against teaching, but that he simply did not want to be put in the position of giving a stand-up, formal lecture. He was also uncomfortable presenting himself as the guru on advertising. He was reluctant to set himself up in front of senior marketing executives who consider themselves to be experts and tell them how to advertise. Russell cleverly discovered ways to address Pottasch's concerns.

First, he proposed that the course title be changed from "Advertising and Creativity" to "The World of Advertising According to Allan Pottasch." This simple change in title recognized that the program was built around Pottasch's opinion: "You can do advertising any way you believe is most effective, but I am going to tell you how *I* do it." This freed Pottasch to tell his story in his own way and be as provocative and controversial as he wanted to be. Second, Russell customized the program delivery format to play to Pottasch's strengths. The group would be kept small (fifteen or fewer participants) to ensure an atmosphere encouraging discussion. Russell framed the design to Pottasch in the following manner: "Your job will be to introduce topics, and then I will work with you to figure out great examples of all of your points in each topic and summary overheads." The great examples would be of both advertising successes and failures so that Pottasch did not feel that he was setting himself up as the advertising wizard. Topics would be general enough—such as the use of celebrities in ad campaigns—to ensure wide participation.

This story illustrates the crucial role of the designer in making these programs work. Designers are as important to the process as the executive. For example, one of the principle reasons why the PepsiCo programs work so well has to do with Paul Russell himself. Several critical characteristics about Russell enable the programs to work. Companies wishing to have a similar impact would have to ensure these qualities were present in their counterparts to Russell.

First of all, Russell has access to senior executives throughout the company at the highest levels. Having cultivated a strong network of relationships with top corporate and divisional management allows him both access and candid feedback on programs and on possible instructors. In essence, they serve as an informal board of directors for the company's leadership development initiatives. He can bounce program ideas off them as well as obtain their suggestions about possible candidates for teaching.

Second, he has an ability to create truly comfortable teaching designs for his executive teachers. He understands the psychology of their reactions. For example, when interviewed about how he enlists executives to conduct these programs, Russell describes the phases of reactions that most of his potential instructors typically experience. An initial reaction is, "There is no way I can do that." Most feel that their schedules are already enormously busy and so are reluctant to take on further responsibilities. Others doubt that they really have something unique to teach. After a bit of reflection, both groups begin to realize that they are being considered as company role models. They also start to see the unique opportunity being presented—the possibility of having a broad impact on the corporation beyond their own group. But then comes a reaction of doubt, of not feeling competent to teach their expertise. The thought is, "I don't know how to tell people what I do. I just do it." At this point, Russell steps in to explain that his role is to help them prepare and develop the material they will teach.

Third, Russell is an effective coach of high-level talent. Some of his executive teachers have natural ability, others need coaching. He has a talent at putting executives at ease so that he can provide them with candid and nonthreatening feedback: "One of my many roles is, during breaks, to talk with Roger Enrico about what he calls his stagecraft. He realizes that he is on stage. He looks to me to candidly tell him what I think he should do more of, less of, what is working."

The program designer must be prepared to address and coach on certain common problems. For example, the executive often feels a burden to carry the full weight of the program on his or her shoulders. Part of the designer's task is to convince executive teachers that effective learning occurs best when the participants are involved. In other words, guided discussions are better than a straight lecture. Also executive teachers often must learn to allow the group to reach its own conclusions rather than simply feed it information. To assist in coaching, Russell typically sits through the first two runs of any new program. During breaks, he provides the executive with feed-back on style, how discussions are progressing, course design, and so on. He at times suggests ways for the executive to more effec-tively involve participants in a discussion. Another challenge is that on the first run of a program the executive teacher may miss mate-rial or move too quickly or slowly through sections. In-depth dis-cussions on one topic may delay another topic. Because of this, program schedules are designed to be highly flexible. Still, key learn-ing points and experiences must be clearly spelled out so that they are always covered. Exactly when they may occur in the program, however, may vary. In addition, it is important that portions of the program simply be left open for general discussion with no fixed agenda. After each first run of a program, revisions are inevitably made in its content, design, and style. From feedback, it will become clear that certain topic areas need more time and attention and that others require less.

3. Corporate Ownership Supersedes Division Ownership

Many socialization initiatives are driven by the corporate centers of companies. This occurs for a number of reasons. They may have fewer resource constraints for large-scale educational initiatives. Programs are often developed out of concerns held by the CEO or other executives who fear that important values, behaviors, and mind-sets are being poorly reinforced in different divisions. More-over, corporate-level human resources executives may possess a big-ger-picture sense of their organization's long-term needs. Finally, it is easier to share the cost of a program across twelve divisions than for only one to bear it. Because of these factors, we tend to find socialization initiatives driven at the corporate level.

There are clear advantages to corporate ownership. In tough times, corporate centers are often more immune to cost cutting. One divi-sion may be suffering but three successful ones provide the corporate center with the resources to continue a program. It is not uncommon for the corporate level to end up the guardian of a company's vision and values. So it is only appropriate that it be the source of educational initiatives that promulgate them. Finally, support from the very top powerfully reinforces what is valued in an organization.

But there are tradeoffs to program ownership centralized at the corporate level. For one, programs owned by a division can more effectively tailor their learning content around the particular market and organizational issues of the operating unit. For example, action learning projects can be focused on resolving actual problems facing the operating division. In contrast, corporate-level projects may feel too removed from a manager's world or too general in nature for participants to see an application for themselves as leaders. With program ownership at the divisional level, leadership competencies can be tailored to the specific needs of the division, unlike the more universal models offered by corporate center programs. By bringing work units into a program (which is more characteristic of the divisional approach), participants have a far greater number of opportunities to strengthen their working relationships and dialoguing across functions. In addition, after programs end participants frequently encounter each other in the workplace, creating numerous windows for reinforcing program learnings. For these reasons, we feel that some level of divisional ownership is crucial to program effectiveness. There are a few exceptions, most notably programs such as Motorola's Vice Presidents' Institute, which seeks to instill a corporate viewpoint.

4. Organizational Downturns or Challenges May Undermine Programs

Hard times may lead companies to cut back on their educational programs. It is not unusual in a downturn for training budgets to be among the first to be cut. As a result, the socialization initiative gradually dies out. As importantly, a symbolic message is sent throughout the firm that in the end those values and leadership behaviors were not as essential as employees were led to believe. In sharp contrast, Motorola, for example, opened its university in the midst of a recession to demonstrate that education was of primary concern even in the toughest of times.

Crises can also produce events that undermine the very behaviors and values companies have been attempting to socialize. For instance, one of the companies we studied experienced a rapid reversal in its fortunes that caused it to seek outside help from a consulting firm. The consultants implemented a major reengineering effort to streamline company operations, which not only resulted in major layoffs but also produced an exodus of the company's leadership talent. Both dramatically negated the impact of the company's socialization program. As one senior manager explained to us, "The layoffs were so poorly handled. The consulting firm implementing them really did not understand our culture. As a result, the event ripped out the soul behind the leadership program. Everyone lost someone they cared about. How can you talk about trust and teamwork and leadership after something like that? Whatever we learned became meaningless."

In conclusion, we believe that socialization initiatives hold great promise for leadership development despite design challenges and problems. They are potentially a very powerful means of reinforcing a company's vision and culture and of developing cadres of leaders who value and live them out. But socialization programs may not be enough in themselves, given how rapidly today's competitive environments change. As we noted earlier, a common pitfall of these approaches is that they often fail to help organizations adapt strategically. One answer to this challenge is addressed in Chapter Six, where we look at leadership development initiatives that focus on facilitating and accelerating strategic changes within an organization.

5

How Federal Express and PepsiCo Socialize Vision and Values

F ew companies have had such a dedicated interest in developing the leadership abilities of their front-line managers as Federal Express.

A Case Study: Federal Express

Playing a vital role in that process is the company's Leadership Institute, founded over a decade and a half ago. The mission of the Institute is to develop leadership talent at FedEx through coursework that examines and applies the principles and practices of successful leadership. It is also an important vehicle for socializing the corporate philosophy of Federal Express and its way of conducting business. In many ways, FedEx is an outstanding example of the socialization approach to leadership development.

Interestingly, much of what is socialized centers on the company's values concerning employees. As Steve Nielsen, the Institute's managing director, explained to us, "You come to our courses, and you are essentially spending the week experiencing the people values of FedEx. Our aim is to infuse our managers with the theory and philosophy and beliefs that the company has held to and practiced and benefited and grown from over twenty-five years. We want to infuse these into our leaders and have them go out and do the same to their employees because we believe it works."

The Institute's approach to training can be said to be a marriage of philosophy and practicality. By using company managers as instructors and designing classroom activities around participant exchange, program content is driven by concerns about how to employ company values and philosophy in day-to-day management actions.

Founded in 1984, the Institute began with a single course on leadership for front-line managers. The success of that initial program led to today's broad array of offerings for managers, senior managers, and managing directors on topics such as team and individual development, communications and relationship skills, and diversity. In addition, there are seminars on ethics, coaching, and Stephen Covey's Seven Habits. The Institute also broadcasts numerous programs each year on topics of leadership and management over the company's FXTV internal television system. The Institute, however, has its broadest impact through three mandatory core courses (Management Principles I, II, and III) designed for distinct levels of management, and through an elective course (Exploring Leadership) that examines the interpersonal issues and partnerships involved in leadership.

The Institute's Origins

Concerned about a formal channel for employees to voice management-related problems, Federal Express in 1981 established the appeal process described in Chapter Four, the Guaranteed Fair Treatment Procedure. Soon after implementation of the GFTP, the Appeals Board began to query offending managers about why they had treated a particular employee in a seemingly unfair fashion. The answer they frequently heard was, "Nobody ever told me that I should treat them this way. . . . There is nothing written down in the Policy and Procedure Manual that says that if they did this or if this was delivered to me late that I should do this . . . or that if my subordinate talked back to me that I should do this." CEO Fred Smith, Jim Barksdale, the company's chief operating officer at that time, and Jim Perkins, senior vice president of personnel and chief personnel officer, realized that part of the problem could be traced to a lack of clear and explicit guidelines about effective leadership behavior for front-line managers. Steve Nielsen paraphrased Barksdale's thoughts at the time: "At Federal Express, if you have the title of manager, that means you also have to be a leader . . . because all of our managers are responsible for people. You've got to listen to that voice [of leadership within]. It's called common sense. It's called conscience. It's called the right thing. We at Federal Express have given you that special trust and confidence as a leader. We need to get this message out to company managers."

Roy Yamahiro, vice president of human resources at the time, accepted the challenge of conveying a clear set of guidelines and formulated the idea of a Leadership Institute to address the problem. By 1984, the Institute and its first course, Management Principles I, was launched. In the spirit of using internal management resources, the course designers were company managers who also served as instructors.

Institute Preceptors

As described in Chapter Four, a most unusual feature of the Leadership Institute is its source of instructors or facilitators called management Preceptors. Drawn from the ranks of senior managers and managing directors who are themselves recognized as company leaders, Preceptors are chosen to teach and facilitate in Institute programs. Yamahiro believed that the best instructors would be practicing managers. The goal was to have Preceptors who mirror the values and philosophy of the company in their own track records. In other words, actual company leaders would be teaching leadership. Over the years, Institute director Nielsen has refined and enhanced its selection process so that the caliber of Preceptors today achieves that goal.

The Preceptor design has several unique advantages. For one, instructors are role models. By using practicing managers, the Leadership Institute ensures that classroom learnings generally remain grounded in the reality of the current workplace. As one Preceptor explained to us: "As a Preceptor, you are constantly looking back on yourself and seeing the mistakes you made at work as well as what worked. And how much learning material there is for the classrooms. This is part of what you end up sharing in the classroom. It keeps the discussions very much grounded in reality and in real solutions."

Second, the Preceptor system creates a two-way educational experience. Through their facilitating, Preceptors themselves learn more deeply about the principles of effective management and leadership. They return to management positions with a much broader perspective on the corporation and a better sense of how to develop their own people. In many ways, the Preceptors learn more than their participants. A typical comment we heard in interviews was, "Since becoming a Preceptor, I have a much greater understanding for the operational side of the business—out in the ground operations and in the hubs. I had worked as an engineer in a hub which is totally different from being out in the operations. I now have a much greater respect for what they do—such as the time limitations they have to deal with. . . . It is an invaluable experience because not only are you teaching but you also have an opportunity for self-development." Another Preceptor commented about skills they learn: "When I walk out of here in sixteen more months [and return to management], not only will I be back as a manager, but I will know far better how to develop my people. It is not only to my benefit but the company's as well. I feel like I have gotten a masters degree in facilitating. When I give a work group meeting, it is going to be far more powerful."

Finally, Preceptors have a limited term—twenty-four to thirty months at the Institute. This continual rotation introduces new mind-sets and ideas into curriculums. At the same time, the Leadership Institute today maintains a permanent staff who assist in logistics support and training design while ensuring continuity despite an ever-changing Preceptor staff.

The limitations of the Preceptor system have much to do with the temporary assignments, however. For example, managers who might make ideal Preceptors may be reluctant to leave management ranks for two years. Their superiors may also be concerned about losing valuable talent to the program. Other potential Preceptors simply do not want the demands of relocation. Some 60 to 70 percent of managers must physically relocate to Memphis, Tennessee. Moreover, there is the uncertainty of what company position will be available when the Preceptor's term ends. The company guarantees a job after the Preceptor's assignment, but not which job. Finally, as Preceptors become experts in the instructional process, it is time for them to leave. Talent is lost on a continual basis. The Leadership Institute must constantly invest in the development of Preceptors as they rotate in and out.

In addition to these tradeoffs, there is the particular challenge of who gets selected. Preceptors are chosen because they are role-model managers. This puts a heavy onus on the Leadership Institute. To guard its reputation and the credibility of what it teaches, selection must be conducted very carefully. And indeed it is, as we described in detail in Chapter Four.

Training of new Preceptors is largely through observing the more experienced ones in action. The first three months in the role essentially involve a great deal of observation and feedback. The new Preceptors first attend classes as actual participants prior to sitting in as observers. For all courses, they study facilitators' manuals that provide guidelines, activities, and learning objectives. After participating and observing, they are ready to join an experienced Preceptor as a cofacilitator for an ongoing course. During this experience, the institute's permanent staff are on hand to provide guidance and coaching. After each class session the new Preceptor and the staff review the session, pointing out positives and negatives about how the class was led. In addition, there is participant feedback to Preceptors for all of the Leadership Institute's courses.

Program Content and Learning Formats

Designed for the company's approximately 5,500 front-line managers, 1,000 senior managers, and 300 managing directors, the Leadership Institute's coursework centers largely around the three mandatory courses, each tailored to an employee's transition to a new level of leadership. Generally, these courses employ several essential leadership models that are shared by the three courses and taught largely through experiential learning experiences. Depending on the course, anywhere from 50 to 95 percent of the learning is experiential.

One popular exercise is a simulation involving a rescue operation after an earthquake in the Memphis hub of FedEx. Participants are provided a list of individuals trapped in the facilities. This gives details about work performance, race, gender, personal lifestyles, age, and so on. The participants must decide in what order the trapped individuals should be removed, knowing that additional damages and further earthquakes will not allow those last on the list to be rescued. This ranking is done individually and then as a group. When completed, two "reporters" arrive on the scene who are in actuality Leadership Institute Preceptors facilitating the course. The Preceptors then interview the leaders about the selections they have made and how they managed through the crisis. This exercise deals directly with diversity, emergency responsiveness, and how pressure may alter how a leader deals with individuals and relationships.

A second example is called the "checker's game," designed to teach the importance of delegation. In this exercise, participants are divided into three groups. One group represents experienced players of checkers, the second has little or no experience, and the third are experienced players but designated to manage the other two groups. The first group of experienced players take the black squares on the checkerboard and are placed around the outside of a horseshoe-shaped set of tables. On the inside of the horseshoe are the inexperienced players who take the red squares. The black-square players are instructed that they cannot make a move until their manager from the third group arrives and tells them where to move, nor are they allowed to challenge or question the move proposed by their manager. The red or inexperienced side has a manager as well, but one who plays an advisory role so that the "subordinates" or players can choose to heed advice or ignore the advice given or to simply discuss options. The red players can also move their pieces if their manager is not able to arrive on time. This latter rule becomes quite important because there is only one manager for each side, and the game operates under a strict time limit. What inevitably happens, of course, is that the manager of the black side always arrives late to moves and with little memory of what has happened beforehand. As a result, the black side of more experienced players ends up losing the majority of games. By having the more knowledgeable side fail because of autocratic leadership, the game teaches the importance of delegation, empowerment, and participative decision making in leading others. Both the checkers and rescue exercises essentially convey people-related leadership values.

Theory about leadership is taught largely through three models used by the Institute: the transformational, situational, and servant models. Each is designed to convey a core learning message to participants. A brief summary of each model follows.

The Transformational Model

Developed by political scientist James McGregor Burns and organizational psychologist Bernard Bass, this model essentially argues that the more effective leaders are those able to motivate subordinates to performance levels that exceed both their own and their leader's expectations. Transformational leaders accomplish this outcome by raising the importance or consequence of organizational goals, by demonstrating the means to achieve them, and by inducing subordinates to transcend their self-interests for the goal's achievement. In the process, they meet subordinates' higher-order needs for meaning and self-expression, which in turn generates commitment, effort, and ultimately greater performance. Federal Express has taken the Burns and Bass model and distilled it down to the three behavioral dimensions of charisma, individual consideration, and intellectual stimulation. To these are added another six dimensions that were identified by a corporate task force as descriptive of successful leaders at Federal Express. This in essence serves as a competency model for effective leadership behaviors at FedEx.

Situational Leadership

Whereas the transformational model teaches FedEx managers the essential behaviors of effective leaders, the situational model teaches that managers must vary their style with individual subordinates. Some subordinates need more hands-on guidance, others less. Developed by Paul Hersey and Kenneth Blanchard, the model revolves around a two-step process. In the first step, the manager assesses the readiness of their subordinate or group to perform a particular task. (Readiness is defined as a combination of the individual's ability and willingness to undertake the task.) After assessment, the manager must then take the second step, which is determining a leadership style most appropriate given this overall state of readiness. The model has four possible outcomes.

If the subordinate is unable and unwilling to perform the task, the most appropriate leadership style is to "tell"—in other words, for the manager to provide very specific instructions and to closely supervise performance (high task, low relationship). If the subordinate is unable but willing, the leadership style is to give detailed instructions with opportunities for clarification along with encouragement (high task, high relationship). If the subordinate is able but unwilling, the effective style is to promote participative decision making where the leader shares ideas and facilitates rather than directs the decision-making process (low task, high relationship). Finally, a situation where the subordinate is both able and willing requires a leadership style where the manager turns over responsibility for both decisions and implementation to the subordinate (low task, low relationship).

Servant Leadership

If situational leadership teaches one to vary approaches to leadership and the transformational model teaches core competencies, then the servant model is mostly about attitude. Based on the ideas of a former AT&T executive Robert Greenleaf, servant leadership is a philosophical model built on the premise that the most effective leaders are in essence servants to their subordinates. These leaders work for their staffs, not the other way around. Greenleaf's central premise is, "A new moral principle is emerging which holds that the only authority deserving one's allegiance is that which is freely and knowingly granted by the led to the leader in response to, and in proportion to, the clearly evident servant stature of the leader. Those who choose to follow this principle will not casually accept the authority of existing institutions. Rather, they will freely respond only to individuals who are chosen as leaders because they are proven and trusted as servants. To the extent that this principle prevails in the future, the only truly viable institutions will be those that are predominately servant-led." The model, in essence, can be represented by turning the traditional hierarchical pyramid upside down thereby placing customers and employees at the top and the president and CEO at the bottom.

The model has been grounded in actual managerial behaviors by an in-house study entitled the Federal Express Best People Practices that searched for managers who value employees as professionals, coach them in their work, help out when called upon, care about the long-term success of the group and the well-being of subordinates, and communicate reasons for changes in the operations. These have become the behavioral dimensions of servant leadership for FedEx managers to develop.

Participant Learnings

In interviews with program participants, it is clear that learning occurs around six categories: awareness of leadership concepts and principles, awareness of the skills required to implement those concepts and principles, the critical importance of constructive relationships in leading others, coaching skills, feedback on one's personal leadership style, and a heightened awareness of the Federal Express culture and company values and philosophy.

For example, in interviews with new managers in the Management Principles I course, we often heard them describe a central learning or two about leading their staff. Here are some representative comments:

"I realize now that I am not delegating enough. When we did the situational leadership exercise, I saw that I don't allow myself to see the opportunities to delegate. . . . Right now I have an employee in this kind of situation. I am trying to let him manage a particular situation. He knows exactly what to do, and I am using this as an example this week to keep my hands off. I have told him to let me know if he needs any help from me, but otherwise this is his opportunity."

"I think what you really remember is the importance of developing relationships. Having a relationship with people so that they feel free to talk to you about things. This is one of the key things you take away. If you don't have good relationships with people, you don't get things done."

"I need to focus on the minimal achievers in my work area. I have been hearing success stories from other people in this program about how they focused on the lowest rung—on the unmotivated, the low achiever. They got a little bit of a positive reaction from them and then just watched them grow. It has taught me that I need to focus on that. It is easy to interact with the star and good workers. My real challenge is to work with those who are less motivated."

Still, participants are quite realistic about the limitations of learning to be a leader in a week-long course: "Nobody is going to learn to be a leader in five days. . . . Nobody is going to walk out of here and practice everything that we have been taught. But what is going to happen is that some small part of it has sunk in somewhere in us, and at some point, you are going to run into a situation and something is going to click."

The Power of Reinforcing Systems

As we noted earlier, one cannot understand the impact of Federal Express's Leadership Institute in isolation from the company's culture and certain organizational systems. For example, the culture of Federal Express is relatively open and participative. It is guided by a belief that front-line employees possess a great deal of knowledge in terms of understanding their operations. Therefore they must be involved in implementing redesigns of their work. As a result, changes in company procedures are routinely discussed beforehand with employees to obtain their perspective. Many of the executives at the top of the company are role models themselves, and the culture itself is generally supportive of the leadership and people principles being taught in the classroom. In addition, Federal Express's well-articulated vision and its company programs such as the Guaranteed Fair Treatment Procedure, the LEAP program, and the Survey-Feedback-Action process reinforce leadership behaviors at multiple levels.

Case Study: PepsiCo's Building the Business Program

Among the more innovative programs for socializing senior-level managers is one run by PepsiCo entitled "Building the Business." What is most unusual about the program is the principle instructor: company CEO and chairman Roger Enrico. Tailored to be an intimate learning experience, only nine PepsiCo senior managers attend each session. Beforehand, they have each chosen a significant business-building project in collaboration with the president of their division that will serve as an important learning vehicle.

During the course of the program, each participant develops and refines a personal vision for their project, as well as an action plan for its implementation. In addition, there are educational sessions where participants learn about the fundamentals of leadership in

PepsiCo and receive 360-degree feedback on their own leadership style. The five days of the program are devoted to learning about PepsiCo leadership fundamentals, receiving personal feedback, and honing their projects. Enrico will follow up after the program with a personal visit or call to each of the participants.

The program has been so successful that its designer, vice president of executive development Paul Russell (who is responsible for the company's top nine hundred executives), has launched additional programs using other corporate executives as instructors. When we interviewed Russell, his PepsiCo Learning Center had eight programs running and several in the works. The current programs include Enrico's on leadership as well as a series of functional excellence programs on key topics in marketing, research and development, and human resources. A similar program targeted at finance is in the design stage. Sessions for each program are generally held two to three times a year. A major new program is in the final development stages and will reach all of PepsiCo's top nine hundred executives by 2001. It will consist of detailed coverage of the key levers of customers, consumers, and competitors that drive the business to profitable growth.

Program Origins

Building the Business had its origins in 1993, when at the age of 48, Roger Enrico was chairman of PepsiCo Worldwide Foods and was seriously contemplating a second career teaching at a university (Tichy and DeRose, 1996). Wayne Calloway, PepsiCo's CEO, and Enrico's close associate Joseph McCann, senior vice president for public affairs, set out to convince him to stay at PepsiCo. Why not become a teacher at PepsiCo instead?

Calloway was deeply concerned that leadership talent in the company would soon be in short supply given future growth prospects for PepsiCo. His division presidents, however, were not responding aggressively to the magnitude of the problem. They were even reluctant to spend funds earmarked for leadership development. Instead they reclaimed half of these monies annually to improve their final profit picture. PepsiCo had for a long time considered itself to be one of the top producers of executive talent in the United States and deeply believed in its system of challenging job assignments and cross-division transfers as the best means to develop leadership talent. These beliefs had led to inertia on the part of division executives and to reluctance to invest their resources in training and development programs. But in 1991, Calloway criticized them for such shortsightedness. He explained that fewer than 20 percent of company executives would be in the same position five years later— meaning that demand would move them forward rapidly. He added that though PepsiCo then filled some 86 percent of its executive vacancies from within, the coming crunch for talent would soon compromise this promote-from-within policy. The risk was that a large surge of outsiders might undermine the cultural fabric and operational standards of the company. His message to the division presidents was simply to get going on executive development, and hastily.

To supplement the divisional efforts, in February of 1993 Calloway challenged Paul Russell, then director of executive development, to develop "the world's leading executive development program" for use across the corporation. One day in discussions about his early design of a potential program, the senior vice president of personnel commented that Roger Enrico had expressed a strong interest in doing something similar. At that time, Russell did not know Enrico. Not wishing to compete with any efforts of Enrico's, he decided to pay a visit to Enrico to discuss the possibility of a partnership. Beforehand, Russell called Enrico's assistant and requested speeches from the last year. Russell read through these and distilled a de facto model of Enrico's perspective on leadership as preparatory homework. During their visit, Enrico explained his desire to return to others what his mentor Don Kendall, PepsiCo's cofounder, had done for him. Part of Pepsi's history was that executives often had one or two individuals who served as important mentors for up-and-coming executives. Enrico wanted to expand his circle of mentoring to more than just one or two key players, however. A course might be the ideal vehicle. He also told Russell that his message was a personal one, and that he wanted a small audience with whom he could build a mentoring relationship. He was reluctant to simply become a stand-up instructor before large audiences. Instead he wanted something quite different, though he was not certain how to put it all together.

Sensing mutual interests, the two agreed to collaborate. Calloway had urged Enrico to use the program as a vehicle for generating new growth ideas for the company, which fit nicely with Enrico's belief that managers often suffered from the "tyranny of incrementalism"—ideas that only built marginally upon existing businesses. With growth ideas and leadership as the central building blocks, Russell and Enrico worked toward a final design drawing on Enrico's philosophy of leadership and the work of noted leadership theorists. Time with Enrico, however, was often so tight that at one point Russell had to resort to flying with him on a business trip to Spain and Portugal, working in airplanes and hotel rooms to finish the program.

One day while in Madrid and close to the program launch, Russell observed that Enrico seemed to be losing his excitement about the program. When asked about it, Enrico explained that he was concerned about teaching a program based on models of leadership developed by others. Wouldn't it be better to simply hire business school professors to teach the program? Russell's response was emphatic: this was a program for PepsiCo people by PepsiCo people. At that moment, the two men decided to scrap their existing design using other people's models of leadership. The program instead would be built entirely upon Enrico's own ideas about leadership that would be translated into a five-point framework.

Program Objectives

The program has several crucial objectives related to PepsiCo's future and its leadership needs. First of all, it aims to be a watershed event in the careers of very-high-potential executives. It is a transition marker of sorts, saying that the company is formally recognizing them as one of its best bets for PepsiCo's future. It is also a vehicle to assist in that transition by providing participants with a practical leadership model, tools, and a chance to learn about leadership from a world-class leader. The choice of a Build the Business project has several aims. One, it socializes participants into understanding that the greatest value a leader can add to their organization is to become a change agent, to build the business in some significant way. Drawing on Enrico's guidance to assist in refining and implementing their projects, a second goal is to dramatically improve executives' ability to make an impact. The concern is simply to help them launch their ideas. Finally, the experience helps executives improve their understanding of how things really get done at the executive level.

Program Instruction

Many management programs involve company executives as guest speakers, but it is extremely rare to see them as full-time instructors. In Building the Business, Enrico plays the full-time lead role as instructor, but he is indirectly supported by several other executive teachers. Video commentaries from the division presidents are used for instruction, and each of the five themes of Enrico's model is illustrated by comments from four or five division presidents. As Russell explains, his objective was "to create a feeling through the videos that the program is team-taught. As a participant, you really get to know the division presidents and their viewpoint on what leadership is and what is important in driving change. And while their styles can be widely different, their underlying philosophies are quite similar. By the end of the week, even though you have not personally met any of these people, you feel you know them well." In addition, Russell is on site to provide assistance to both Enrico and the participants during the program.

This diversity of leaders shown as models is helpful in addressing a desire of Enrico's not to appear to be trying to build clones of himself. This potential problem was identified early on in the program design when Russell canvassed line managers across PepsiCo to get reactions about the program idea. A small percentage of individuals had expressed cynicism that perhaps Enrico was trying to create mirror images of himself. This was in reality the opposite of Enrico's true intention. To the contrary, his message to participants is that everyone needs to leverage the special skills they possess to "find the leader in themselves" and to develop their own style. In other words, there is no one best style for leading. So while the personalities and leadership models of the division leaders vary widely, it is in their shared values that participants can learn about leadership. Here we return to the notion of socializing key values. Elaborating on this idea, Russell comments, "We believe there is a common set of values in this company that should be subscribed to. These values are broad enough to give our people tremendous flexibility and room to move. Our executives should be able to fully develop their style into a strong leadership style in whatever way is best for them and still live within these values."

Program Description

Program Prework: The major prework for participants is to identify a business project that will serve as an important learning vehicle. The mandate from Enrico is that the project must be "big." This means that the initiative must affect the division's product quality, costs, customer satisfaction, or revenues in a dramatic fashion. One central aim of the course is to help participants accelerate their progress in the initiative's implementation. Examples of past projects include strategies to combat private-label businesses, a Frito Lay joint venture, and a family meals campaign for Kentucky Fried Chicken in Australia, which was later rolled out worldwide.

Sunday Night: The opening by Roger Enrico sets the challenging tone for the week: "The good news is that somebody believes in you enough to feel that you belong in this program. The people we are looking for in this program are the people that the division presidents think could be future division presidents themselves. The bad news is that it carries with it an extra burden. Simply put, we expect more from you. We think that you will go farther, and consequently we are going to push you harder and expect more from you. No more can you point upwards and say 'Those folks at the top don't know what they are doing.' Because as of right now, you are one of them." The message is "accept the mantle of leadership being handed to you" as of this program.

That evening or the very next morning all participants must deliver an "elevator speech." Enrico explains, "Imagine you have just gotten into an elevator. You have three minutes to the top. In that three-minute period, you need to convey the essence of your project and why it's so important to the group who you are imagining in the elevator with you." This exercise is used by Enrico to drive home the notion that unless an individual can articulate the essence of their project in less than three minutes then they need more work to crystallize their vision. Generally, half of the group has a difficult time achieving this outcome. It also sets up a discipline early in the seminar that crystal clarity of purpose is of the essence.

Monday: The second day begins with Enrico sharing his own elevator speech about why he is conducting the program. The essence of his message is that he is here to help the group see things that they have not seen before, to open their eyes to see that they are leaders. Enrico's message is straightforward: "This is how things get done. You don't wait for somebody to tell you to do something. You don't even have to wait for someone to tell you it is okay to do something. You figure it out and you make it happen. It is time to get your own agenda and to figure out how to drive it." He then goes on to describe his career and the mentors who shaped it.

His stories about mentors contain certain important lessons that Enrico wishes to convey. For example, his experiences with various mentors highlight themes about the obligation of leaders to develop leaders. Other times he will use it to highlight points in his model of leadership. For example, under the ability to "think in different terms," he describes being called in to see a former CEO of PepsiCo.

He assumed that the appointment concerned a project that he had been working on. So he arrived with a presentation in hand ready to explain himself and the project. Instead the CEO began to discuss the opera, world politics, and an upcoming trip to Russia. It was a broad, sweeping discussion. As it ended, the CEO asked Enrico to schedule a meeting with him once a month to talk about such issues. As he left the office, Enrico realized that the CEO was simply making certain that he was building a broader thinker for the company.

Enrico then covers the purpose of the program. His goal is to accentuate the leadership skills that the participants already have. This is not a remedial course but a "take-it-to-the-next-level" course. His goal is to graduate a group of change agents who understand that the biggest value they bring is driving productive change. The purpose of the course is to give them some new ways to think about how to effectively drive change.

Central to the learning experience is the opportunity to simply hear and learn from Enrico. Questions to him are an essential part of the learning. No question is off limits, and discussions are direct and candid.

After this introduction, Enrico then focuses on how the division presidents describe "running their businesses" versus "building their businesses." Videos of each division president are shown describing the differences in their own words. Running the business is the role of managing; building the business is the role of leadership. This contrast is used to establish an important distinction between managing and leading early in the course. Although both are essential (in fact, if you cannot do the former, you do not even get a chance to do the latter), the program is designed to learn about building the business.

Afterward, myths about leadership are explored. For example, the notion that leaders are individuals with high IQs and that they are invulnerable is explored and debunked. This is reinforced by the division presidents, who in their videos talk about the importance of admitting mistakes or setting a vision or empowering. Following this, the leadership model of the five themes is presented and discussed.

In the afternoon, Enrico meets individually with each participant for a half hour to discuss any leadership subjects they wish to discuss. The discussions with Enrico tend to focus on each participant's project. What barriers are they facing? Are they really thinking big enough about the project? Participants will have a second individual session with Enrico three days later. This one tends to focus more on the personal side where they discuss career issues, problems they are having with leadership, or challenges they are facing with their boss.

Concurrently, Russell meets with the participants one on one to discuss their feedback from the 360-degree assessment. This provides them with self, boss, peer, and subordinate feedback on the set of leadership competencies. In addition to helping interpret their results, Russell covers what each participant is likely to gain from the course relative to their developmental needs. Given that he has reviewed feedback reports of several hundred top managers at PepsiCo, Russell is able to interpret and discuss each participant's feedback relative to the population of senior managers. In addition to the leadership survey, participants also receive feedback on a management styles inventory and on a climate survey, both of which draw upon self and subordinate assessments. The latter looks at issues such as subordinates' levels of satisfaction, communications within the participant's work group, the clarity of the unit's goals, teamwork, and the clarity of performance expectations.

Those who are not working with Enrico or Russell are busy preparing an exercise called the "Fortune magazine article." This exercise has them write an article projecting the outcome of their project several years hence. Later in the program, the articles serve as a point of discussion and learning. In summary, Monday is devoted largely to exploring the importance of new business ideas— where they come from, how they are developed, and how they are crystallized into concrete projects.

Tuesday: This day focuses on how individuals ensure that their growth ideas are good ones and determines which ones to ultimately pursue. Enrico lays out the basic ideas here. For example, before drafting an idea into a formal, written proposal, it is best to talk to others and get their reactions. Test it on the boss, peers, and anyone else who will listen. In the process, reflect on the language you are using to describe the idea. Language, Enrico argues, is important to create a positive emotional response and to get others' commitment. So in addition to assessing the idea, assess how to communicate it and gauge others' reactions to it. This process is essentially testing the notion of whether the person has a compelling proposition or not.

Much of the Tuesday discussion is centered around the importance of language. Enrico draws on a personal example where he took over the helm at Frito Lay and used the expression "take back the streets" to emotionally convey the necessity of Frito overcoming its eroding market share. "Take back the streets" soon began to show up in managers' speeches and on the company's stationery. It evoked an emotional response and became a rallying cry.

Then the emphasis turns to measuring the vision's progress—how best to benchmark and what kinds of metrics to employ. The late afternoon is spent sharing the "Fortune articles" that everyone has written. They learn that they still require further refinement in terms of the ideas and the language used to convey them. As a group, participants listen and critique each other's articles, acting as consultants to help with improvements.

Wednesday: A day off from the classroom.

Thursday: This day is devoted to understanding how to gain commitment to a new vision. Issues such as dealing with resistance, understanding the needs and concerns of key stakeholders, and how to enlist others are covered. Again a series of videos are employed with comments drawing on the experiences of the division presidents—their success and failure stories about actual initiatives. A discussion follows where links are made to the participants' own projects. In sessions such as these, Enrico will guide the discussion and provide summaries at the end where he shares the key lessons that everyone needs to understand.

The final part of the program is devoted to lessons on how to make change happen. So the focus is squarely on execution. Participants on this day have their second one-on-one with Enrico and prepare a final presentation on their project.

Friday: The presentation is shared with the group in a ten-minute overview of what they will communicate back to their key stakeholders at the office. This is followed by a discussion of the overview. The program concludes with a discussion of the legacy each participant wants to leave at the end of their career.

6

Strategic Leadership Initiatives

Business leaders today face a marketplace characterized by change and growing complexity. Numerous books, articles, and studies document the scope of this change and offer insight into the forces that create it. We all know the story line: an increasingly global marketplace, rapid technological innovation, industry deregulation, privatization pressures, not to mention a resurgence of merger and acquisition activity, all have converged to create the treacherous corporate white water that today's business leaders must navigate. Unfortunately, many leaders have discovered in the midst of this sea change that they are ill-prepared to respond to—let alone lead—this change. Schooled on the calmer waters of a more stable past, many executives and general managers have reluctantly come to realize that their existing leadership skills may be insufficient to meet the demands of the hypercompetitive, rapidly changing business environment of the twenty-first century.

There are strong indications that learning how to manage the speed, direction, and intensity of strategic and organizational change will be the key driver of corporate success in the years ahead (Verlander, 1992). Moreover, this learning will be required not only of the organization's most senior leaders but of leaders throughout the corporate hierarchy. No longer will senior leaders be able to rely on the top-down command-and-control tactics of the past, for these work only when the organization's environment is relatively stable and when directives can be well defined. In today's world of short-ened product life cycles, international economic integration, and deregulated markets, a more visionary and collaborative form of leadership is needed. Important components of this new form of leadership are the capacity to think critically, to plan strategi-cally, and to draw upon the insights of others. Leaders throughout the organization—not just at the top—must be able to create strat-egy and lead change. To do so, however, requires that leaders share a common understanding of what it means to be strategic given the organization's immediate and long-term goals. In other words, lead-ers must develop a collective understanding of the organization's environment, the challenges it presents, and the firm's vision for responding to those challenges. Only then will the firm's leadership be able to achieve the coordinated action necessary for driving large-scale change.

Given the ubiquity of change and the increasing importance of an organization's capacity to adapt to it, many organizations have begun to see a critical role for executive education in their strate-gic change efforts. These companies realize that executive educa-tion can serve as one of several key process levers that can help align an organization to its strategic imperatives. For these leading-edge firms, leadership development represents a strategic interven-tion that is able not only to affect change but to build many of the organization's core competencies. In essence, leadership develop-ment serves a dual purpose: it builds critical capabilities while at the same time achieving real-time business needs. In this chapter, we examine the role of leadership development as a strategic inter-vention and examine several design elements that have come to characterize this form of development. We describe representative programs and highlight features that make them effective. We also identify a number of problems that can undermine a program's impact. We begin our discussion by examining how and why many of today's leaders lack the capabilities needed to guide their firms through sig-nificant change.

The Challenge of Change
and the Legacy of Management

The discrepancy between today's business challenges and the capabilities of many of today's corporate leaders can be attributed to two related phenomena. At the macro level, many leaders are largely a product of the times they grew up in. Like all of us, leaders develop capabilities consistent with the demands of their surroundings. Thus, to better understand their capabilities and deficiencies, we need to examine the history and demands of the business environments within which they were raised.

What we find in looking at the history of most industries is a common evolutionary pattern. It looks something like the following (Kanter, Stein, and Jick, 1992). First, industries initially form when new technologies make it possible for activities that were previously difficult or fragmented to be performed efficiently on a large-scale basis. After an early round of competition among firms experimenting with various approaches, a few dominant players emerge as victors. A network of suppliers grows up to service these survivors, a set of customers typically comes to depend on their products, and industry standards are established. Competition tends to stabilize at this point, with the surviving players competing largely among themselves for relative position within a well-defined, sometimes geographically bounded space.

Prior to the 1980s, this was the environment within which most corporate executives learned to lead and compete. Concerned mainly with protecting existing advantages in established markets, these executives learned to manage their firm's internal growth, improve efficiency, and manage add-ons and enhancements to existing products. They learned to manage incremental change because the changes they had to deal with were indeed largely incremental.

A second, related phenomenon adds additional insight to this evolutionary account—this time from a more micro-level perspective. In this case, the emphasis is not on industry dynamics per se, but rather on the organizational cultures that have emerged in light of these dynamics. As industries evolve and dominant organizations emerge, the primary challenge for many firms becomes the management of a growing bureaucracy. According to Harvard Business School professor John Kotter (1996), the organization's need to deal with its growing bureaucracy causes it to focus primarily on monitoring and managing internal operations rather than adapting to external demands. An emphasis on management—the set of processes that keeps existing systems running smoothly—rather than leadership—the set of processes that initiates and adapts the organization to significant change—becomes ingrained in the very fabric of the corporate culture: "After a while, keeping the ever-larger organization under control becomes the primary challenge. So attention turns inward, and managerial competencies are nurtured. With a strong emphasis on management but not leadership, bureaucracy and an inward focus take over. But with continued success . . . the problem often goes unaddressed and an unhealthy arrogance begins to evolve. All of these characteristics then make any transformation effort much more difficult" (Kotter, 1996, p. 27).

Such was the case for many companies in the 1990s. These firms discovered that their managers had become stronger in management skills than in leadership skills and that many had become overly confident and somewhat complacent. Arrogant managers—though perhaps good at managing internal processes—also often overestimate their firm's competitive position in the market, listen poorly, and learn slowly (Kotter, 1996). They tend to respond to bureaucracy by creating bureaucratic cultures that place a premium on processes such as planning, budgeting, organizing, and controlling over communicating, motivating, and inspiring. These cultures, in turn, perpetuate and reinforce an inward focus and further retard individual efforts to respond to changing conditions. Together, these forces not only smother individual efforts to initiate change, they hamper the learning and development of competencies needed to

lead change. Environmental conditions eventually become less stable and a critical gap emerges between internal capabilities and
external demands.

Such a gap has become painfully apparent in the leadership
structures of many of today's corporations. Many CEOs realize that
their individual leaders and organizational capabilities are not up
to the demands of their business strategy. Because change depends
on the new use of information, which often means that information
must be acquired from the world outside (MacDonald, 1995), the
myopic managerial cultures of the past have thwarted critical learning opportunities. As Kotter notes: "The combination of cultures
that resist change and managers who have not been taught how to
create change is lethal" (1996, p. 29).

A New Role for Leadership Development

Recognizing the change imperative and the executive's role in leading corporate transition, many firms have begun to invest in a new
form of leadership development in order to address the skills gap
just mentioned. This new approach tends to be more customized,
learner centered, and integrated with the organization's immediate
strategic agenda than past efforts. No longer just a forum for teaching abstract concepts or functional skills, development programs are
increasingly used as opportunities to recast the worldviews of executive teams and to align the organization to a new direction. These
programs facilitate efforts to communicate and implement the corporate vision, to build strategic unity throughout the company, and
to create a cadre of change agents. They simultaneously build the
firm's leadership capabilities while facilitating progress toward key
corporate objectives.

To understand how these programs differ from more traditional
development efforts, it is helpful to examine their objectives. In contrast to traditional development programs—which seek to impart

generic leadership skills or enhance functional knowledge or socialize values—leadership development programs aimed at strategic
intervention seek to advance five very different objectives:

1. To facilitate a unified, collective understanding of the firm's
   strategic vision
2. To expedite large-scale change
3. To ensure the immediate application of useful knowledge
4. To build depth of leadership talent
5. To achieve measurable results that meet the "bottom line"

Let us look at each of these in turn. First, the most distinctive
feature of this new development approach is the focus on the firm's
strategic vision and change agenda. Without question, development
programs aimed at change must focus first and foremost on developing a clear understanding of the firm's strategic priorities and on
providing the knowledge, skills, and support systems needed to
interpret and execute these priorities across all levels of the corporate hierarchy.

Because of the emphasis on the firm's strategic vision, this new
breed of leadership development can play a major role in an organization's transformation efforts. Firms see these programs as a critical tool for creating dialogue around a new corporate vision and
for building consensus on how the vision should be implemented.
Such programs are often desperately needed and incredibly useful
because they can surface underlying assumptions and reveal conflicting perspectives that might otherwise fester in the background
and impede change.

Indeed, without structured opportunities to learn and grapple
with the firm's new strategy and without time to discuss changes in
roles, responsibilities, and expectations that ensue, many managers
find it difficult to embrace a firm's new direction. This is to be
expected because a new vision is often vastly different from how

managers have operated in the past and from what they have previously worked to accomplish. It is critical to get these interpretive differences out in the open and to identify conflicting opinions early on. Otherwise, leaders may fail to develop ownership of the new vision and may end up working at cross purposes. By providing organizational members with well-constructed occasions for collective reflection, innovative leadership development programs can play an important role in minimizing political battles and interpretive standoffs. Structured exercises, well-focused topics, and process assistance can all help to enhance dialogue and facilitate collective decision making. The best programs, in fact, work to disseminate communication and collaboration processes throughout the firm. To the extent they are successful, they perpetuate the benefits of open dialogue and build adaptive flexibility into the organization's very culture.

In addition to building a unified commitment to the firm's strategic vision and expediting large-scale change, leadership development and intervention programs work to accomplish the other three objectives listed. It is important to note, however, that the first two objectives—facilitating vision and change—largely drive the remaining three. As such, the desire to expedite change consistent with the firm's vision requires that programs provide knowledge and skills that are immediately useful and relevant to implementing the vision. If, for example, identifying and building new business opportunities is a necessary competency for achieving the firm's vision, then new business development takes center stage in the educational experience. If strategy implementation skills are of paramount importance, then they become the primary focus of the learning effort.

One of the most important distinctions of programs designed to facilitate strategic transformation is their inclusiveness. No longer designed solely to groom the corporate elite, these programs recognize that large-scale change depends on buy-in from more than just the senior leadership. Widespread involvement is a necessity. All managers and employees must take ownership of a new vision and apply it to their daily decisions. If lower-level staff are expected to make decisions consistent with the firm's new priorities, then these individuals must be shown the logic of the strategy and be able to interpret it to fit their local conditions. Moreover, if these individuals are expected to implement the new vision, they must be given skills to design supporting initiatives, integrate and communicate these initiatives to their staffs, and motivate and inspire others to make the vision a reality. In short, strategic thinking capabilities must be distributed throughout the corporate hierarchy. In today's faster-paced environment, those firms that reserve strategic capabilities solely for their upper echelons will find themselves, in effect, "hobbled at the knees." They will lack the foresight to anticipate change and the strategic horsepower to adapt to change quickly and continuously. Thus, the fourth objective is to build a depth of leadership talent throughout the firm.

Finally, development programs aimed at change tend to emphasize results that meet the bottom line. As corporate cost-cutting has become commonplace throughout industry, budgets for executive education have been placed under greater scrutiny. No longer just a reward for past accomplishment or preparation for future responsibilities, these programs are evaluated according to their cost-to-benefit ratio. This results-oriented approach has heightened efforts to tailor programs to specific strategic needs and has increased the frequency of in-house, customized program designs. Firms have discovered that working closely with a select group of university professors or facilitator-consultants allows them to maintain greater control over the content of their offerings and to contain costs. Indeed, it doesn't take long to determine that hiring five faculty members or consultants to design and teach an in-company program for several hundred managers is less expensive than sending each of those managers to a one-week session at a prestigious university or commercial program.

As with the two other leadership development approaches we have examined in this book, leadership development programs that seek to facilitate strategic change have a number of common design elements. These elements include a well-articulated strategic framework, sophisticated assessment processes, content customized to promote strategic objectives, learning organized around executive cohorts, curricula designed to elicit collective dialogue, trained facilitators, and active feedback processes. Before we examine each of these in turn, let us first take a look at a typical program in context.

A Case Study: Philips Operation Centurion

Starting out as a manufacturer of incandescent lamps in 1891 in the Netherlands, Philips had transformed itself over the decades into a global producer of lighting and electronics. In the early 1930s, it laid the groundwork for its successful growth by transferring production from the Netherlands to local countries to overcome barriers created by a world trading environment that was highly protectionist. Its operating philosophy became "local factories making local products, for local markets, under local management control" (Ellis and Williams, 1996).

Though this design ensured some four decades of remarkable growth, by the 1980s shifts in the competitive dynamics of the industry began to undermine its effectiveness. Specifically, Japanese electronics companies had begun to coordinate their own efforts through clearly defined, integrated global strategies. With more centralized operations, they became better positioned to take advantage of economies of scale in both production and sourcing than Philips. Philips had little ability to leverage its technology, marketing, and managerial talent across national borders. In addition, the narrow view of a single marketplace caused country managers to underestimate the threat posed by Japanese manufacturers. By the 1980s, the company's growing lack of competitiveness began to show itself in the balance sheet. For example, its product margins lagged significantly behind those of the 1960s. In 1990, senior managers predicted a strong upturn in performance but were instead greeted with a crisis. That year, Philips posted record losses. Senior management determined it was time for a radical intervention.

In 1990, a new chairman was appointed, Jan Timmer. He called a special three-day retreat of his top one hundred managers to discuss the future of Philips and to mobilize their leadership in new directions. He began the retreat by circulating a copy of an article from the *Wall Street Journal* declaring that Philips had announced it would enter bankruptcy proceedings. Though his executives quickly realized that the article was a hoax, it nonetheless drove home Timmer's point. The company was deep in a crisis. In that retreat, Timmer built consensus among Philips's senior executives that they would have to take responsibility for changing their troubled organization. They were now enlisted to lead Philips out of its current predicament.

Under Timmer's leadership, Operation Centurion was launched. Centurion had several critical objectives that had been significantly shaped by C. K. Prahalad, a strategy professor at the University of Michigan. The program's goal was to revitalize the company in two phases of activity. The first involved a short-term restructuring phase aimed at rapidly bridging performance gaps with the competition. Sales organizations were streamlined, factories closed, product lines pruned, headcounts reduced, and major assets disposed. The streamlining activities were to be followed by a longer-term initiative, the Philips Quality Drive.

The challenge for Philips was reaching its 244,000 employees working in 272 production centers in 52 countries. Three activities were used to bridge this enormous company. The first was a leadership initiative built around translating the corporate vision into local goals and programs. Some thirty thousand managers representing four of the company's most senior levels were brought together in groups of thirty to seventy for a three-day Operation

Centurion program. With the exception of the corporate level, groups were formed with members from within the same division. These leadership team meetings set out to translate the company's vision of the change process into actions and goals for the business units and product divisions.

Each of the three days represented a separate learning module. The first day was designed to confront participants with the current state of Philips's business by benchmarking the company against their "best in class" competitors. This was followed by the groups working to identify the key challenges facing their business. The second day focused on how major transformations had unfolded at other large companies. On the final day, groups devoted their attention to action planning and setting stretch targets and goals for their business units. All told, some six hundred change projects were initiated.

These were followed by some twenty-two task forces examining important aspects of the company's strategy, marketing, corporate governance, management skills, research, products, and assets. Their aim was to identify and address issues that managers believed were key drivers for the future vision. Each task force was given a champion who had a track record of performance in the area being examined (see Exhibit 6.1).

Whereas the first initiative focused on a top-down cascade of communications, the second came from the opposite direction by reaching some two hundred thousand employees. Town meetings of up to four hundred people were held at each plant to discuss the implications of the change process for individual work environments. They served both to convey information about the change initiative and to identify local plans.

Two days were devoted to interactive satellite discussions for the entire European workforce. One occurred in 1992 and the other in 1994. Their principal purpose was to discuss how Philips could become more customer focused and quality driven.

In conjunction with these activities, the Group Management Committee created a code of conduct for the company known as

Exhibit 6.1. Philips Centurion Taskforce Clusters

Assets
- Stock management
- Accounts receivable
- Fixed assets

Product
- R&D effectiveness
- Miniaturization
- Purchasing/supplier base

Marketing
- Customer first
- Brand/channel management
- Corporate image

Strategy
- Strategic direction
- Alliances/standards

Governance
- Management skills
- Shared values/corporate governance

Source: Based on "Some basic issues relating to Europe's future in electronics," Philips internal briefing document, 1992, p. 54. Reprinted by permission of Philips International B.V.

the "Philips Way," which included values such as "surpass customer expectations," "inspire a passion for quality," "encourage entrepreneurial behavior at all levels," and "achieve premium return on equity." Exhibit 6.2 lists its core values.

Centurion's impact would be felt in the company's overall performance as it steadily improved over the next few years. But as with all such programs, unto themselves they are not enough. They are but one or two of the many steps that must be taken over a continuous period. For example, performance across the entire company has not been con-

Exhibit 6.2. The Philips Way

Customer first	Surpass customer expectations
Demonstrate leadership	Inspire the passion for quality
Value people as the company's greatest asset	Respect for each other; teamwork
Encourage entrepreneurial behavior at all levels	Strive for excellence
Achieve premium return on equity	Improve continuously

Source: Based on "Philips Quality," Philips internal document, 1993, p. 13. Reprinted by permission of Philips International B.V.

sistent. Several divisions continued to struggle, such as Grundig, the company's consumer electronics division, which has now been sold.

After the company's performance began to turn around, the sense of urgency necessary to drive change diminished. Jan Timmer himself resigned from the board in 1997 after leading a six-year restructuring effort. Nonetheless, the initiative did enlist thousands of leaders at all levels of the corporation in reexamining existing strategies, structures, and systems and in reinventing these to fit a new business reality. It facilitated a unified, collective understanding of the firm's new vision and of crucial shifts in its competitive world. The company has also reversed its fortunes with improved profitability in recent years. At last report, the new CEO, Cor Boonstra, is launching a new initiative.

The Philips case illustrates the demands of such leadership interventions. They are logistically complex and require a concerted effort at all levels of an organization to have a truly positive impact.

Common Design Elements of Intervention Programs

Leadership programs built around strategic interventions appear to be growing in popularity. Organizations ranging from major automakers to software producers to the U.S. Army have used and benefited from programs designed to enhance leadership capabilities and simultaneously facilitate significant strategic change. Yet though these programs have become more prevalent, they have not become any easier to execute. They continue to require intense planning, elaborate logistical support, and careful attention to follow-through and reinforcement. Neglecting any of these can cost the organization dearly in terms of time, money, and the support of some of its most valuable employees. When executed well, however, the benefits of these programs are tremendous. They can galvanize leaders across all levels of the organization into a unified force for change. Part of their strength lies in the fact that they compel those sponsoring and designing the effort to be very clear about its focus. To the extent that senior management has a clearly defined change agenda and a good sense of the leadership requirements needed to carry it out, these programs can be extremely effective mechanisms for building a shared vision that is meaningful and actionable for all involved.

During our research, we examined a number of leadership development programs designed to spur strategic change. Not surprisingly, we discovered that certain design elements were common among the more successful programs and were usually necessary to realize the programs' full potential.

1. Strategic Framework Drives Program Content

The single most important feature of any leadership development program designed to facilitate large-scale change is a clearly articulated framework that guides the firm's collective efforts. Leadership development programs that bring about effective change do so in large part because they provide structured experiences that focus participants on the firm's strategic agenda and improve employees' understanding of how that agenda can be implemented in local, day-to-day activities. Because development programs bring together many of an organization's most influential players, they have the potential to be powerful events. If the firm's strategic agenda is well thought out and carefully crafted, programs can enhance a shared understanding of the firm's objectives and accelerate progress toward their achievement. If, however, the strategy is vague or clouded by competing initiatives, the development effort will simply surface underlying conflicts, create frustration, and ultimately increase opposition to the change effort. In short, these programs can be a double-edged sword and should be undertaken when there is consensus around a clear strategic agenda. If programs work, there is a significant upside: enhanced capabilities, shared vision, large-scale change. However, if programs fall short (which they often do), there is an equally significant downside: strategic confusion, dashed expectations, loss of confidence in senior management, and the potential alienation of some of the organization's most highly valued employees.

One firm that has developed a very successful program to enhance leadership and facilitate large-scale change is Ernst & Young (our Chapter Seven case study), one of the largest and fastest-growing audit, tax, and consulting firms. Its Leadership 2000 program was successful in large part because the firm had a clear strategic framework that drove its program design. The firm's overarching strategy dictated the goals and content of its leadership development program and provided a clear focus for program participants. Faced with consolidating markets, a shrinking customer base, and growing competition in its tax and audit businesses, the firm realized that it would have to make some major changes to survive the consolidation beginning to take place among "Big Six" firms and many of their markets. To be successful, Ernst & Young determined that it would have to penetrate high-value markets by offering superior industry-specific services. Numerous initiatives were put into place across the firm's many practices to move the vision forward. The firm's chairman, Phil Laskawy, however, realized that achieving such an ambitious and complex vision would require that managers and partners throughout the firm understand how these strategic initiatives fit together and be able to take actions consistent with the firm's overall thrust. Only then would they be able to achieve the unity and coordination needed to bring the vision to fruition.

As an important first step in building this understanding, Laskawy and his staff created Vision 2000, a strategic framework that formally tied together the various strategic plans in the firm's tax, audit, and consulting practices. Corporate publications and communication briefs explained the framework, and schematic diagrams were created to illustrate it. More importantly, the framework provided a concrete focus to the organization's leadership development agenda. Because Vision 2000 aimed to build market share in high-priority industries by offering tailored, integrated services to dominant firms within those industries, the Leadership 2000 program sought to provide a learning experience that would foster leadership development and industry strategies that would advance its targeted growth objectives.

This was done in two ways. First, because the nineteen area managing partners and their leadership teams would have to customize the firm's vision to fit local conditions, the program brought these leadership teams together to learn about visioning processes and implementation strategies that would facilitate their efforts. A business school professor was brought in to teach concepts on vision formation and vision implementation. Through several highly interactive sessions, the professor drew participants together to collectively discuss and reflect on the concept of vision and to examine techniques for communicating and instilling vision throughout the organization.

Second, the program involved the area teams in facilitated group exercises designed to enhance team leadership, collaboration, and a common team understanding of the firm's vision and its implications for their local practice. Each group was composed of the leadership team from a given geographical area who worked together on a regular basis. An experienced facilitator guided each executive cohort through a series of structured exercises designed to promote collective discussion, clarify roles and responsibilities, and facilitate decision making and commitment around the new strategic agenda. The exercises were purposely experiential and intended not only to enhance the development of communication and teaming competencies but to jump-start each group's strategic implementation efforts. Guided by the facilitators, each group spent approximately half of the two-day program in break-out sessions discussing how the firm's larger vision could be adapted to local conditions and implemented in specific operations and markets. The firm's clear strategic framework provided both the focus and the flexibility that leaders needed to simultaneously experience and learn. Without this overarching conceptual structure, the program would have lost the direction, content, and relevance that made it both instructional and compelling—not to mention strategically important.

2. Up-Front Assessment of the Organization's Learning Needs

To be effective, strategic intervention programs must be preceded by an in-depth assessment of the organization's learning needs. This ensures that program designs directly address critical obstacles and dilemmas facing the implementation of the firm's strategic goals. Again, Ernst and Young's Leadership 2000 initiative provides a nice example. Although the national organization had begun to promote the firm's new strategic vision, implementation had been uneven at the local level. In an attempt to address this problem, Sallie Bryant, director of the Leadership and Organizational Change Group, and Mike Powers, vice chairman for professional and organization development, launched a series of interviews with leaders across the firm. Based on interviews with more than a dozen senior officials, Powers and Bryant identified several critical issues that appeared to lie at the root of the firm's implementation problems, including the following:

- Roles and responsibilities of area leaders were not clearly defined and lacked consistency.

- Many leaders felt overwhelmed by the number of initiatives that had to be implemented in a short time.

- Some area leaders felt the firm lacked a well-understood set of values to drive behavior consistent with the vision's goals.

- The new vision's goals often seemed at odds with existing measures.

- Many leaders lacked team leadership skills.

The interviews indicated that managers had been overwhelmed by a barrage of competing initiatives and burdensome, often repetitive, reporting requirements. Not until the firm clarified its priorities and coordinated its initiatives, asserted the local leadership, would its regional and area leaders be able to implement the firm's vision effectively.

As Bryant and Powers reviewed their findings, they realized that leadership needs within the firm had changed. No longer could partners and managers resort to the top-down command and control tactics of the past, for these tactics worked only when directives were well-defined and the environment was relatively stable. The firm's broader, more abstract vision required a more collaborative leadership approach. Not only would leaders have to interpret and adapt global strategies, they would also have to build consensus and commitment to strategies, create energy, and make the firm's vision real. In essence, they would have to build ownership of the vision throughout the firm—a process that would entail communicating values, developing people in ways consistent with these values, and aligning support systems to reinforce strategic objectives.

Out of this assessment, Bryant and Powers developed the Leadership 2000 initiative. This initiative, they decided, would be aimed at developing a clear understanding of the firm's priorities and would provide education, tools, and methodologies to interpret and execute these priorities at the local level. As local area offices—in particular the area managing partner and leadership team—were the main conduit for transforming the firm's vision into action, the initiative would focus on developing the effectiveness of the leadership teams. Because many of the areas were newly formed during the firm's recent restructuring, many area leaders had never worked before as a team. As a result, the initiative would pay special attention to developing effective team relations. Ultimately, by improving these relations, the initiative hoped to increase the firm's ability to implement its vision faster and better. Moreover, it would enhance its leadership capabilities for handling other initiatives that would inevitably arise in the future.

The assessment phase then clarified the broad objectives of the program. Three objectives emerged from the assessments: clarify the firm's overall vision and facilitate its interpretation and implementation at the local level; improve the areas' ability to manage an increasingly complex matrix; and enhance the level of two-way communication within each area and between the areas, regions, and national organization.

To personalize these objectives and to provide feedback that could potentially motivate and direct the learning of individual teams, a leadership effectiveness survey was conducted. Sent to all partners within a given area prior to the leadership initiative, as well as to the area leadership team itself, the survey assessed how effectively leaders of each area had been working together to manage operations. Partners answered questions about how well their leadership team communicated the firm's vision, involved others in planning and decision-making processes, and worked across organizational boundaries to align systems and eliminate barriers to implementation. The survey was completed anonymously and leaders saw only their personal results presented in relation to overall mean scores. The results of the survey further directed the design of the leadership program and also provided information to each leadership team about where they, in particular, needed to improve.

Without preassessment measures, it is unlikely that program designers will understand the fundamental leadership challenges with which their leaders struggle most. In many cases, the CEO or other sponsoring official will also lack the proper vantage point to fully assess the barriers to change within the organization and the development needs of leaders at relevant levels. Leaders themselves may be limited in the extent to which they can articulate specific leadership challenges. For all these reasons, it is critical that program designers collect input from multiple sources throughout the organization. They must understand the organization's most pressing short- and long-term business issues and the strategic priorities implicit in its overarching agenda. They must understand the views of both subordinates and superiors and be able to link these to specific development objectives. Careful preassessment helps ensure that resources are directed where they can have the greatest impact on both the change agenda and on the leaders who must implement it.

3. Programs Structured for Executive Cohorts Around Specific Learning Objectives

Many strategic intervention programs ultimately cascade to lower levels of the organization, but most begin at senior levels where an organization's overall vision is set. It is crucial that senior leaders build a shared vision at the top before asking those below them to act in support of it. Otherwise, strongly divided opinion concerning the firm's direction will cause greater confusion as subsequent operational initiatives begin to unfold. Indeed, decisions throughout the organization—not the least of which relate to skill requirements, key appointments, and resource allocation—will be difficult to make in light of larger uncertainties surrounding the vision.

Getting senior leaders to work closely to agree on and enact a shared vision is difficult. Executive cohorts rarely function as true teams, and day-to-day demands on senior leaders have a way of distracting attention from longer-term thinking. It is particularly difficult in very large or fluid organizations where senior leaders are distributed around the globe or move to new positions frequently. One strength of the initiatives described in this chapter is that they can serve as powerful vehicles for team building and for driving consensus on critical long-term objectives. They can help surface values or assumptions that need to be reevaluated and to reaffirm or redirect strategies that are no longer appropriate. In the process of collectively scrutinizing these difficult and complicated issues, leaders may develop critical strategic thinking skills, a better understanding of their own implicit assumptions, a better understanding of the assumptions held by those they work with, and greater insight into the organization as a whole. They will learn about each other and from each other. And ultimately, they may develop better ways of working together in the future.

The strengths of these programs are nicely illustrated by an important leadership development initiative conducted for senior noncommissioned officers of the U.S. Army. In the early 1990s, the Army faced significant change in its technical, institutional, and social environments. The end of the Reagan administration had brought about major reductions in military spending and a dramatic downsizing of military forces. Despite these reductions, however, the scope of military responsibilities continued to shift and expand. With less threat from the former Soviet Union and more uncertainty in developing countries, the meaning of national security had changed from its previous focus on military means for containing communism to dimensions beyond military power. The purpose of military capabilities had begun to move away from waging war and deterring the threat of war toward deliberate activities aimed at preventing or limiting war and maintaining peace. In addition, the scope of activities no longer centered on a few traditional points of vital interest (such as the Persian Gulf) but rather had extended to the world at large.

Like other military personnel, the Army's noncommissioned officer (NCO) corps faced a number of strategic challenges in the wake of these changes. As a result of budget cuts, major reengineering and restructuring efforts had significantly reduced the number of active military NCOs and reshaped the distribution of NCO positions across occupational specialties. These changes created additional and different leadership responsibilities for the smaller forces that remained. In addition to reductions among noncommissioned officers were significant reductions in the officer corps. Though traditionally officers and NCOs had worked in separate but parallel hierarchies—with officers responsible for planning and policy making and NCOs responsible for leading day-to-day operations and directly overseeing soldiers—fewer officers meant that NCOs were increasingly being asked to assume more officer-like responsibilities. Moreover, with the end of the Cold War and an increase in civil unrest in countries such as Bosnia and Somalia, Army leaders began to see an increase in the tempo of their operational assignments. They were deploying more frequently and leading smaller, more mobile efforts that differed considerably from the military defense missions they had led (and been trained for) in the past.

Army leaders began to have serious concerns about the impact these changes were having on the training and development of the Army's future leaders. Concerns were particularly strong among NCOs whose operational responsibilities increasingly prevented or detracted from traditional development efforts. For example, with fewer people and less time between missions to prepare for deployment, commanders were frequently reluctant to release NCOs for scheduled development efforts. Moreover, as senior NCOs began to assume more officer responsibilities, there was less time available to them for mentoring junior NCOs. Together, these changes highlighted a critical need to reevaluate the existing NCO leadership development system. An important goal of this effort would be to identify ways to strengthen and modernize the development of NCOs to meet future demands. This, in turn, would require an understanding of these demands and a clear vision of what they held to be central to their mission.

The Command Sergeant Major of the U.S. Army Training and Doctrine Command and the Sergeant Major of the Army determined that a special program was needed to begin defining a vision for the NCO corps and instigating appropriate changes in NCO leadership development. The professional development of officers and soldiers is one of the most important missions of any military service. Unlike leadership development in many commercial organizations—which is often regarded as tangential to the firm's primary business—leadership in the Army represents a core competency and central focus of the entire organization. As such, creating a vision and implementing change to the development process would constitute a significant strategic change. It would require buy-in from the entire NCO corps on an issue that most saw as central to their core ethos and heritage. Ironically, rethinking the development system would also require NCOs to engage in the very type of critical strategic thinking that all NCOs would have to develop and that would have to be incorporated into their future leadership development system.

Recognizing the opportunity to simultaneously build crucial leadership skills and facilitate change, the two Sergeants Major, together with their staffs and help from the RAND Corporation, designed a program that would bring together noncommissioned officers from across the Army to reexamine the NCO leadership development system and craft a vision for its future. Because a primary objective of the workshop was to build consensus on the strengths and weaknesses of the current system, a cross section of the Army's most senior noncommissioned officers, in addition to a subset of NCOs from other levels, were invited to a week-long Noncommissioned Officer Professional Development Workshop. The sixty-four NCOs chosen to attend were well-respected individuals nominated from across all levels and occupational specialties throughout the corps. Careful attention was given to selecting individuals representing all major constituencies. This helped ensure that all felt they had a voice at the table and that commitment would build among the corps' most senior leaders.

Concurrent with the need to build an agreed-upon change agenda was the need to stimulate strategic "out-of-the-box" thinking. As leadership development of NCOs happens almost exclusively within the walls of the Army and is largely conducted by NCOs themselves, the workshop faced an interesting challenge. The very leaders who used, operated, and had been raised within the system were now being asked to reevaluate it. On the one hand, only experienced NCOs knew the system well enough to know its most important components. On the other hand, being steeped in the existing system limited their ability to see its weaknesses and generate alternatives. Thus a key learning objective of the workshop was to provide a developmental experience that would help participants learn to think more critically and strategically in their efforts to plan and effect change.

In order to achieve its dual objectives, the workshop used an assumption-based planning exercise to facilitate both the learning process and the change agenda. Participants were broken into five groups of twelve to thirteen NCOs who met regularly over the course of the week to work through structured exercises and present their results to other participants for further discussion and debate. Each group was paired with two trained facilitators, an instructor from the Army's Sergeants Major academy (also a former NCO) and an outside facilitator who was familiar with the Army (though not necessarily the NCO corps) and trained in the methodology.

The purpose of assumption-based planning is to help existing leaders surface important assumptions on which current organizational concepts, plans, and operations are based. By identifying important assumptions—specifically those whose negation would lead to significant organizational change—leaders can begin to assess the extent to which these assumptions are vulnerable and identify "signposts" indicating changes in vulnerability (Dewar, Builder, Hix, and Levin, 1993; Winkler and others, 1998). The approach is useful for planning in very uncertain environments because it helps leaders look critically at existing practices, identify the assumptions that underlie them, resolve current problems that derive from inappropriate assumptions, and watch for changes that may render other assumptions invalid. Facilitators play an important role by leading participants through a set of questioning exercises, challenging their rationales for why certain practices exist, and keeping the communication process flowing.

Having leaders come together as a cohort to struggle with focused learning objectives embedded in important real-world issues can produce a number of benefits. In the case of the NCOs, a clear understanding of the strategic leadership skills that NCOs need but lack was immensely useful for structuring an appropriate learning experience. Because leaders needed to develop the ability to question and critically reflect on current practices and to reevaluate them in light of new demands, a facilitated group process organized around the surfacing of implicit assumptions gave participants valuable experience and simultaneously produced needed insight. Bringing together leaders with similar responsibilities and common ownership provided a unique opportunity to build collective knowledge that no single NCO could have discovered on his or her own. Shared experiences, common interests, and similar challenges fueled the motivation to learn. Differences in vantage point, approach, and style provided the variation needed to develop new insights.

This structured learning process, removed from the pressures of daily demands, not only builds important learning but creates the strategic focus and commitment needed to jump-start large-scale change. Carefully planned exercises, well-focused topics, and dedicated facilitators help to surface underlying assumptions and to air differences of opinion quickly and efficiently. They help leadership teams collaborate more effectively to discover critical issues and then work quickly toward their resolution.

Finally, the team-building aspects of these initiatives should not be underestimated. We found that time away from everyday hassles often allowed senior teams to develop a deeper understanding of each other. Where relations had been good but perhaps distant or fragmented, focused time together encouraged members to learn more about each others' goals, expectations, and personal leadership styles. It fostered among them a better understanding of the challenges and responsibilities faced by other members of the leadership team and the problems or obstacles that made achieving their goals difficult. Equally important, it allowed them to develop a better understanding of how others view the business, their role in the organization, and how the business itself could be improved.

An important by-product of the mutual understanding that team building allows was that it often enhanced a group's ability to communicate effectively, discuss issues openly, and consider a broader range of potential solutions to their problems. In some cases, this proved to be one of the most important outcomes of the leadership development effort. As a participant in one initiative stated: "[Our leadership team] is such a cynical group that nothing you do pleases everybody. So, to me, to get this team to the point where we're honest with each other . . . is a major step. That's why I think . . . what we're doing is such a good thing. Because it's getting . . . the people that represent the leadership team to be candid with each other and support each other and change their behavior a little bit."

4. Curricula Designed to Elicit Collective Dialogue Between Units and Across Levels

Collective dialogue refers to a process whereby individuals come together, share their experiences and backgrounds, and jointly construct a common interpretation of the information and events around them. This enables managers to make shared decisions more rapidly and with greater information. It also allows them to make strategically consistent decisions when acting independently.

Collective dialogue across functions and between levels is particularly important for developing a common understanding of a firm's larger vision, and in turn a shared interpretation of how that vision can be adapted at the local level. Because strategic planning efforts require a complicated transition from abstract ideas to clearly defined directives and goals, collective dialogue is essential for determining how an organization's vision or strategy can unfold to become an effective course of action. Collective dialogue enables a more successful transition process because it increases the probability that participants speak the same language—listen to and hear each other and interpret comments and suggestions as they are mutually intended.

The importance of collective dialogue is perhaps best demonstrated in its absence. When leadership initiatives fail to incorporate dialogue processes in their design, leaders across the organization are less likely to develop common frameworks and ways of interpreting the firm's vision. It follows that they are also less likely to develop a shared understanding of their role in fulfilling it. Without the common language or understandings that develop through dialogue, leaders often struggle to communicate ideas to their colleagues and to understand the ideas their colleagues hope to communicate to them. As a result, they are often not able to fairly evaluate different perspectives or consider as wide a range of alternatives. By bringing leaders together and structuring their interaction to create opportunities for dialogue, leadership development initiatives can provide the appropriate context and process assistance to help leaders not only build consensus on strategic topics, but also—more importantly—build ways of working together in the future.

We saw in the Philips example how intact work teams were brought together to talk about the company's vision, to discuss obstacles that might impede it, and to offer solutions that might expedite it. Ernst & Young's Leadership 2000 process similarly facilitated collective dialogue by focusing leaders on issues designed to manifest conflicting expectations about the firm's vision and implementation tactics. Program sessions, for example, introduced participants to leadership strategies and tactics that had been used successfully to facilitate change in other companies. The models and concepts presented in these sessions began the dialogue by provoking focused thought and discussion. Break-out sessions furthered this by encouraging participants to use their newly acquired models to structure and articulate their own strategic priorities. Each group was asked to create an "Area vision" for implementing the firm's overarching agenda at the local level. Because many leaders had previously approached these problems only from a particular functional or industry perspective, common models and concepts improved their ability to communicate and collaborate as a team. Said one: "I think what Leadership 2000 . . . really did is it probably served as a catalyst (a) to develop the dialogue that needed to happen as a foundation for [the change process] and (b) to ensure that everyone was on the same page, so that we could implement . . . effectively."

Any number of creative tactics can be used to facilitate collective dialogue. Participants can be given structured exercises designed to evoke their views on relevant and important topics. They can be asked to come up with a plan of action or strategy for overcoming a controversial problem. They can be asked to develop a new policy or to consider a new business initiative. The critical factors to consider in creating dialogue are that the issues must be viewed as important, must involve or affect all participants in a significant way, and must be perceived as real and as having nontrivial consequences in the foreseeable future.

One creative mechanism for facilitating collective dialogue is an approach undertaken by Ernst & Young. Known as the "little red book," the concept was introduced to area leaders during the plenary session at the Leadership 2000 kickoff event. A professor speaking at the plenary illustrated the importance of visioning tactics by showing a communications booklet devised by Jan Carlzon, the CEO of Scandinavian Airlines, describing a simple but powerful tactic he had used to convey his company's strategic vision. It was a concise and easy-to-read statement in a pamphlet Carlzon called the "little red book." It was distributed to all employees and reportedly has been remarkably effective.

Hearing the benefits of this approach, many leaders at the kick-off became convinced of its merits and decided to adopt a similar tactic in conveying their own visions. How well the tactic worked for them, however, depended on the extent to which they used the little red book to stimulate collective dialogue. In some cases, the book was simply used as a one-way communication device to convey a vision developed solely by the senior leader or a small leadership group. This approach did little to develop a shared understanding of the vision and even less to build buy-in. In more successful cases, the little red book was used not so much as a repository for words and ideas but as a mechanism for enacting the vision through dialogue and interaction. This method involved far more people in shaping and reviewing the vision. The leadership team would often spend several day-long sessions or conduct off-site retreats to hone and draft a concept that would be distributed to all area partners for review. The leadership team would then meet with the partners to discuss the draft, listen to their concerns and suggestions, and then incorporate their ideas into the final document. The dialogue created during this effort was a critical element in building not only a sound vision but also a true understanding of it and commitment to making it happen. One leader described the rationale for the dialogue process:

> The rationale was very simple: we wanted to make sure that we could take some of the things that we were trying to do as a leadership team and communicate them to the broader population. One of the things that I think is very difficult to do is to take the results of all that interaction and dialogue [the discussion generated during the various leadership meetings] and pass it on in a meaningful fashion. I mean, I can't explain to you the conversations that happened. And if I give you the end result, you really have no capability to buy into *why* it's the end result because you didn't [get to see] the whole thought process that led [to it]. And so what we tried to

do is say: "There's a whole lot behind these goals. If we get everybody to understand the direction that we're going in and the goals that we're committed to, it will explain the behavior that they're going to see from us because we're all going to do everything . . . based on these goals." And if it doesn't fit, people should have a reason and a willingness to say: "Hey wait a minute, I don't understand how that fits in view of the goals that you've given us." That's their challenge point, if you will.

What differentiated the more effective little red book processes from the others was that less effective leaders used the book primarily as a vehicle for conveying information, thereby reducing dialogue, whereas more effective leaders used it as a vehicle for stimulating interaction, thereby increasing dialogue *and* conveying information.

5. Trained Facilitators Provide Critical Process Assistance

Given that much of what occurs in these programs is through dialogue, well-designed programs tend to employ trained facilitators. With discussions centered on issues that are complex and charged, facilitators serve to keep participants focused and their meetings on track. In the programs we studied, most participants felt that the process assistance that facilitators provided helped to make meetings more fruitful and, in many cases, more efficient. They were instrumental in organizing and codifying group discussions and kept groups from getting sidetracked on unproductive tangents. One facilitator summed it up nicely:

The most significant thing I do for them is meet with them and help them through a structured process to come to decisions. So, I think the right description would be decision facilitator. They do lots of stuff where they debate and then don't make decisions. Then they leave the room and go about their day-to-day responsibilities and it's a waste of time. I don't let them get away with that. I kind of stop them and say, "Okay, as I understand it, you've just authorized Herb to go spend a million dollars to recruit these kinds of people." And they'll go, "Oh . . . geez . . . wow . . . wait, wait." And we don't walk away until we've agreed specifically who has authority to do what and by when. It's teaching them a process, as well as making them work responsibly as a leadership team.

At their best, facilitators not only enhance group process but challenge and push teams to think in different ways. Because many are outside consultants, they can challenge the status quo when company participants may be unable or uncomfortable to do so. As they are not embedded in the corporate culture, they tend to take little for granted and question existing practices more readily than those who have grown used to them. In contrast, many leaders who have spent years in the organization (or one that is similar) are blind to the differences between fact and choice. They assume that current practices exist because they have to or are the best available. Facilitators can help dislodge these taken-for-granted assumptions and encourage leaders to think more broadly and creatively.

Revealing implicit assumptions was a key objective for facilitators in the Army's NCO leadership development program. In that effort, facilitators not only helped structure discussions, they served to identify and challenge underlying assumptions. This was done by asking leadership teams to describe in detail specific elements of the processes they were evaluating. For example, one team spent a day detailing where NCOs learned their leadership skills. Where were skills formally trained? Where were they learned informally? What sites were used? What facilities? What was the role of unit versus centralized training? Throughout the process, facilitators questioned leaders about why things were done the way they described. When given an answer, the facilitators continued to push, probe, and question the underlying rationale. By asking these difficult "why" questions, they revealed important assumptions under which the current system was developed, helping leaders recognize that existing systems were built on fundamental premises that were perhaps no longer valid. More importantly, the facilitators encouraged leaders to think more critically about the status quo and to scan the horizon for potential threats that might render existing practices obsolete.

Facilitators can also encourage participants to step back and examine group dynamics. For example, they can encourage teams to examine their decision-making practices and interaction styles, thereby stimulating important self-reflection and learning. Facilitators may improve group process skills by role-modeling effective practices themselves (Bandura, 1977). In the very best cases we studied, the facilitators' attention to group dynamics often ended up rubbing off on participants. For example, company leaders experienced firsthand the benefits of well-facilitated interaction. In one company we examined, senior leaders drew on their experiences in facilitated break-out sessions to develop subsequent communications strategies back in their own divisions. These leaders recognized that face-to-face conversations, team-based decision processes, and collective dialogue produced far greater understanding and buy-in to a new vision than did more generic communication mechanisms such as documents, memos, or e-mails.

In addition to providing process assistance and enhancing self-awareness *within* teams, facilitators can expedite learning *across* teams as well. For example, in one initiative, facilitators of the different teams met regularly to discuss the progress of the various groups they had been working with. They shared their experiences and discussed the practices and strategies their teams had been using. Mechanisms that worked particularly well in one group were shared with the facilitators of other groups, who in turn conveyed these more effective strategies to the teams they worked with. This cross-unit sharing of best practices was an important mechanism for organizational learning.

In some cases, facilitators can add value by carrying out parts of an implementation effort themselves. Having participated in initial dialogues, and often having met with leaders individually, facilitators frequently have unique insight into the change initiative and a broad understanding of the program's purpose and potential trouble spots. We found that facilitators can assist in at least three aspects of implementation. First, and most important, they can be deployed after a program ends to work with groups struggling with their implementation goals. Second, in some cases they can help design communication strategies. For example, facilitators working closely with members of one team helped to design a communication strategy used in rolling out the vision to the rest of the staff. Third, facilitators often work with special task forces created to address unique problems considered especially important to the organization's implementation efforts.

In short, facilitators provide value in multiple ways. They provide process assistance that helps to maintain focus and momentum. They stimulate different ways of thinking and encourage self-reflection. They model effective team facilitation skills. They provide direct assistance and technical expertise. Most importantly, though, they serve as a nonthreatening conduit of information across the organization. Where effective strategies are rarely shared because no one has explicit responsibility for it, or because competition among units discourages it, facilitators can bridge gaps and disseminate information broadly. As a result, they can leverage important lessons from one area to another and greatly enhance organizational learning.

6. Learning Experiences Cascade Across Multiple Levels

The best strategic intervention programs design initiatives that cascade across all levels of the organization. A multilevel approach is necessary because it ensures that all levels of the organization have a consistent understanding of the company's strategic direction, the leadership demands in light of the direction, and the implementation steps essential to moving the organization forward. Cascading initiatives help build consensus about what a particular vision or change initiative means to leaders at each level. They also ensure better integration among levels when leaders from the upper echelons actively participate in conveying their understandings to those below. Perhaps most importantly, cascading learning downward helps build leadership depth throughout the organization.

Cascading initiatives also help translate the corporate vision into local actions that make the vision a daily reality. Our research suggests that senior managers are generally too far removed from day-to-day operations to determine the best ways to implement the vision in every unit, function, or situation. As such, it is difficult and often inappropriate for them to take responsibility for determining local structures, crafting local strategies or tactics, and making many operational decisions. These activities are usually best suited to those actually conducting the business.

Cascading designs also increase the likelihood that the overall initiative will have buy-in throughout the organization, especially when sessions are structured to help local management develop locally tailored solutions. For example, Philips discovered during its Centurion program that business units that had not cascaded their efforts downward typically experienced greater difficulties in implementing their goals. Because local levels were not involved in opportunities to translate proposed goals into their own objectives, they felt little ownership and therefore less compulsion to make things happen.

Beyond the effects of participation, cascading initiatives build ownership and commitment by having senior management directly and visibly involved at each stage. There is both a substantive and a symbolic component to this involvement. First, almost by definition cascading initiatives build in forums for managers at senior levels to convey the organization's new vision or change agenda to levels directly below them. Each successive level typically plays a substantive role in helping those below translate the vision at their level. This works nicely because each level of management is helped by the level above to understand the vision in its own terms and context. Because the initiative cascades downward, higher-level managers have already struggled through the process and have formed a collective understanding of the vision's implications for what they must accomplish. This makes them ideal coaches for guiding the process at the next level; they understand the initiative, have wrestled with the concepts, and are familiar with the next level's responsibilities and how they must contribute.

Second, there is also symbolic importance to leader involvement. In one company we examined, an in-depth investigation had determined that significant cultural change was needed for the company to remain competitive. A leadership program was created to mark the beginning of the company's commitment to cultural change, process management, and continuous process improvement. The program employed a cascading design whereby managers at each level were brought together in groups of fifty to participate in a three-day workshop held at a central location. Starting with the CEO and his direct reports, each session was organized so that senior line managers would convey the new change agenda directly to the managers below them. The workshop was a highly symbolic event, not only because of the level of participation from senior management but because of how they participated. For example, during an initial session, the CEO and his senior leadership team served dinner to their direct reports to emphasize their commitment to open communication and teamwork. The act sought to symbolize the view that senior management depended on those below them to think critically about the organization's practices and to make significant process improvements at each level. Similar acts were carried out in subsequent sessions, with managers at each level demonstrating their commitment to a more open and empowered culture.

In sum, cascading initiatives can help to localize the larger change agenda and build ownership. Leaders develop a better feel

for the organization's vision not only by receiving direct coaching
from the leaders above them but also by having to stand up, support, and explain the vision to those below them. By discussing the
vision, encouraging comments, answering questions, and incorporating feedback, company leaders demonstrate their commitment
to the change agenda and to making it happen. This not only signals their own confidence in the vision, it can inspire confidence
in others to initiate new strategies as well. Most notably, by practicing open communication and encouraging interaction these leaders become role models for others to emulate in their interactions
with employees down the line. A participant in one of the programs
that we examined summed it up nicely: "I think the more that leaders are around better leaders, the more good leadership rubs off on
them. So, I continue to encourage the frequency of our leadership
interacting with us. The more support, direction, and leadership I
get from upper management, the more courage, the more vision,
and the more will I have to do all the things [the vision requires]."

7. Active Feedback Mechanisms

Another feature of highly effective initiatives is the extent to which
they incorporated active feedback mechanisms into program design.
These are specific ways for program designers and sponsors to mon-
itor the views of program participants and to track the program's
progress in meeting objectives. There are probably many ways that
programs can capture important feedback. We touch on a few of the
more common and easily implemented ones.

One of the most important feedback mechanisms is direct interaction between program participants and the program's main sponsors. This often means that the company's chief executive officer or
other high-level official participates in some part of the development initiative. The sponsor's participation may be brief, but it
should ideally involve some type of direct, unscripted interaction
with the leaders participating in the program. Typically this comes
in the form of an informal question-and-answer period, though

there are sometimes good reasons to design longer, more intimate forums.

Open two-way communication between leader-participants and the senior officials sponsoring the initiative provides each with a feel for the others' goals and concerns. It signals the program's importance, establishes a certain tone, may enhance its credibility, and can also convey important information. For example, one program we studied was structured to allow extensive interaction between the organization's new CEO and the top 140 or so leaders that made up its Senior Leadership Council. As the CEO was new to the firm, the program aimed to provide an experience that would allow him to get to know his new senior leadership team better and let the team get to know him better. Each day-and-a-half-long session involved a group of eighteen to twenty leaders with a variety of functional backgrounds and experiences from different corporate operations. During these sessions, leaders would break into three separate subgroups to discuss designated topics related to the organization's key problems and need for change. After a day of discussion among themselves, the senior executives met with the CEO to discuss the issues they felt were most important and to provide suggestions for how to move forward with needed changes. While one group discussed their ideas with the CEO, the others observed; at the end of each discussion the conversation was opened up for all to participate. The discussions were intended to be informal—no presentations, slides, or flipcharts, and no team spokesperson was to be appointed. The idea was to have an open, participative dialogue that allowed the CEO and senior leadership greater insight into the issues and problems that each perceived.

Our interviews with participants of this program indicated that the two-way dialogue provided important information to all involved. For the new CEO, it provided information about key issues and barriers blocking the organization's performance goals and cultural turnaround. Interacting directly with executives from across the firm's many business units, he gained a broader awareness of the critical problems facing the organization as a whole, in addition to specific issues facing business units individually. Perhaps more importantly, though, it allowed the CEO to develop a better understanding of how his senior management approached problems. It gave him a direct window into the range of strategic thinking capabilities they possessed. And it gave him a good sense of who held particular strengths and where improvements were needed. For the participants, the program provided important insights about their new CEO. In contrast to a more formal forum, the structured dialogue sessions allowed the senior leadership team to get to know the CEO at a more personal level and to better understand his view of the world. It demonstrated to them that he was willing to listen and wanted to learn about key issues from their perspective.

Interactive sessions with program sponsors also provided useful feedback in Ernst & Young's program. In this case, the amount of interaction within the two-day program was a two-hour question-and-answer session between the firm's chairman, deputy chairman, and area leadership teams. Even this short exchange provided important feedback. As one of the program's chief designers described it: "Phil [the CEO] would say that it gave him . . . and everybody in a way . . . an increased understanding of how the matrix was and wasn't working and what some of the real dynamics are. You can theorize about an organizational structure and you can draw it out and so on, but it's like when you design a new airplane or something—what is on the drawing board and how the thing really flies, you kind of just gotta wait and try to fly it."

Again, direct interaction between the program sponsors and participants gave the CEO critical feedback about how specific change initiatives were "flying." The feedback proved to be so useful that the CEO decided to discuss Leadership 2000 issues in a similar format during his regular quarterly leadership meetings from then on.

Another way to ensure active feedback mechanisms is to incorporate ongoing follow-up and information gathering into the program design. We talk about the importance of follow-up and reinforcement in the next section, but we touch on one essential type of follow-up here: proactively seeking structured feedback. The more successful programs we examined carefully coupled program delivery with well-timed feedback from a representative sample of participants. In one, a program designer and corporate manager conducted interviews with all senior officials from each team participating in the initiative. The interviews took place approximately eight months after the program originated. Having a program sponsor and designer jointly interview the leaders allowed a more comprehensive evaluation and signaled that the program remained an important corporate initiative. The main objective was to audit the program to determine what aspects had value, what was progressing well and—in those instances where the program had derailed—what needed to be done to get it back on track. The interviews provided valuable information about the strengths and weaknesses of the program and provided actionable ideas for improvement. For example, through the interviews it was learned that many leaders felt the program's sponsor had moved on to other things—that the change initiative was no longer a key focus. The feedback provided a necessary wake-up call and spurred corporate management to take actions that visibly signaled its continued commitment.

In sum, active feedback mechanisms are critical for tracking a program's progress, strengthening and maintaining its credibility, and ensuring that it stays on course. Feedback mechanisms may take a variety of forms, including direct interaction, follow-up interviews, surveys, and the like. Methods that allow a greater flow of ideas and information are probably best. However, regardless of the form, it is important to gather feedback from a representative set of participants from across the organization. This ensures that the information gathered forms an accurate picture of how the program is actually being received. Increasingly, technology may also play a role in the feedback process. On-line discussion groups, listservs, and intranet sites may all serve to facilitate an active feedback process and may promote an active flow of information among the initiative's various participants.

Common Problems and Pitfalls

Programs designed to enhance leadership capabilities and facilitate strategic change tend to be extremely complicated and demanding. The greatest risk they face is that they will be seen as simply an event rather than as part of an ongoing change process. Moreover, they raise expectations. Employees leave with a sense of hope and momentum that places an onus on the program's sponsors and designers to maintain its energy and focus. This can be extremely difficult to do. For example, early successes may rob the initiative of its sense of urgency. Shifts in the firm's environment may lead senior executives to plan additional initiatives that all too quickly supplant the first and leave company managers skeptical about the importance of the next. Subsequent layoffs or a radical change in strategy may ultimately undermine the entire effort. These are but a few of the challenges that program designers and corporate leaders must face in the wake of these very demanding interventions. Here we list some of the more common pitfalls we discovered in our research.

1. Poorly Articulated Links Between Development Program and Strategy

In some programs, serious problems arise because the links between the firm's overall strategy and the program's role and expected contributions are not clearly spelled out. Thus participants and their work groups end up spinning their wheels in endless debate over what they are and should be accomplishing through the program. Entrenched managers may use this confusion to stalemate future efforts. They will leverage uncertainty about the program's contribution as an excuse to avoid change, perhaps blocking the progress of work group meetings and reducing the impact of the initiative overall.

In one organization, we witnessed the challenge of getting company leaders to see and internalize the links between the program objectives and the organization's strategy. The firm's many initiatives looked strategic when viewed from the corporate offices, but to the business units they appeared confusing and disruptive. The leadership initiative drew the links for participants, but company leaders nonetheless had a difficult time internalizing them. As a result, the initiative at times fell victim to a perceived disconnect between program goals and the strategy. For example, initially the program's focus on leadership, communication, and teaming made sense. How could anyone argue against better leadership? Certainly, few could contest the need for better communication. Most participants readily conceded that leadership, alignment, and communication were desperately needed to implement the firm's vision quickly and effectively. Agreement turned to enthusiasm as the plenary sessions described and illustrated how leaders in other corporations had developed and communicated meaningful visions that had led to inspired action and then results. The vision, the leadership concepts, alignment, and communication all resonated with company managers as they reflected on their own experiences. These principles were important and they needed to happen.

But as the working groups moved to break-out sessions and started to grapple with the leadership concepts in very real terms, their enthusiasm quickly dimmed. In many cases, coming up with a local vision that represented a compelling interpretation of the firm's strategic framework seemed to cause more confusion than it resolved. Differences in interpretation emerged and broad concepts dissolved into difficult distinctions and dilemmas. In one group, for example, members struggled with the distinction between vision, goals, strategy, and mission. This was important, they argued, because although a vision or mission needs to provide direction it also needs to provide meaning and purpose. How much latitude did the team have in modifying the firm's larger vision? Could it infuse the vision with local goals and values? Or was it only to proffer the corporate values? According to participants, the single greatest barrier working against the initiative was the ambiguity surrounding its objectives. Commented one:

> I think one of the problems with the leadership initiative is that there's a real lack of understanding at the local level [about] what the real objectives are. . . . I think there are a number of leaders who, in hindsight, have no idea [what the program was about]. . . . It was hard to push back on the concept that we need more communication, better teaming, and we need to help develop leadership skills in our people. I think at forty thousand feet they understood that these kinds of things are good things to do, but I think—specifically what they thought was going to come out of this—I think they were, you will find, in the clouds and just leaving it up to the local managers and designers to help them sort through it.

Managers who were less supportive of the program used the uncertainty surrounding its goals to rationalize their difficulties in adopting its principles. They often argued that the initiative added little that was new or different to their implementation efforts. As a result, these individuals failed to change their behavior, and their groups saw little difference in their ongoing operations after the program ended.

Poorly understood links between the corporate strategy and the program also created problems for facilitators. Whenever an initiative's objectives were unclear, participants often turned to their facilitators for clarification. Yet facilitators in these cases often struggled to clearly explain the program's goals and, as a result, tended to guide the work groups to issues and tasks that were more tangible and well defined. So, for example, they might focus the group on developing a communications plan rather than providing them with a better understanding of the program's purpose relative to the corporate strategy.

2. Poor Modeling by Corporate Leaders

By the nature of their focus on leadership, these programs tend to raise expectations of the company's senior leaders. Because programs typically present and discuss many best practices of leadership, they provide external benchmarks or standards by which to measure the behavior of the organization's current managers and executives. As a result, they raise expectations that senior leaders will model the very behaviors the program is attempting to instill. If they fail to do so, frustration and cynicism can quickly arise. Thus it is crucial that senior leaders attempt to visibly model the various practices the program teaches. In addition, immediately following a program company employees will watch to see what initiatives emerge from the executive suite as tests of the senior team's true commitment. Executives would be well advised before a program is even launched to have on the drawing board follow-up actions that are highly visible and consistent with the program's themes and philosophy. By engaging in these symbolic actions—and acting consistently over time—senior managers demonstrate their commitment to the larger change agenda.

To illustrate the problems that can occur by failing to "walk the talk," consider the following example. Like many in our study, one organization had recently begun a major transition designed to shift its corporate vision. As is often the case, the organization structure, roles, and responsibilities changed; multiple initiatives were put in place; and confusion ensued. After a great deal of self-reflection and investigation, the organization determined that a leadership initiative was needed to improve understanding of the new vision and to enhance communication up and down the corporate hierarchy. Directed at the organization's senior operating managers, the initiative incorporated discussions with the CEO, who emphasized his commitment to two-way communication. Group exercises structured around key implementation issues were used to build communication skills.

Through their participation in the leadership initiative, which allowed them to experience the power of active two-way communication directly, many of the operating managers became convinced of its benefits. They returned to their jobs committed to improving communication in their units and set forth to do so. But much to their surprise, communication with the corporate offices remained one-way, flowing from the center out to the units. Given the leadership initiative's emphasis on open discussion, distributive leadership, and two-way information flows, the managers were dismayed. The initiative had raised their expectations and increased their ability to discriminate between good and bad communication. Moreover, their follow-up efforts had demonstrated that effective two-way communication could produce significant benefits. As a result, they became increasingly aware of deficiencies at the corporate level. They became frustrated when corporate executives failed to coordinate their initiatives and were quick to notice when senior leaders did not provide adequate direction or feedback.

Ultimately, many operating managers became skeptical about the authenticity of senior management's claims. Did they really want to increase the flow of information or were they really interested in improving communication only within the business units— in essence, exempting themselves? Was all the talk just a ploy to build buy-in at the lower levels? Because the corporate leaders neglected to model the principles and behaviors emphasized in the leadership initiative, they undermined their own efforts. Moreover, operating managers were quick to point out that the senior leaders' actions undermined communication at the business-unit level. Midlevel managers felt less compulsion to be models. Like a river whose waters shape the shores of each community through which they flow, behaviors of the senior team can reverberate throughout an entire organization, affecting interactions and trust at each level.

3. Entrenched Managers and the Legacy of Past Relations Limit Program Impact

Some people always support change, and some always resist it. Leadership programs are no different. Because strategic intervention designs rely on local managers and their work groups, recalcitrant managers can block the impact of learning initiatives in their units.

Among the leaders we observed, those most resistant to change tended to be highly entrenched and reliant on a very directive and autocratic management style. They were usually quite reluctant to change their practices and openly skeptical about the changes they were being asked to make. Unfortunately, such leaders tend to have profound influence over those who report to or work with them. They usually play a major role in determining assignments, conducting performance reviews, and making compensation decisions. Moreover, because they tend to make important decisions on their own, have substantial authority, and rarely listen to the views of their teams or colleagues, they invariably stifle communication within their units and destroy both motivation and the capacity to change.

Such leaders can create intractable problems for an intervention initiative. They often have a history or pattern of past relations that prevents the interaction and dialogue needed to effect learning and change. In one company we studied, the two least-effective groups also had the worst attendance at the original event. The senior leader in one group participated in fewer than half of the sessions. In the other group only half of the team attended. Because critical team members essentially boycotted the original event and often failed to participate in subsequent events and meetings, remaining team members concluded that independent efforts to develop a vision or create a communication strategy would be futile. In all likelihood they were right. Without key decision makers present and with only partial participation from the rest of the team, plans for going forward likely would have been ignored by those who were absent.

In rare cases, highly skilled facilitators can increase leader self-awareness by carefully guiding team discussions so that the leader may ultimately see the negative repercussions of his or her behavior. Unfortunately, these efforts are extremely difficult and depend not only on the skill of the facilitator but on the extent to which the group trusts the process. In most cases, however, facilitators are limited in their ability to influence recalcitrant behavior. As outsiders, they simply lack the political knowledge and credibility needed to reach these difficult individuals.

Moreover, these initiatives are not really designed with the individual in mind. Interventions are designed to facilitate strategic change, not to provide individual feedback and personal development. They focus on teams, interaction, and the construction of collective vision, not on evaluating individual behavior, feedback, or skills. Indeed, given the relatively short duration of events and the limited amount of interaction time with facilitators, it would be unreasonable to expect significant change in any one leader's behavior. Such change requires significant evaluation and practice. Thus, although strategic change initiatives may emphasize the importance of concepts such as open communication and active involvement, they seldom provide opportunities for practice and feedback. As a result, even if they heighten the perceived need for such things they rarely do much to improve them.

4. Competing Initiatives Detract from Sponsor Support

As time passes, the initial momentum created by a program may begin to wane. Senior leaders may turn their attention elsewhere even if they think the program important; they may have little time to direct its planning or to keep communicating its importance.

As the firm's leadership becomes less directly involved in the initiative's implementation, the execution of the program can begin to change in subtle yet noticeable ways. For example, managers may see that the program is losing momentum and that it seems less connected to the firm's vision. Sensing a growing disconnect, they may begin to question the program's relevance and ongoing importance. Is it actually changing anything? What should it accomplish? How can we know its objectives have been met? Soon, other initiatives take precedence. Opportunities to describe the links may be overlooked, which further aggravates the problem. For these reasons, program sponsors must continually communicate their commitment and demonstrate it through follow-up initiatives. Otherwise, employees down the line will interpret the process as simply a one-time event or, worse, a fad or whim.

5. Lack of Consistent Reinforcement

Ideally, we would have liked to have included systematic follow-up and reinforcement in our discussion of good design elements. But though we saw many follow-up plans and good intentions, we saw few plans being implemented. Designers at one organization we interviewed clearly recognized that their strategic leadership initiative was likely to lose momentum without continued reinforcement. Several follow-up events were designed into the overall program as well as a follow-up survey. Ultimately, however, they never materialized. Leaders were too busy with the change itself and felt that the initial excitement of the initiative had worn off. Yet one could argue that it is under exactly these conditions that a follow-up event is needed most.

For a number of reasons, even the most well-designed programs typically fall short in their follow-up. First, there is a whole set of organizational realities that can get in the way. Program sponsors or designers may be promoted, transferred to other assignments, or leave the organization. Second, the daily challenges and time demands of operationalizing the change agenda, added to those of one's regular work, make people less supportive of subsequent events that require additional time and energy. And third, the natural rhythms of the business cycle, as well as unexpected events in the external environment (such as the merger of competitors), may divert attention to other, more immediate pressures.

Another, perhaps more dangerous, obstacle is top management's disregard for—or naïveté about—the importance of follow-up. In some cases, senior managers may be more interested in the program's immediate product than in its long-term impact. In other cases, they may simply not recognize that a lack of follow-through and reinforcement can have serious repercussions. In a program we described earlier, a key objective had been to provide the new CEO with an opportunity to get to know his senior managers, their strategic thinking capabilities, and their perspectives on the organization's problems. The highly interactive two-day forum that was created allowed senior managers from across the organization to dialogue directly with the new CEO about major obstacles to change. By all accounts, participants left the sessions believing the forum had been a valuable and productive experience. They had been able to air critical issues openly and had developed a better sense of the CEO's priorities and approach to problems. The open dialogue signaled to many of the managers that their new CEO was willing to listen and that he valued their perspective.

Unfortunately, this initial optimism and renewed hope gave way to disappointment. Because there was little follow-up and no communication about how the CEO had decided to use their input, most managers ultimately felt that the forum had little impact. In fact, many managers concluded that by bringing to light a number of major issues, raising hope and optimism that something would be done, and then taking little action and providing no follow-up, the program had actually made the situation worse. Their false hopes only led to greater disappointment and alienation. Perhaps the CEO actually acted on the input he received at the forum, but with no follow-up with the managers, they were unable to determine whether subsequent actions were in any way tied to their input.

In reviewing the initiative, managers invariably stated that it could have been greatly improved had the CEO simply reinforced his initial interest with adequate follow-through. Specifically, a follow-up summary of key themes and issues would have reinforced that managers had been heard, and periodic updates would have provided reassurance that their efforts had not been in vain.

A final reason that adequate reinforcement is so rare is because it often requires systematic change across a number of important support systems. Incentive systems, job assignments, performance measures, reporting relations, training, and organizational structures may each need to be realigned to support the larger change effort. Political dynamics and prior investments may stand in the way of these. However, only when there are proper alignments to key support systems will developing leaders have the incentives and capability to transfer their learnings from programs to effect change.

6. The Limitations of Facilitators

Despite the many benefits that facilitators provide, their influence—by definition—has limits. It is important to remember that much of facilitators' value comes from being outsiders, apart and separate from the system. This status allows them to question existing assumptions, challenge traditional practices, and remain free from political influence and the potential ramifications of threatening the status quo. But because they have no formal authority and only a temporary role, their power to influence is limited. Moreover, they are in a precarious position—their fees are paid by the client they are facilitating. If they challenge too strenuously, they may jeopardize their own employment. Their jobs are also frustrating because they are typically asked to resolve issues that are particularly difficult, yet they are given few resources or formal power. Other times, they are the scapegoats for unresolved problems or failed expectations; it is not uncommon for the facilitator to personify the company's initiative and take the brunt of resistance against it. Also, many initiatives concern strategic challenges, but facilitators are rarely strategy consultants and so are generally limited in their ability to help teams develop a more strategic mind-set. In one case we studied, however, just the opposite occurred. The organization hired strategy consultants to act as facilitators. Their problem was an inability to facilitate. Instead they joined in with their own solutions and minimized the learning opportunities of the working groups.

Other problems can arise in the use of some facilitators, but these can often be avoided with certain precautions. For example, for some program participants, facilitated discussions are a new experience. Though a manager or work group member might understand the facilitator's role in principle, they may be less comfortable with the facilitator's role in practice. This leads to a common problem: managers who are hesitant to use their facilitators because they lack an understanding of *how* to use them. This can be rectified to an extent with some work ahead of time in which the manager and facilitator explore how best to use facilitation. The problem is magnified when formal team leaders are reluctant to give up control over the group dynamic. In fact, in our research we found that the more controlling leaders were the least likely to allow facilitation yet at the same time those who needed it most.

Other times, facilitators are at a disadvantage because they simply do not know the history behind the many issues being debated nor important political dynamics. Without such knowledge, they may miss certain clues in discussions or have difficulty understanding why participants and team leaders chose to handle an issue one way and not another. Thus it is imperative that facilitators be extensively briefed beforehand by highly knowledgeable company insiders on the history and politics behind the issues to be discussed. It is also important that the selection of facilitators be partly based on their willingness to develop a baseline understanding of their client's industry and markets.

Facilitators must also be very clear about the program's larger, long-term objectives. Because facilitators represent such an integral part of the initiative, any uncertainty about a program's objectives is particularly detrimental. Not only will its evidence frustrate participants as they seek to utilize the facilitators' services, but it can also seriously undermine their trust in the program itself. If the initiative's primary messengers cannot clearly articulate the program's purpose, how can the firm expect to carry out its change agenda?

7. Customized Programs May Limit Out-of-the-Box Thinking

Some of the very strengths of these programs—for example, their customized design and company focus—may at times prove to be limiting. For example, because much of the project work is conducted in cohorts of company employees, out-of-the-box perspectives may rarely emerge. Instead, existing paradigms deeply ingrained in the corporate culture may be perpetuated. Though facilitators may challenge existing ideas and uncover implicit assumptions, in reality they may not be in a position to sufficiently encourage unconventional thinking because they lack an essential familiarity with the company culture and the industry to know what are truly new ways of thinking. Though interaction with senior leaders is an essential part of these programs, the use of internal leaders to guide and direct work groups can also serve to reinforce traditional views and approaches. These individuals may bring with them experiences based on existing and older paradigms of the company and its marketplace. In sharing their perspectives, they may simply encourage traditional approaches to company challenges, thereby stifling more novel and innovative ways of thinking.

As readers can see, there are many challenges and pitfalls that programs designed to facilitate strategic intervention may face. Nonetheless, when designed and conducted well, they still offer an unusual opportunity not only to accelerate the pace of strategic change but to build widespread ownership and commitment. As importantly, they can create a cadre of leaders who are able to translate corporate-wide strategies into local initiatives—in turn, enhancing the probability that new strategies will successfully take hold deep within the organization. At the core of these programs is the notion that learning must be oriented toward solving practical challenges and problems. In other words, it needs to be action oriented. In Chapter Eight, we will explore in depth other approaches to using actual company challenges as a vehicle for leadership development through formats called action learning.

7

Ernst & Young's Leadership 2000 Strategic Leadership Initiative

E rnst & Young's Leadership 2000 program shows how one firm used a leadership development program to strengthen and accelerate its progress toward strategic change. Designed to propel its Vision 2000 strategy, Leadership 2000 not only improved the firm's leadership capabilities, it also produced a better understanding of the guiding vision for partners and associates throughout the firm. This collective knowledge, in turn, improved the strength and consistency of individual efforts to implement the vision across Ernst & Young's nineteen national business units.

Strategic Context: The Impetus for Change

During the mid to late 1980s and continuing into the 1990s, the professional services industry began to face a number of strategic challenges. Consolidation in many primary markets posed perhaps the greatest challenge. A globalizing economy and roaring stock market had fostered a wave of mergers and acquisitions across the business world. As a result, an accounting firm's clients could vanish overnight into the hands of competitors serving acquirers. Facing consolidation in many of its key client markets, and fierce competition both at home and abroad, Ernst & Young LLP, one of the largest and fastest-growing of the then Big Six accounting firms, realized that the firm's past success in its two primary lines of business—audit and tax—would not guarantee its future success (the firm's consulting arm was not involved in the initiative).

Clients had also begun to change, demanding increasingly more in the way of services. They needed superior services to remain competitive, and aggressively demanded these services from their suppliers or else moved on to other providers. Unlike in the past, when clients had viewed tax and audit services as a professional specialty, today they saw these offerings more as commodities and looked for other value-added services that could be used to differentiate among potential providers.

Specifically, clients increasingly demanded higher-quality information and more of it. Not only did they need tax and audit services, they also needed information on business processes, transactions, controls, and technology. No longer were they satisfied with simple tax compliance services or incremental improvements in the audit process; now they demanded insight into business issues and wanted to be warned of potential problems. Moreover, clients that were moving into international markets required expertise in international tax, transfer pricing, financial instruments, dispute resolution, mergers and acquisitions, and other specialized services. And they wanted these services to be integrated and customized.

Consistent with more demanding clients, increasingly responsive competitors posed a major threat to the firm's business. Facing the same consolidating markets, some of E&Y's traditional competitors took the offensive. They reorganized, implemented new technologies, and integrated service offerings. E&Y found itself a member of the pack rather than the industry leader. To alter this situation and gain a dominant position, Ernst & Young reasoned that it would have to provide additional value to its clients by offering them superior, customized services responsive to their changing business needs. Furthermore, the firm recognized that if it hoped to do this from a position of strength, it would have to act quickly before its competitors did the same.

Vision 2000:
Ernst & Young's Strategic Framework

Like other firms seeking to compete in an era of consolidating industries and growing expectations, Ernst & Young realized that the key
to its success would be its ability to penetrate high-value markets.
This would be accomplished most effectively by meeting and exceed-
ing the demands of clients in those markets. Vision 2000 represented
the firm's stated vision for achieving this goal. Formally stated, Vision
2000 aimed to attain "a position of dominance in . . . eight National
priority industries and in serving entrepreneurial companies" by the
year 2000. In a special report to the people of Ernst & Young in Jan-
uary 1996, Phil Laskawy, the firm's chairman, described Vision 2000
as the "strategic framework that encompasses our firm's strategic
plans" in tax, audit, and management consulting.

In 1992, consistent with the goals of reducing costs and providing
greater customer value, the firm undertook a major restructuring. It
reorganized its operations from thirty business units in seven regions
to nineteen units in two regions. Business units, commonly referred
to as "areas," consisted of three to five local offices organized around
clients in a particular geographical location. Shortly after the reorganization, the firm also established a new industry structure. The
new industry focus was superimposed on the existing functional and
geographical structures, effectively creating a three-way matrix. The
operating unit became the area, with functional and industry goals
established within and across each area. Management responsibilities were transferred from the local office managing partners to
an area managing partner (AMP) supported by an area leadership
team (ALT) typically composed of the area director of Assurance
and Advisory Business Services (ABBS), the area director of tax
(ADOT), the area sales director, a set of area industry leaders
(AILs), and in some cases the area director of human resources, area
director of finance, and local managing partners (LMPs) from each
office.

Though the reorganization simplified the firm's geographical structure, it also elaborated the matrix and thus complicated existing reporting relations. The functional push to develop new products, coupled with the implementation of the new industry emphasis, created confusion over various responsibilities including hiring decisions, engagement staffing, client continuance decisions, and—most important—the revenue planning process. Despite these initial growing pains, the reorganization served to promote and facilitate the firm's larger vision in three important ways. First, it increased the firm's focus on area markets. Second, it improved the transfer of knowledge within and across the firm. And third, it streamlined service delivery by improving area coordination and empowering areas to make strategic trade-offs in deploying talent.

In addition to the restructuring, Vision 2000 focused on three broad yet integrated strategies designed to further enhance customer value. These strategies sought to strengthen the firm's functional expertise, build in-depth knowledge of targeted industries, and develop a coordinated market approach, supported by an aggressive sales culture, to penetrate key industries. Together these strategies were designed to enable the firm to improve its services and beat back the competition.

Despite important early successes in the vision's implementation, Ernst & Young recognized that the long-term key to implementing its vision rested in the hands of its people. They would have to drive change and struggle with its challenges, including (1) developing strategic goals in line with the demands of particular industries, (2) leading in a more complicated matrix structure, (3) sharing critical knowledge across multiple functions and business units, and (4) integrating knowledge in the delivery of more customized solutions.

It quickly became apparent that the success of Vision 2000 would largely depend on the firm's leadership. In particular, area leadership would be pivotal because areas represented the critical leverage point for successful implementation. Indeed, given the scope and purpose of the vision, area leadership teams would have to do a lot more than simply implement a well-defined strategy. They would have to interpret the firm's vision to fit their local conditions, design initiatives to support it, integrate and communicate these initiatives to their staffs, and provide the information and motivation that partners and staff would need to make the vision a reality. In short, partners—who in many cases had spent their entire careers managing audit and tax procedures—would now be asked to lead a major change initiative that required strong strategic planning skills. As a result, the original objectives of Vision 2000 led to a fourth objective: to enhance the quality of leadership development within the firm and embed leadership capabilities deeper within the organization. An intervention entitled Leadership 2000 would be designed to directly address this objective.

Leadership 2000: Developing Strategic Leadership Teams

To emphasize its connection to the larger vision and its focus on strategic leadership, the company's Leadership 2000 program would consist of three overlapping phases and involve the leadership teams from each of the nineteen areas. Region and national management would also participate. The first phase of the initiative would entail data gathering and assessment. This phase would essentially benchmark the existing leadership dynamics within each ALT and identify strengths, weaknesses, and problems. The second phase would consist of a two-day workshop organized around (1) discussions of the firm's progress and priorities, (2) a series of leadership case studies and videos presented by an expert on leadership, and (3) facilitated break-out sessions designed to structure and guide team communication on critical leadership and strategy concerns. Finally, the initiative's third phase would provide ongoing reinforcement designed to maintain the momentum generated during the kickoff. In sum, the program would have a conceptual component as well as an experiential one, and would be supported by a dedicated staff of facilitators to ensure appropriate follow-through.

Preassessment

Once Sallie Bryant, director of the Leadership and Organizational Change Group, and Mike Powers, vice chairman for Professional and Organizational Development, gained the approval of senior management and secured their support, they began to assemble their planning teams. Six area managing partners selected for their knowledge of the firm were asked to serve as an advisory committee. Because Bryant and Powers needed these partners to provide direct and honest feedback about potential program features, their advisory roles remained confidential. In addition to this advisory committee, Bryant and Powers drew on members of Ernst & Young's Professional and Organization Development (P&OD) team—an internal consulting group focused on personal and professional skill development and organizational change. This group helped to craft the program design and hone its content. Seven outside consultants were also brought in to work with the leadership initiative. These consultants would be used to facilitate the workshop sessions and provide ongoing process support. They were selected from five different consulting organizations with the express purpose of bringing in different methodologies and leveraging multiple approaches to enhance innovation.

The first order of business was to map the leadership structure of each area and to examine the dynamics of the various leadership teams. Interviews with area managing partners (AMPs), region managing partners (RMPs), and other area leaders provided information about who comprised the ALT, how well members functioned as a team, and issues that affected their performance. Focus groups were held with area industry leaders and the area sales director, and a conference call collected input from local managing partners. Together, these interviews provided information about how the ALTs communicated with the local offices, involved industry groups, and worked with other areas and the larger regions. Best practices were examined, as were process issues.

Confirming Bryant and Powers's earlier meetings, these interviews revealed that the composition of the leadership teams varied from area to area. Because of all the restructuring and the creation of new positions to drive the industry and sales strategies, roles and responsibilities had become somewhat vague and priorities and accountability were often unclear. Though AMPs were expected to work closely with industry, functional, and local leaders, most had yet to fully orchestrate and effectively lead their teams. Indeed, some teams were teams in name only because new assignments and geographical distances meant that some members had never worked together nor, in some cases, even met before.

To better assess the effectiveness of the various area leadership teams, the P&OD group supplemented its initial scoping effort with a comprehensive "Area Effectiveness Survey." This survey was sent to all partners within an area, as well as all leadership team members and relevant regional managing partners. Designed to quickly evaluate how well the leadership teams had been working together to lead area operations, the survey asked partners to evaluate how well their area leadership team communicated the firm's vision to the line partners and staff, involved others in planning and decision-making processes, and worked across organizational boundaries to align systems and eliminate barriers to implementation. The results of the survey provided a general overview of the main issues challenging leaders across the firm and a relative assessment of which areas were doing particularly well or poorly. This information, coupled with feedback from the advisory committee, would help the Leadership 2000 planning group design a kickoff event targeted to the firm's most pressing leadership needs and implementation issues.

The Program

The second phase of the initiative consisted of a two-day team workshop. Three or four ALTs attended a workshop at one time.

Full team attendance was heavily emphasized, as developing effective team relations depended on having all team members present.
The workshop began with Mike Powers presenting a general
overview of Vision 2000 and its progress. The vision, he explained,
had thus far been very successful. Functional excellence, industry
specialization, and an aggressive sales culture had all taken hold.
However, implementing the vision had not been without its growing pains. The firm's streamlining efforts had produced a highly
matrixed structure that often led to conflicting demands and difficulties in prioritizing key initiatives. However, though partners and
directors often wanted a detailed blueprint, no one approach would
lead to effective implementation in all nineteen areas. Instead, the
vision had to be adapted to each area's markets and resources. Successful implementation would thus depend on strategic thinking
and effective leadership throughout the firm. Nowhere would this
leadership matter more than at the area level, where abstract concepts would have to be transformed into concrete action.

Following this general overview, a professor from a well-known
business school led a discussion on the differences between leadership and management. Using a case study approach, leadership principles were illustrated through a series of rich case studies and
videos. The examples emphasized how leaders developed ownership
of a shared vision through involvement and extensive communication. Integration and teaming were cited as key components of the
leadership process.

Next, teams were divided into break-out groups. Each area team
formed a single break-out and struggled with the challenges that
faced its business unit. A trained facilitator moderated the discussion and provided process assistance. The facilitator led the team
through a number of exercises designed to clarify key issues revealed
during the preassessment stage. One exercise, for example, had team
members discuss the various roles and responsibilities associated
with each leadership position. Prior to the kickoff, Bryant and
Powers had worked with the firm's Operating Committee to define

the key responsibilities for each area leadership position (AMP, AIL, ABBS, ADOT, and others). These roles and responsibilities were compiled into a one-page document used to guide discussion during the break-out sessions. The document was intended to encourage role consistency across the various areas, but at the same time allow flexibility where needed. To jump-start the exercise, the facilitators had team members walk around and silently match responsibilities to roles listed on whiteboards scattered throughout the meeting room. Team members then discussed their different perceptions and how conflicting interpretations should be resolved. By making implicit assumptions about roles and responsibilities explicit, team members collectively defined who should be responsible for carrying out or supporting specific tasks. This allowed teams to clarify decision-making authority, accountability, and support processes throughout the area.

A second and even more important exercise concerned clarifying the overall vision for the firm at the area level. Again this was accomplished through facilitated group discussion. This time the team's task was to discuss how Vision 2000 should be interpreted at the area level. Should the larger vision be adapted in some way? Or should it be implemented exactly as the firm laid out? How should the vision be communicated to partners and other area staff? What role should the area partnership play in shaping the local vision, and what could be done to build ownership? The break-out sessions provided a forum for airing these issues, and the facilitators provided structure and guidance to bring them to collective resolution.

In most cases, the two-day workshop simply planted the seed for future thought and discussion. Essentially, the break-outs provided the teams with a taste of the work that lay before them. From there, the teams would have to take the tools and techniques presented at the workshop, incorporate them into their planning and implementation efforts, and then hone them to fit their needs. Together they would have to collectively create their own vision, then implement and instill it in the beliefs and values of the area culture.

Reinforcement

The final phase of the initiative was, in fact, not a phase at all. Rather, it entailed ongoing follow-up and reinforcement. The L2000 team sought to design support systems that would assist ALTs in their efforts to implement the Leadership 2000 principles. The most significant reinforcement mechanism was the use of dedicated facilitators who continued to work with area teams after the kick-off was over. Facilitators provided process assistance to area teams who embraced the effort and subtle prodding to those who did not. They also moderated group planning sessions, challenged existing practices, and monitored group dynamics. They played an important role in transferring best practices across the firm.

Not all areas, however, utilized facilitation to the same extent, and not all leaders appreciated the same facilitation styles. For example, some AMPs preferred facilitators to provide process assistance, whereas others wanted facilitators to challenge their ideas and help them to think more strategically. Some areas relied on their facilitator extensively and others chose not to use a facilitator at all. Unfortunately, the areas that may have benefited most from facilitation were often the least likely to use it. As with the other follow-up activities, facilitation practices varied considerably from area to area, as did the outcomes that ensued.

To maintain the program's momentum, plans were made for follow-up sessions. These events were intended to be periodic events that would reconvene area leaders to discuss their efforts to implement the firm's vision and their progress in doing so. According to the initiative's designers, these events would take the form of short workshops or review sessions and would provide valuable insight into area dynamics and ongoing problems. The L2000 team also thought that the events might help to keep tabs on how the firm's major constituents viewed the initiative's value. However, they never fully materialized as they were initially conceived due largely to competing demands on the time of partners.

In addition to ongoing facilitation and follow-up events, a 360-degree assessment tool was developed in parallel with the Leadership 2000 program to provide feedback to area leaders on their leadership effectiveness and development needs. The assessment system was piloted in two areas approximately six to eight months after the kickoff event and then slowly rolled out to other areas on a voluntary basis. Though plans for executive coaching were also discussed as a possible follow-up measure, the team decided to delay these plans until it could determine whether coaching would facilitate performance improvement and whether area leaders would value it.

Many reinforcement practices—such as the little red book (communicating area visions) and the roles and responsibilities exercise—were adopted broadly by most groups. Leaders used the processes they learned at the kickoff event and incorporated them within their own practices at home. The actual processes by which follow-up tactics were carried out did, however, vary across the areas. For example, as mentioned previously, more-effective areas involved more people in crafting the book and the vision within it. Less-effective areas, in contrast, invited area leaders and partners to provide input or feedback, but still relied solely on the AMP (perhaps assisted by a few confidants) to determine what the vision would ultimately entail. In a similar vein, more-effective areas tended to meet more frequently to discuss the vision. In many cases, they arranged off-site sessions devoted entirely to reviewing the vision and assessing the area's progress toward fulfilling it. Less-effective areas met less frequently and rarely evaluated progress toward their strategic targets.

To date, Leadership 2000 has been largely successful. However, like all large-scale change efforts, it has run into its share of stumbling blocks and problems. Participants on balance believe the program has improved their leadership, their understanding of the firm's larger vision, and their ability to implement it effectively. Many report that the program has changed the way area leaders interact with partners, managers, and staff, and in some cases it has significantly enhanced area communication and commitment. E&Y is now embarking on an individual leadership development initiative aimed initially at all partners with a longer-term goal of cascading to all staff members. Much of top management's support and the buy-in of area management is due to the Leadership 2000 initiative. It developed an understanding of leadership, a sense of its constructive power within an organization, and a thirst for more.

Part II

The Future Is Now
Building Twenty-First Century Leaders

8

Action Learning
The New Paradigm for Leadership Development

Today, more and more leadership development takes place in action learning formats where company-based projects serve as the principal learning vehicle. The projects themselves center around important challenges facing the organization and so ensure that the learning experience serves both the individual and the company. Grounded in actual organizational dilemmas or opportunities, learning is viewed as far more useful and therefore more appealing. The experiences in turn push participants to develop skills and worldviews that prepare them for expanded leadership roles.

Over the last decade, these developmental experiences have become enormously popular, driven largely by two forces. The first is a strong desire on the part of companies to see their investments in education produce tangible outcomes. Learning experiences therefore revolve around projects that address key issues facing the company today or in its future. Often these projects translate into company initiatives that grow markets, cut costs, streamline operations, and build leadership talent. The second force is a growing appreciation for the learning requirements of adults. Advances in the fields of adult education and cognitive psychology over the last two decades have substantially increased our knowledge of how adults best learn. Specifically, research has shown that adults are most motivated for learning when it is immediately relevant to their lives. With an emphasis on acquiring knowledge useful to address

11

work-related challenges, action learning formats have strong appeal
and utility for participants.

Given these forces, action learning has been widely embraced
by corporations across North America. Within a decade, it has gone
from being relatively rare to common in most in-company leadership programs. In light of action learning's growing appeal, we
explore the opportunities for learning afforded by this method and
delve into the design elements that make for more effective learning
experiences. We also examine common shortcomings we have discovered in programs.

Action Learning: The Basic Features

The term action learning is often used loosely to describe any educational experience that includes action. So, for example, some
describe experiential exercises as action learning because participants are active in the learning process. But we prefer a much
stricter definition. For us, action learning describes educational
approaches where managers learn using issues from their own companies. These formats involve a continuous process of learning and
reflection built around working groups of colleagues, more often
with the aim of getting work-related initiatives accomplished. Most,
therefore, emphasize learning by doing, are conducted in teams,
address company issues, place participants into problem-solving
roles, and require that team decisions be formalized into presentations (Noel and Charan, 1988, 1992). For example, a typical action
learning project might involve participants in conducting a team-
based field investigation of new markets for company products. The
learning outcome would result in a presentation containing findings and recommendations to company senior management. For
instance, at General Electric, programs are built around consulting
projects provided by the company's business units, seeking ideas in
return for their cooperation. The company's locomotive division
has had teams investigate markets for leasing train engines. The

European Plastics division has had teams assess the division's overall strategy and marketing plans for plastic applications for automobile bodies. In the more elaborate action learning programs, managers might be sent to foreign countries where they conduct market surveys, meet government officials, interview potential clients, and immerse themselves in culture and language courses.

The stages of an action learning experience are fairly standardized across many companies. The schematic shown in Exhibit 8.1 illustrates the flow of one representative action learning experience undertaken at Citibank. Typically, after receiving project assignments and reviewing background materials, action learning teams travel to the headquarters of their assigned businesses—domestic or foreign—to perform further diagnostic research. They have access to key managers and can review essential financial and marketing information as well as visit the field and customers. As their findings and recommendations progress and materialize into drafts, they are reviewed by outside consultants who identify gaps in the analyses and assist in mapping out strategies for overcoming internal resistance to the team's recommendations. The conclusion of their efforts results in presentations to a senior group of executives from the business units concerned. In follow-up sessions, participants also have opportunities to learn about the successes or problems that their recommendations have encountered as they were implemented by the businesses. In this way, participants learn firsthand about the implementation challenges facing their ideas and draw important postproject lessons.

The Advantages of Action Learning

In our interviews with participants in action learning programs, most report positive to very positive learning experiences. In contrast to traditional classroom learning where lessons are separated from work, participants find the experience of hands-on learning through the application of theory and principles to work-related

Exhibit 8.1. Citibank's Team Challenge: Roadmap of an Action Learning Process

Selection of issues and participants	Team building and orientation to issues (off-site, 3–4 days)	Data gathering (2–3 weeks)	Data analysis and development of recommendations (1 week)
Issues recommended by business heads or CEO • Really significant • Cut across businesses and impact total Citibank performance Participants • Recommended by business units • Based on "talent inventory review" process • Done on a worldwide basis	Purpose and objectives Introduce coaches Team-building exercises: • Diverse (business, geography, and function) teams of 6–7 people Overview of issues and deliverables Background presentations • Experts, best practice companies, existing data, and so on Team planning time	Travel both inside and outside Citibank • Customers • External best practice companies • Internal best practices • "Experts" • Focus groups (internal and external) • Senior Citibankers or those closest to the issue	Data analysis and development of recommendations (1 week) Debrief data gathering Formulate recommendations Draft presentations Coaching

Presentations	Debriefing and reflection (1 day)	Senior management follow-up (within 1–2 weeks of presentations)
CEO and business heads • 90 minutes per team (30-minute presentation, 60-minute discussion)	Structured debrief with coach • Recommendations • Team process • Individual development opportunities Individual learnings and action plans Celebration	Decision on actions to be taken Assignment of responsibility for implementation Continuous update on project status

Source: Dotlich, D. L., and Noel, J. L. Action Learning. San Francisco: Jossey-Bass, 1998, p. 22.

projects extremely helpful. They are able to test the utility of frameworks and techniques on tangible problems and are able to see for themselves what can be usefully applied. By being placed in unfamiliar surroundings—in terms of businesses and often geography—and by encouraging individuals to stretch beyond their existing comfort zones, participants can at times feel deeply challenged. Because projects are often conducted in cross-functional teams, the mix of individuals exposes participants to different business models and expands their perspectives. Working closely with people from other backgrounds forces participants to learn about different ways of doing business. In addition, it encourages them to view their home operations in a new, more generative light. Participants particularly value this exchange of experience and the way it helps them examine their own businesses more critically. As a result, they often report that the process strengthens their understanding of their company as well as what the various business units do, how the company and the units are organized, and what products the organization makes. The learning process further helps participants to better understand the organization's competencies and how corporate and other functions add value. In addition, these experiences facilitate a deeper understanding of the organization's overall corporate vision and strategic direction.

Those who participate in action learning experiences in foreign countries describe additional learnings—for example, better and deeper understanding of cross-cultural business practices, the infrastructure and cultural peculiarities of a country's markets, and thus greater insight into how to introduce products into other nations. They learn how to locate and collect needed information. And they develop a keener sensitivity to cultural differences that could have an impact on the market penetration of their products.

Although broadening perspectives and developing expertise are two important aims of action learning, another is the development and honing of analytical ability. In our research, we discovered that participants varied with respect to the analytic skills they actually developed during their action learning experience. Some, for example, reported improved analytic capability—learning how to develop business plans, conduct customer segmentation analyses, or create analytic models for evaluating alternative business scenarios. Others reported simply applying skills they already possessed. The extent to which participants developed their analytical skills depended largely on the expertise they brought with them and their prior training. Those with more recent business school training or those who already employed the techniques taught in a program tended to learn less than those without such training or responsibilities.

In addition to participants' descriptions, research in adult learning confirms the power of action learning experiences when it comes to developing complex skills such as leadership. For example, we know from studies in cognitive psychology that knowledge comes in essentially two forms. One is *procedural knowledge,* the other is *declarative knowledge* (Clark, 1992). As we shall see in our descriptions of the two, action learning focuses primarily on the development of declarative knowledge, the more conceptual and complex of the forms.

The ability to develop principles and concepts to explain complex events is at the heart of declarative knowledge. For example, in a business context, we use declarative knowledge when leading individuals through organizational change, formulating strategy, or developing new product ideas. These are complex situations with lots of contingencies, and no one situation is likely to be identical to the next. Step-by-step techniques and formulas are of little use. Rather, one must detect patterns, make creative connections, and formulate in-the-moment theories of action. In contrast, procedural knowledge involves tasks that can be accomplished through standardized formulas and step-by-step learning. So, for example, accounting techniques and financial formulas are forms of procedural knowledge—in other words, they are tasks that can be accomplished according to a clear set of procedures.

Declarative and procedural knowledge require different types of learning. How people learn procedural knowledge is fairly well understood (Clark, 1992). Behavioral psychology has taught us that traditional training methods are best suited for procedural knowledge—applying knowledge in practice sessions spread over time and using corrective feedback and appropriate incentives to direct and motivate learning. In other words, we give accounting students a series of exercises, have them practice applying the rules of accounting, and then provide them with detailed feedback on what they did right and wrong. The closer the training experience replicates the actual problems and experiences to which it will be applied, the more likely it is that procedural learning will occur. So we teach accounting by providing problem-solving exercises that mirror situations managers would experience back at their jobs (VanLehn, 1996).

How people learn declarative knowledge is less well known. Learning declarative knowledge requires developing a set of concepts and principles that permits creative connections to be drawn between events. The ability to create and use appropriate analogies to connect several domains of knowledge is particularly important to the process. The more frequently individuals can successfully link events that are seemingly unrelated but actually similar to the new problems they are addressing, the more they will be able to produce creative solutions. In essence, action learning formats and the case method of instruction achieve this outcome by presenting learners with complex situations that parallel events they will encounter in their work. As such, action learning is an ideal pedagogy for declarative knowledge. The only dilemma is that often the learning in these programs is based on a one-time experience—a single program. To truly develop declarative knowledge, however, learners require repeated or multiple exposures. This is because individuals need exposure to a large enough set of case experiences to begin developing a reliable repertoire of principles and a valid conceptual understanding of what they are experiencing. So it would be a mistake to assume that a single action learning program is sufficient to build declarative knowledge in subjects as complex as leadership or strategy formulation or global marketing. Therefore, in the ideal world companies would need to send participants from their action learning programs directly to job assignments that build upon program lessons and in turn perpetuate the learning process. By not doing so, the learning process stops prematurely.

The Design Features of Effective Programs

In a rush to adopt the latest educational experiences, many companies institute action learning projects without fully understanding the necessity of having crucial design features in place. We found at times a mistaken belief that action learning is in itself a magic bullet of sorts, and as a result sponsors often gave insufficient thought to critical political issues and follow-up steps. For example, in several of the cases we studied, the benefits of these formats were completely undermined by poor designs, a failure to obtain broad buy-in, a lack of follow-through and appropriate reinforcement, and weak connections to overall company strategies. In this section, we look at the design factors that increase the learning potential of these formats.

1. Careful Selection of Learning Projects

In the ideal case, action learning experiences should create learning not only for individual participants but for the organization as a whole. As such, the selection of projects should always seek to attain this goal. This is not easy, because the interests of the organization may not match the interests and needs of individual participants.

From the sponsors' viewpoint, it is always important that the projects have a direct link to some business imperative. As Dotlich and Noel (1998) point out, the business imperative of the project must also be characterized as a situation where current approaches are widely recognized as insufficient to address the upcoming challenge. In addition, it is essential that the sponsor of a project be motivated—"genuinely concerned to get something done" (Revans, 1980, p. 293). Those providing projects must see themselves as equal learners in the process along with the participants themselves. The sponsors must also be comfortable involving outsiders who are frequently junior managers addressing their problems. For these very reasons, it is often best to start with a sponsoring group that is already motivated and has a tangible initiative in mind. If the project outcomes prove quite useful and translate into initiatives that show positive payoffs for the sponsor, it is then easier to involve other more skeptical groups. In addition, this line of thinking leads to the importance of allowing sponsors to chose the initiatives they most value rather than compromise initiatives that attempt to meet some combination of needs of the corporation *and* the sponsoring group.

From the perspective of participants, we found that the most valued experiences were those where the teams were given primary responsibility for initiating a significant change or new venture. Such experiences provide not only learning but motivation. In addition, it is important to structure projects so that they provide participants with a good chance at success. One participant summarized the outcomes when this happened: "Nothing matters more in terms of experience than being involved in a very difficult challenge and being successful at it. Because you learn how to be a winner. Having a win, at least once in a while, especially under difficult challenging circumstances, gives you the confidence to know that you can stretch yourself. You can stretch your organization. You can be an effective leader."

So in the ideal case, projects would be chosen where individual development could be addressed while simultaneously tackling the business imperative. For example, as General Electric expanded globally, there was a realization that the company needed to understand the markets for its products in emerging nations and to develop a cadre of globally minded leaders to capitalize on opportunities. GE action learning projects therefore focused on sending managers into foreign countries to learn firsthand about the challenges of opening new markets for the company's products and to develop their capability to manage across cultures—successfully addressing both an organizational and a developmental objective.

In addition, projects need to be sufficiently open-ended such that there are a range of alternative solutions or issues, and they need to be a learning "stretch" for participants and a broadening of one's perspective. Revans (1980) captures the quality of the stretch when he proposes that "[the projects] of action learning are to be problems, to excite the interest of the participants in what they *cannot see* rather than enhance their skill in elaborating what they can see already" (p. 292). Here we return to the notion of declarative learning—that participants should be solving problems that require the development of often fundamentally new perspectives and in turn new principles and concepts—versus the application of existing skills to solve difficult but familiar problems.

Finally, in selecting projects it is important that they have an identifiable owner or individual sponsor. This person need not necessarily be the senior leader, but must be part of or closely linked with the executive coalition running the business. It is crucial that they have political clout. This is essential given that action learning projects often engender resistance. For example, operating units may be reluctant to send their more talented managers off for extended learning periods. Projects usually challenge the status quo of an organization, forcing participants to "confront their own failings, the failings of others, and the failings of the organization" (Dotlich and Noel, 1998). Because of potential obstacles like these, the sponsor must have a base of political power. But if the project owner is at too high a level, say the company CEO or COO, this can cause problems. Because of the multiple pressing demands of their role, they may simply not have the time to devote ongoing attention and help to projects. Reflecting on several decades of experience with action learning, Revans (1980) adds that in the ideal case the sponsoring individual not only has power but is knowledgeable about the issues and has demonstrated the motivation to address the issue publicly: "There are three . . . qualifications for [an effective] client [sponsor]: [1] that he is well informed as to why the problem is a thorn in the flesh of the power structure, [2] that he should be well known across the enterprise for his readiness to see that something is done about the trouble, or that, once the trouble has been defined and resources got together for attacking it, [3] he has the power to put behind the shoulders of those ready to make the first shove. Understanding, eagerness, and force are all called for" (p. 293).

There are lesser factors to consider in selecting projects. For example, some projects may require far greater classroom or instructional education in order for participants to address initiatives about which they have no prior knowledge. This is likely to be the case with learning about strategy formulation, the application of advanced functional knowledge, or dealing with entry challenges in foreign markets. These considerations will shape how many and what kind of human resources are needed from the outside, such as university professors, consultants, or other experts. Some projects hold a greater probability of being implemented by a business unit. As a result, they are more likely to ensure learning among participants, because the outcomes and implementation challenges associated with their recommendations can also be examined. Some projects lend themselves to follow-on action learning initiatives that can build one upon another and so deepen and perpetuate the learning process.

2. Objectives and Outcomes Must Be Clearly Defined

Before a program begins, there must be widespread agreement on objectives and outcomes. Otherwise, participants will find themselves in conflict over what to produce. For this reason, it is essential that the sponsors of action learning projects be very clear up front about their expectations. Deliverables and objectives must be spelled out and consistently communicated by all program sponsors. This requires mutual agreement prior to participant selection. In the cases we studied where teams felt a lack of clarity around expectations, much of it could be traced back to confusing messages from sponsors. Problems were generally more pronounced in the case of joint sponsors, say a combination of a corporate and a business unit sponsor. Each party might convey differing expectations or have conflicting notions about what the other's responsibilities entail. In one case, a participant commented to us, "The corporate sponsor was somewhat unclear and largely unavailable to give feedback. . . . They seemed to think that establishing the action learning project was their contribution. And, having done that, they were now going on to the next thing." As a result, this individual's group turned to its internal facilitators to play a stronger role in establishing the overall structure of the project and guiding members. But like the participants, the facilitators were either unaware of sponsor expectations or ill-suited to carry them out.

In some cases, there may be too many objectives or else objectives that are hidden or in dispute among the sponsors. One company we studied had decided on three primary objectives: (1) to identify and develop an entry strategy into an emerging market deemed strategically important; (2) to develop strategic synergies among business units where silos or barriers had traditionally existed; and (3) to develop the strategic thinking capabilities of the participants as well as their knowledge of the various business units. In our investigations, however, we found that participants felt there were at least two other somewhat unspoken objectives. These included (1) directing business unit attention to a growing corporate emphasis on the future importance of Asian markets and (2) resolving differences of opinion that existed among company executives concerning how best to enter into certain emerging markets. As a result, there was considerable confusion over priority. This spread to the criteria participants used to make decisions and their beliefs about how the project would be evaluated. Several participants felt that the business units viewed the projects, first and foremost, as a vehicle for personal development and for determining broad strategic direction. Corporate, however, viewed the projects' role as one of directing business unit market strategies for entering into these markets. They wanted the project teams to be integrally involved in developing an ultimate entry strategy. In addition, the business units did not particularly welcome outside assistance—especially from relatively inexperienced managers—in determining which strategies they should be using. As a result, the business units were far less committed to these projects as a vehicle for guiding specific market entry strategies and hence their view that these were purely projects for individual development. These conflicting priorities ultimately hampered both participant and organizational learning.

3. Multiple Opportunities for Reflective Learning

One of the advantages of action learning environments is that they remove participants from the day-to-day demands of their work and provide what would otherwise be rare time for reflective learning. At the same time, part of their attraction is that they are task-based—in other words, they are all about achieving important projects by a certain deadline. As a result, the accomplishment of the task can potentially overwhelm the process of learning. The better-designed programs powerfully blend reflective learning experiences with the pressures and deadlines of a significant undertaking.

Action learning projects are vehicles for learning, with feedback and reflection as the primary mechanisms by which the participants actually learn. Without these, action learning would be no different from a normal day on the job. Feedback is essential because managers receive so little direct feedback on their own performance and learning. Moreover, an individual's personal interpretation of feedback can be ambiguous, and sometimes actually the *wrong* lessons are learned from experiences (Davis and Hogarth, 1992). Therefore, it is essential that active and disciplined feedback be provided by objective sources. Coaches, facilitators, company managers, and teammates are all sources of useful feedback in action learning experiences. They can also foster and reinforce reflective learning in how they structure sessions with participants. For example, a good facilitator employs feedback techniques that promote discussion and reflection. They use questions and discussions rather than statements and lectures to guide learning.

Feedback and reflection should be focused around the many different levels of learning that are occurring for the participant and their organization. In the better-designed programs, reflective learning opportunities are not only targeted at what was learned through the projects themselves but also on the personal approaches and styles of the individual team members. Here are several topic areas for reflective learning that should not be overlooked:

- How do our findings confirm or disconfirm our existing notions of our marketplaces (competitors, customers, suppliers, governments)? our existing notions of our organization and its capabilities and shortcomings?

- What am I learning as a participant about business strategy, leadership, organizational change, innovation, global markets, and so on?

- How effective are our group's processes for accomplishing the project task?

- How effective am I as a team member in terms of my personal style, contributions, teamwork, initiative, decision-making approach, and so on?

- What am I learning about how other functions, business units, and the corporate center operate, and their distinct needs?

- (When the project is completed) What could we as a team and I as an individual have done differently to make the process more effective? How could I have improved my own contribution and performance within the team setting?

Reflections should be staged regularly. Unfortunately, in some programs, reflection on learnings is held in only one session on the last day of a program. This is a serious mistake. Instead there should be daily opportunities where participants reflect on learnings to that point in the program or on that day's work. This type of daily reflection has two advantages. First, it forces participants to reflect more directly on immediate moments and events, and so learning tends to be richer and more around specific incidents. This fits with what we know from research on feedback: it is most useful to learners when focused on recent events. End-of-program reflections miss the smaller moments of learning and can overlook events and stages that in hindsight appear to be far fewer and far less memorable. We also know that in looking back retrospectively we often distort our perceptions of an experience. The more reflections are tied to immediate events, the lower the likelihood of distortion. Second, by instituting daily reflection, a program is modeling what we hope managers will learn to do for themselves—to reflect on their actions and decisions day-by-day.

How can a program be structured to ensure that critical reflection actually occurs on a regular basis? There are several approaches that action learning experts recommend. For example, Dotlich and Noel (1998) recommend pairing team members with one another to provide one-on-one feedback. Each participant might be asked to give the other a single behavioral change they wish to have made as an outcome of the program. Another device is to have participants write observations about each other on sticky notes and then place them on a wall for all to read. Their observations are shaped by the request posed: "Describe what you think your team member should do more of, less of, or continue as is." Names are not attached to the notes, but members choose the one that they feel most applies to them. In turn, participants ask for examples of their behavior and its effects and solicit general feedback. Journals or daily diaries can also be used as sources of reflection and learning. Finally, it is helpful at regular intervals to schedule team meetings where time is devoted solely to providing group process feedback. Ideally, these sessions would be moderated by a facilitator for maximum impact.

4. Active Involvement by Senior Management

The importance of active senior management direction, support, and feedback in action learning cannot be overemphasized. Participants join these learning initiatives with high expectations and often excitement. They assume that their enthusiasm will be similarly matched by their senior leaders. They are also subjected to high levels of stress. Often, participants are relocated for the duration of the project and may spend significant time traveling overseas and battling deadlines. They come to expect some form of special recognition for their personal investment. Moreover, members feel they have an important and visible role to play in developing solutions for a project. All are aware that presentations on project findings and solutions can potentially provide great opportunities for enhancing one's visibility. As such, many see it as a rare opportunity to be seen and heard by the company's senior-most leaders. Given these dynamics, a lack of active support from senior management can seriously dampen the motivation to learn and can even stifle the transfer of learnings back to the workplace. For example, in one company we studied, it was estimated that only 15 to 25 percent of the action learning teams' recommendations were adopted by business units. At the same company, members of one team expressed considerable frustration over the fact that senior management had given them the go-ahead to develop an entry strategy for a business unit that was then sold three days prior to their final report. On top of this, the CEO did not attend the final presentation. As a result, this organization realized little on its investment, failing to truly harness project learnings and in turn losing its opportunities for institutional learning. Disappointments like this can have extremely negative consequences, not only for the individuals involved but for the organization as well. They may be so frustrating and demotivating that some of the organization's highest-potential leaders may choose to leave the firm, taking their talent and training investment with them.

Without a question, then, senior management's attention to action learning experiences and their involvement in critical reviews has significant symbolic and performance consequences. Such involvement signals the importance of programs, rewards participants for their efforts, and conveys to the larger organization that such programs are valuable and valued. The lack of involvement conveys a similarly, though perhaps unintended, strong message. Therefore corporate sponsorship must be explicitly defined, and company executives need to be actively involved in programs. Frequent interaction and feedback with both corporate and business unit executives is therefore critical for improving the program's chances of furthering organizational learning.

5. Expert Facilitation and Coaching

Because a large portion of the learning process occurs in team-based discussions, facilitators, coaches, and instructors play a crucial role in helping teams to learn and reflect. In our research, facilitation proved to be one of the most critical success factors for action learning programs. For one, participants often find themselves bombarded with information from field visits and company presentations. They generally experience some difficulties in making sense out of all of the data and its complexity. Facilitators and instructors can assist teams to consolidate and learn from information. They can provide needed structure and analytic frameworks early in the process. As one participant noted, "Facilitation served to bring order to the chaos we were experiencing from the rapid pace of visits to the various operations and the volume of information." Facilitators can also help teams organize their approaches before field visits. They can focus the group's efforts by crystallizing the questions the team would like to have answered in its field work and the points to consider in formulating final recommendations. Sessions with facilitators are also essential to demonstrate how concepts and frameworks can be applied to design thoughtful recommendations. At the same time, facilitators must be well informed in advance about what factors or impediments may undermine the action learning process so as to maximize the probability of successful implementation of project recommendations.

One important issue to be decided up front is whether to employ facilitators who are members of the organization or to use outsiders. The advantages of internal facilitators are their existing knowledge about the organization and their ability to be on call after programs end. As well, they are generally a less expensive option. But external facilitators possess several advantages. They may bring with them special expertise not available within the firm, little or no personal investment in the organization's paradigms, and a greater willingness to challenge, as their careers are not invested in the firm. It is also important to select facilitators based on an initiative's learning aims. For example, where teams lack a certain expertise that the project demands, it may be most appropriate to pick consultants or instructors who possess a depth of knowledge in this area.

In several cases, we observed firms using management consultants to facilitate the learning process. How successful these efforts were depended largely on the expectations established up front and the type of learning involved. Generally, consultants were effective facilitators to the extent that the following were true:

1. A goal of the program was to impart strategic thinking capabilities and provide models for approaching strategic problems.

2. They had demonstrated expertise in the area for which learning was needed (such as market entry strategies in a particular foreign country or product branding).

3. They were committed and skilled at facilitating and teaching and not simply at prescribing solutions.

Consultants were far less effective when the following were the case:

1. Expectations for learning were not clearly established and agreed to before a program was undertaken, and there was greater interest on their part in doing and explaining rather than in teaching.

2. They failed to provide models, structures, and simplifying frameworks to help learners digest the often enormous quantities of data that participants encountered.

3. They failed to provide roadmaps of where the project was going and of how to approach problems, collect information, and analyze data.

Problems and Pitfalls

To the extent that action learning initiatives are well managed, they have the potential to produce significant business results. To the extent they are poorly managed, they have the potential to demotivate some of the organization's best performers and to discourage senior leaders from sponsoring projects or from sending their own managers to subsequent programs.

Given these consequences, it is essential that careful thought be given to anticipating potential problems in advance. For example, in our experience, program designs typically required far more attention to follow-up activities to ensure continued learning than they actually received. In addition, program designs may be a learning experience for the individual participant but fail to achieve the outcome of *organizational* learning. As one participant stated to us succinctly: "If this [the action learning experience] is merely a personal development effort, if that's all we end up getting out of it, it is not worth it. . . . For the money spent, you could do a lot better. But if you could change the behavior of the corporation—the bureaucracy—then it is extremely *inexpensive*." In short, for action learning programs to be of value, they must be executed well with attention to both individual and organizational learning. Here we explore some of the common obstacles we discovered that often derail these popular programs.

1. Operating Groups Are Not Fully on Board

In most of the action learning programs we studied, projects were provided by an organization's operating groups. Not so surprisingly, then, we found that pivotal to the effective execution of action learning projects is strong buy-in at the front end of programs from a company's business units. Otherwise, there is a risk that operating groups will choose the path of "least assistance" in working with project teams. Buy-in basically starts when business units see a high perceived value in project outcomes for themselves given the time and resource investments they must make. This may mean that certain budgets and metrics need to be modified by corporate to encourage business unit support of such programs. For example, budgets might be supplemented or a particular quarter's targets might be adjusted to reflect the absence of key personnel dedicated to the action learning project. Though such changes may be small, they are highly symbolic—sending messages about the importance of these programs. Moreover, if corporate sponsors are also involved, they must provide operating units with a degree of autonomy in the selection of projects. The worst scenario is for a corporate group to unilaterally decide on projects for its business units. This happened in one organization in our research. The corporate group not only chose the projects but focused them solely around a single business unit, ignoring projects proposed in other units. This occurred after the operating groups had been informed that they would be given considerable latitude in the choice of projects. Needless to say, this caused a great deal of animosity, which then spilled over into the learning experience. As one participant commented to us, the action learning teams kept "getting in the middle of all of this crossfire between corporate headquarters and the business units." Because corporate and business unit managers lacked a common vision, the teams received little consistent direction on their project objectives. This impeded not only the progress of the project but participant learning as well: "Each succeeding layer of management above us basically put in their two cents worth, and we were continuously getting redirection or redefinition of what we were supposed to be doing. . . . [They kept giving us] countervailing direction, so we were never really able to march off in one focused thrust for any period of time."

Without adequate buy-in from project sponsors, we found that interest on the part of business units quickly waned. Participants could easily detect this lack of interest and then either stumbled through projects or else similarly lost interest. Either way, learning was minimized. In one case, the business units and the corporate center failed to see eye-to-eye on what the action learning projects should accomplish. To resolve the matter, corporate then took over and established the project objectives. In the end, the operating groups became passive players in the program and offered more resistance than help. We found that resistance from business units typically comes in the form of withholding critical information or making access to it difficult, dragging out the implementation of recommendations, or simply failing to undertake initiatives proposed by learning teams.

In a few cases where buy-in from operating units was weak, participants themselves attempted to sell their home organizations on the value of a project. But we discovered that participants are in a difficult position to gain commitment from their own business units. First, because participants are at a learning stage, they tend to be at the middle and junior ranks of an organization. As such, their political clout and authority is usually limited. Second, participants are likely to be well integrated within their home business units to the point that they are more concerned about the needs and political dynamics of their own unit than the success of the action learning project. Indeed, if an educational program is seen as having little impact on their careers, managers will typically choose to safeguard relationships with their home organization rather than risking those relations to ensure the success of a program that may or may not be valued by the corporation as a whole.

In organizations experimenting with action learning for the first time, we discovered that it takes time to build the trust and commitment of the operating units. In some cases, the trust-building phase took up to three years. The initial year or two are often seen as testing periods by business units—testing corporate commitment and ulterior motives. Some operating units may see these programs as opportunities for corporate to "spy" on operations or to force new initiatives. These are likely to be the reactions when the learning projects focus on problem areas within a business unit.

2. Dysfunctional Team Dynamics

A critical lesson we have learned is that team dynamics can significantly affect the quality of project outcomes. In general, teams that develop strong norms around candor and diversity of perspectives produce more insightful and more creative project recommendations. In contrast, in teams where one individual or a single functional perspective dominates, the group tends to produce outcomes that are far less innovative and insightful. For example, in one situation, the action learning project centered around corporate investments in existing and future businesses. One participant who was on the finance staff at the corporate headquarters led participants to believe that he had superior knowledge, and as a result, the team readily incorporated his recommendations into its proposals. In the end, his team produced a report that supported the status quo and showed limited insight. It is therefore important to have some form of training on teamwork and decision-making processes at the front end of these programs. In addition, facilitators can play an important role by encouraging team norms that support openness of ideas and constructive confrontation. But most importantly, teams should not have participants who are "experts" on the issue being addressed. Otherwise there is a strong tendency to defer to those individuals, and as a result, both team and individual learning can be drastically minimized—if it occurs at all. With no experts on hand, groups are more likely to identify and debate a wider range of ideas and solutions. As Revans (1980) notes, this process can also lead participants to realize that in trying to solve problems their initial tendency is to draw more upon their past experiences than upon the new insights and ideas of others with a different viewpoint.

Team dynamics are of course strongly influenced by the composition of the team and the selection process. Careful selection of team members is therefore crucial to minimizing the possibility of a team derailing. Though it is extremely difficult to control a team's chemistry in advance, there are certain membership guidelines that may increase the probability of greater team performance and learning. First of all, it is extremely helpful to know beforehand how highly motivated potential participants are. In the ideal case, we would naturally pick only those who are motivated and who see themselves wishing to develop their leadership potential rather than simply to hone their expertise in a particular technique (Revans 1980). Given the expense of these programs, action learning is best employed for the development of high potentials—in other words, the organization's next generation of senior leaders. Selection criteria should reflect the project's goals. For example, if the program has an objective of broadening cross-functional perspectives, then it is important that the mix of participants represent multiple functions. If the objective is to instill a cross-cultural perspective, then team members should be drawn from different cultures. If a goal of the program is to facilitate change across multiple organizational levels, then it is advisable to have team members selected from different levels. According to Dotlich and Noel (1998), the best teams also mix together "unlikely specialists"—for example, a systems engineer and a sales executive. This mix of experts may facilitate the learning process by stimulating competing hypotheses that need testing to be resolved. The process causes participants to rethink their basic assumptions and entertain alternative perspectives—that is, to learn about other ways of approaching problems. Finally, selection criteria should always keep in mind the person's career stage and developmental needs. This should be a foremost concern. What are we grooming this individual to be good at? Is this action learning program a good opportunity to accelerate his or her learning in preparation for leadership roles in the near future? Will the person's next promotion most likely allow him or her to build further upon the learnings from the program? These questions should strongly drive the selection process.

3. Failure to Address Follow-Up Learning

Often when action learning projects end, they quite literally *end*. And here we fall into a similar concern voiced about university-based education: there is no formal follow-up. Instead there is an assumption that sufficient learning has taken place during the program itself and that it will be self-sustaining. Nothing could be farther from the truth. Like any form of training, action learning programs need mechanisms to ensure the transfer of learning back to the workplace. For example, participants might be promoted or moved to positions that are directly responsible for the initiatives proposed by the action learning teams. Or they might receive on-going briefings from those who are implementing their ideas. Yet many programs do not involve their participants in either the implementation phase nor hold postimplementation debriefings with action learning teams. In the ideal case, programs would be structured to ensure that participants are involved in implementation. If such structures were not feasible, participants would be kept informed of the implementation through debriefings staggered over the implementation life of an initiative. These debriefing sessions would allow participants to see how the implementation process unfolded and present them with lessons learned, a review of unexpected obstacles, and key success factors.

We can say without hesitation that learning for the organization can only be enhanced by ensuring that participants have opportunities to apply what they have learned to their own work when they return to their jobs. For this reason, the near-term job assignments of participants become a crucial issue. Ideally, we would want to place participants in future assignments that build upon or deepen the particular expertise or perspective taught in an action learning program. Organizations might also create successive action learning experiences that reinforce and expand on learnings from prior action learning initiatives.

As we now turn to our concluding chapter, it is important to realize that we have devoted much of our attention in this chapter and the previous ones to the design factors that either enhance or impede leadership development initiatives. We have spent less time considering the content of the leadership that we are training. Yet naturally, *what* we train and develop is as important as *how* we train and develop it. For this reason, we now need to focus on the content side of development. In the next chapter, we explore the qualities of leadership that we must be developing in our next generation of leaders. It is crucial that we think about these qualities with an eye to the future, because the managers we teach and develop today will have their greatest opportunities to exercise leadership perhaps as far out as ten to twenty years from now. It will do them little good to learn skills and perspectives based purely on today's leadership models, as these will become outdated. Instead, all of the approaches we have been examining, from action learning to socialization programs to strategic interventions, must focus on the organization's leadership requirements in the decades ahead rather than simply those of today.

9

What Matters
Competencies for the New Century

As we near the year 2000, much has been written about the new demands that leaders will face in the twenty-first century and how their roles will change. In this chapter, we address some of these issues and their implications for leadership development. Because change never happens overnight, some of these projected demands may already seem familiar. Forward-thinking organizations, those on the cutting edge of technology, and those that have become fundamentally global may already be feeling some of the pressures that loom in the distance for others. In many cases, these leading-edge firms have begun to grapple with new demands and have started to try new approaches. Indeed, companies are experimenting with novel approaches to learning like never before, making this the most exciting time for leadership development since the 1950s and 1960s. We try to capture some of this innovative thinking by providing examples where new concepts and approaches have begun to surface. We begin our discussion by examining some general speculation on the future dynamics of competition and work, and then address how these dynamics will impose new requirements for leadership.

The Times, They Are A-Changing

A colleague of ours, Stanford professor Jeffrey Pfeffer, describes many of today's books on management as falling into the "breathless" genre of business literature. By this he means that every part of the business world is depicted as being more rapid, competitive, complex, diverse, demanding, and challenging than ever before. He says this while rolling his eyes, and certainly there is a large grain of truth in the cynical picture he paints. Discussions of leadership are no different. Though we step gingerly in our characterization of the future, leaders must, in fact, be prepared to deal with significant change along many dimensions. Dimensions that most scholars and practitioners agree will likely impact the job of leaders in the future include the increasing demographic diversity of workforces, a faster pace of environmental and technological change, and greater international competition (Maltby, 1994). The scope and magnitude of these changes has yet to unfold, though in many ways the true scope is irrelevant. This is because leaders must deal with the perception of change as much as, if not more than, the reality of it. If everyone believes that change is occurring at a breathless pace, then leaders must be prepared to deal with that perception in addition to assessing its basis in fact. Doing both—and doing them well—will always be the leader's challenge, and it will never be an easy one.

Business pundits argue that projected changes in the nature of work, workers, and competition will result in new and different relationships between employers and employees, organizations and their suppliers, government and business, and producers and customers. These changes will ultimately place new demands on tomorrow's leaders. Indeed, in times of great transition and perceived change, leadership becomes critically important. Leaders offer people a pathway of confidence and direction as they move through what may otherwise seem like insurmountable chaos. As the magnitude of change appears to grow and come at a more rapid pace, not only will more leadership be needed, but also newer forms of leadership. To put it bluntly, new demands may render older models of leadership inappropriate for meeting the challenges ahead.

Just as important, our approaches to developing leaders will have to change. The investments that organizations make today in their young managers will not begin yielding significant returns until some two decades in the future. Only then will today's high-potentials begin to have the requisite maturity and rank needed to make a major impact. To illustrate, consider these remarks by General Fred Franks, former commanding general of the Army's Training and Doctrine Command: "The longest development process we have in the United States Army is development of a commander. It takes less time to develop a tank—less time to develop an Apache helicopter—than it does to develop a commander. It takes anywhere from twenty-two to twenty-five years before we entrust a division of soldiers to a commander. . . . [leaders] must continue to grow and to learn and to study [their] profession, to learn by [their] own experience, to learn by study, school, reading and . . . from others. . . . It [requires] total professional involvement" (interview comment on *Charlie Rose Show*).

With such a long development cycle, it is imperative that we take a hard look at the competencies that will be needed by our future leaders and our current methods for training and developing them. It is critical that we do so now because to the extent that our current leadership models are based on the requirements of previous decades, we put our leaders—and our organizations as a whole—at a great disadvantage in the years to come.

How then will the competencies demanded of twenty-first century leaders differ from those needed today? We can think about these differences along two complementary dimensions: strategic capabilities and organizational capabilities. For example, the external world is likely to continue to be intensely competitive and will demand that future leaders possess a keen strategic sense and a relentless desire to be nonstop learners. At the same time, major changes are taking place in workforce demographics that will pose internal or organizational challenges to future leaders. Both external and internal challenges will either reshape or accentuate the need for very specific leadership skills in the future. We begin our discussion by considering the strategic capabilities that leaders will likely need.

The Need for Strategic Leaders

Since the 1970s with the rise of Japan and Germany, competitive pressures worldwide have been mounting. The increased globalization of economic life and its influence on American business is evidenced by a number of indicators such as trade and capital flows and immigration patterns. The most commonly used measure of global competition and its economic impact is the ratio of exports and imports to gross domestic product. In 1960 the ratio was 0.094, but by 1991 it had more than doubled to 0.214, suggesting an increasingly competitive global marketplace. The ratio of exports and imports to GDP in other countries also rose over this period, further illustrating the expansion of world trade and global competition.

With the entry of foreign producers and the deregulation of many local markets, U.S. firms face a very different competitive landscape than in the past. Competitive pressures have escalated into virtual competitive battles as firms have fought for dominance in consolidating markets at home and emerging markets abroad. Fierce competition has meant an ever-increasing scramble for markets through innovative corporate strategies and through higher-quality products and services. From an economic standpoint, fierce competition has, in many ways, been good for U.S. industry: it has increased productivity and improved innovation. Yet competition has imposed significant challenges as well. For example, in many industries, competition has made it *necessary* for firms to develop innovative strategies and products just to survive. It has brought about shorter product development cycles and it has accelerated the pace of technological change. It has pushed companies to search for markets far outside their homelands, and it has increased their vulnerability to geopolitical shifts. Finally, competition (and the advent of advanced information technology) has forced organizations to flatten their hierarchies and to decentralize decision making so that they can respond with speed to their rivals' actions. These market forces—and the changes they have engendered—will have significant implications for future leaders.

Future leaders will be under enormous pressure to find the strategic opportunities that their competitors have missed. To do so, leaders will have to be both creative and comprehensive in their search. They will have to look within the organization for ways to improve quality, services, and prices. They will have to look outside the organization for new markets at home and abroad. They will have to look to other companies for partnerships and alliances that can bring complementary advantages. And they will have to look within their customers' organizations for new opportunities to improve products or services and extend existing markets. Identifying these opportunities will require significant expertise in a number of areas, perhaps the most important of which will be the area of strategic vision. Leaders will need to develop a profound appreciation for long-range thinking, along with a breadth of perspective on future markets, technologies, partners, and competitors. Leaders will continue to be under short-term pressures to innovate, but simultaneously under far greater pressure to look long-range. Although they will need to respond quickly to the speed of change, they must also be able to look into the future to determine the direction that change should take. That is, they will need to be able to envision alternative scenarios in a world that is currently very uncertain and determine which scenarios will put their organization at greatest advantage.

In addition, future leaders will need to be keen data analysts given that the quantity and quality of available information has and will continue to grow dramatically. Thanks largely to technological advances, leaders will literally be swimming in a sea of data of which only a portion will be truly relevant to shaping strategic decisions. As importantly, they must be able to shift their attention to new data points as customers and competitors change the rules of success in the marketplace. Xerox, for example, in the 1960s and 1970s used time-to-repair as a key quality measure for its copiers in an era where copy machines were expected to experience failures. The Japanese by the 1970s had changed their quality measure to track how frequently machines failed. In other words, they focused on building machines that had far lower failure rates. This proved to be the correct data point for customers who by the 1980s wanted reliable machines over speedy repairs.

Finally, in a world where one's external markets are constantly shifting, future leaders must be learners. Bill Gates is fond of saying that Microsoft is always two years from failure. By this, he means the organization must pay acute attention to its customers and competitors and be open to the changes these two forces introduce. In essence, Microsoft must be a learning organization. The ability to instill this learning mind-set into their organizations will become a trademark competency of future leaders. The upcoming generation of leaders therefore has to become a generation of learning evangelists. By stressing the importance of learning and creating a context where employees want to and are able to learn, leaders can strengthen their organizations for the challenges ahead and increase their ability to compete and innovate.

In summary, to lead effectively in this increasingly complex, information-rich, and highly competitive world, future leaders at all levels will need to develop new competencies. In essence, they will have to become all these:

1. Strategic opportunists
2. Globally adept
3. Capable of leading across organizational boundaries with alliance partners
4. Keen data analysts
5. Learning evangelists

If we turn to the first of these, the strategic opportunist, as the principal driver of the others, we need to ask ourselves how well we are currently developing this competence within our future leaders. There are strong indications that today's leadership education has done a poor job in developing the strategic skills and foresight required to sustain long-term advantage. For example, despite a sizable increase in the number of undergraduate business majors, the entry of more than eighty thousand MBA graduates into the work-force each year, and billions of dollars and man-hours devoted to leadership and management training for hundreds of thousands of corporate employees, the competitive position of the United States actually declined through the 1980s and into the early 1990s. Although corporate leadership is certainly not entirely to blame for the slowdown in productivity growth, the fact remains that as more countries become formidable competitors in the world economy—investing and building for the future—the strategic competence of an organization's leadership will become a key determinant of its ability to compete among this larger, more competitive playing field.

When we examine current approaches to developing strategic competence, however, we find that they are woefully inadequate. For example, attention to strategic analysis typically comes late in the careers of most managers, and then only after years of narrow functional experience that often stunts a truly strategic perspective. International experience until recently has been a low-status op-portunity for many fast-trackers—typically removing them from valuable communication and political networks and reducing the visibility of their achievements. Even with today's emphasis on international exposure, most organizations continue to do a poor job of integrating managers' foreign market experience into their subsequent assignments and career plans.

Strategic skills development has been particularly poorly served by formal leadership training efforts. When we look at the training provided by the majority of today's organizations, we see a heavy emphasis on courses oriented toward people management and self-development—the "soft skills." A report by the Carnegie Founda-tion for the Advancement of Teaching (1990, p. 138) noted the following:

> At a time when the world economy is growing and chang-ing rapidly, the management curriculum should be sub-jected to a general assessment. Regardless of the sponsor, there is remarkable similarity in the courses being offered.

In both the public and private sectors, topics recur in program after program, making management curricula more consistently recognizable than many other types of training. "People-management" courses and, for a lack of a better term, "self-management" courses are taught everywhere. The popularity of the two types of courses indicates a widely perceived need. There are, however, questions about their efficacy. . . . Somewhat less common are courses in strategic analysis and basic financial control.

Indeed, though we are beginning to see some strategy and business analysis skills being developed in programs that fall within the strategic intervention category, these programs tend to focus on a single change initiative and a single set of circumstances. They do not provide the diversity of experiences—and range of strategic dilemmas—needed to produce the analytic thinking and deep insight required for analyzing strategic challenges and formulating long-term business strategies. To the extent that leaders do get some exposure to a broad sampling of strategic issues, the exposure continues to be largely through university programs, which provide instruction through a case study approach. Unfortunately, though case study methodology may be effective for teaching generic concepts about strategy, it faces two common dilemmas. The first is that many case studies deal with issues in other industries unrelated to the participant's business. This is the principal reason why we see an increase in the number of in-house company programs or university programs customized to a single company. The second dilemma is that case instruction itself remains one step removed from the actual marketplace. This limits the developing leaders' ability to probe and experiment with different tactics and to form a strategic sense for the systems dynamics of their own industry and markets.

To develop greater strategic awareness and more refined analysis skills, future development programs will have to provide a broader range of experiences in a reasonably short time. They will have to link these experiences to the organization's immediate competitive pressures while simultaneously building insight into the longer-term challenges that will shape their industry. They also need to provide leaders with a more intimate understanding of their customers and markets, and to do so in a way that helps managers see beyond current paradigms and industry practices. A bit later in this chapter, we explore some new avenues for addressing these educational challenges.

We now turn our attention to the important internal or organizational challenges that future leaders will face. This set of forces is the by-product of fundamental shifts occurring in the composition of the American workforce, the rise of electronically networked organizations, and the growth in workforces that span national boundaries.

The Need for Workplace-Savvy Leaders

Leaders today must respond to a workforce that is far more diverse and culturally integrated than ever before. A look at some basic statistics illustrates the point. In 1950, only a third of all working-age American women participated in the workforce. By 1993, that proportion had risen to 58 percent, and projections estimate that by 2005, approximately 63 percent of all women will be working. The ethnic composition of the workforce has also changed. Blacks, Asians, and Hispanics make up a larger percentage of the American workforce today. So much so that between 1992 and 2005 it is expected that almost two-thirds of those entering the civilian workforce will be racial minorities and women (U.S. Department of Labor, 1994). This increasingly diverse group of employees will bring with it a set of needs and concerns that are likely to be unfamiliar to the white males who currently populate the upper echelons of our corporate hierarchies. For example, with more women working and families relying on both parents to provide an income, employees will increasingly require more flexible working hours, leave allowances, and child care benefits.

The workforce is growing more diverse not only in race, ethnicity, and gender, but also in the extent to which employees affiliate with a single institution. As organizations have sought to increase flexibility and reduce labor costs, they have begun to rely increasingly on contingent or part-time and temporary employees. These contingent relations reflect a growing need for nontraditional work relations and provide a number of benefits to both the organization and employee. They present, however, a special challenge to leaders: how to motivate and inspire employees who view themselves as less a part of and less dependent on their organizations. The rise of the electronically networked office where fellow employees connect largely through Lotus notes and e-mail while on the road or from an office at home poses a similar predicament. Personal connections and relationships are often superficial and distant, which may undermine a strong identification with one's organization. These twin forces of the electronic office and contingent workforces will demand that future leaders be clearer and more compelling in communicating their organization's vision so that all employees—no matter how weakly affiliated or distant—are aligned and dedicated to the organization's overarching goals. And they will have to be adept at using all the mechanisms available to them to convey expectations, motivate desired behavior, and instill appropriate controls.

The growing diversity of the workforce will be made all the greater by yet another workforce trend: an increase in the years of schooling attained by today's employees. In 1992, 53 percent of all working-age Americans had more than twelve years of schooling: 26 percent had some college work, and 27 percent were college graduates. Contrast this to the educational composition of the workforce in 1970, when only 26 percent of the workforce had more than twelve years of schooling and a full 36 percent of working-age adults had less than a high school diploma. Today, we have a better-educated and therefore more demanding sector of the work-force. Despite the increase in educational attainment, however, more than 20 percent of all students continue to drop out of high school (U.S. Department of Labor, 1994). This means that tomorrow's leaders will have to manage an increasingly diverse set of demands, equity issues, and development requirements. To take full advantage of their workforces' potential, leaders will have to appreciate and leverage the differences of their employees and provide learning experiences appropriate to a wider variety of needs and capabilities. Moreover, they will have to do so in a social and legal structure that increasingly emphasizes equal opportunity and fair treatment in the workplace.

Societal values—and the legal structures that reflect them—are a force with which leaders have always had to deal. However, as the workforce has become more diverse, society has become less tolerant of leaders who fail to manage this diversity responsibly. Today's employment laws and regulations are more prescriptive and more pervasive than ever before, reflecting the public's greater scrutiny of their leaders' behavior. These laws provide a wider variety of legal rights to more employees, who are protected by a greater number of enforcement mechanisms. This means that leaders will be held more directly responsible for their behavior by the courts, as well as by shareholders, as it is the shareholder who will, in many cases, have to foot the liability bill. One need only look at the growing number of employment lawsuits—for discrimination, sexual harassment, wrongful termination, and the like—for proof that employees today demand less indiscretion and more respect from their leaders. The statistics powerfully catch one's attention. Between 1971 and 1991, employment-related lawsuits filed in the U.S. Federal Courts rose 430 percent, four times the percentage increase in the overall civil caseload during the same period (U.S. Department of Labor, 1994). Estimates at the state level are no less daunting. The American Civil Liberties Union estimates that by the early 1990s approximately ten thousand wrongful termination claims were being filed annually, with a total of twenty-five thousand cases pending in 1994 alone (Maltby, 1994). These numbers suggest that future leaders will have to be far more sensitive to the needs and rights of their employees and will have to ensure that other leader-representatives of their organization respect these rights as well. Those who fail to be interpersonally and legally aware will have considerable difficulty getting anything accomplished and may ultimately have difficulty holding onto their jobs.

As our economy becomes increasingly global, leaders will have to lead workforces located across national borders. They will face cultural demands, legal requirements, and ethical issues that are new and unfamiliar. They will need to make critical decisions that will set strong precedent and, in many cases, attract attention from government officials, human rights organizations, and the media. These decisions will involve difficult trade-offs, complicated moral dilemmas, and political scrutiny. They will be met with demands from opposing interest groups and will cause significant debate within and around the organization. They will also define the company and what it stands for in the eyes of some of its most important constituents—most notably its customers and employees. In the face of such political land mines, leaders will need to be exceedingly competent in the art of persuasion and skilled at communicating and mediating disputes. Indeed, future employment issues will require the leader to be as much statesman as strategist.

Growing expectations about what leaders should demand from their employees and how they should care for and develop them may, in fact, be a manifestation of something more profound and fundamental: the increasing importance of the workplace as a person's primary community in life. For example, just a century ago, an individual's family, hometown, and church or temple played vital roles as sources of community and well-being. Today this is no longer the case. Divorce, increased mobility, civic apathy, urban alienation, and disillusionment with organized religion have all contributed to the decline of the traditional community. As a result, individuals have begun to bring needs that were originally met by one's family, civic, and religious communities to the workplace. Yet even the workplace community has become increasingly turbulent and disconnected as downsizing and mergers and acquisitions disrupt what was once a relatively stable environment. And though the frenzy of mergers may cool off with declines in equity markets, downsizing is likely to accelerate. In light of the changing needs of employees and the increasingly fluid boundaries of the organization, leaders of the future will need to be adept at quickly building a common sense of purpose and belongingness among employees who have never before worked together. They will have to be able to build a sense of community among employees who are less connected to the organization and to each other. And they will have to do this at a time when the workforce is becoming ever more diverse.

We already see indications that successful leaders understand the importance of community and community spirit. For example, Southwest Airlines CEO Herb Kelleher and his senior team have promoted parties and celebrations as an integral part of the company's culture (O'Reilly and Pfeffer, 1995). Each operating station is given a budget for social events for employees and their families. An annual rolling company party is held with Kelleher and his senior managers across several cities. There are chili cookoffs and Christmas parties. From voluntary contributions, the company has built a catastrophe fund to help Southwest employees in need. At Cisco Systems, CEO John Chambers straps on a red apron and hosts a quarterly ice cream social for all employees at headquarters in San Jose, California. As one of Cisco's core strategies is growth through acquisition, the ice cream social provides one of many mechanisms that Chambers uses to get to know new employees and to build a sense of community. Such community building efforts help to build a cohesive culture that strongly emphasizes teamwork and the sharing of ideas. In an organization that typically buys eight to twelve companies a year, such efforts are vital if Cisco wants to retain the talent it acquires and become something other than a loose conglomerate of competing interests.

Finally, as we move into the future and employees become more dispersed and contingent, it will become increasingly important for leaders to be able to build and leverage their organization's architecture so that it encourages and supports desired behavior in the absence of direct influence. They will need to have a global and systemic understanding of the organization—not just the business—and be able to align key organizational systems (such as planning systems, core structures, evaluation systems, performance measures, incentive systems, information systems, selection and training, and the like) with corporate aspirations. Only by understanding the interrelatedness of these various systems and using them to their fullest will leaders be able to build common direction and commitment.

In the face of the challenges we have been describing, it is important to recognize that leaders will not be able to accomplish these objectives singlehandedly. Leaders may communicate a compelling vision and catalyze a sense of community, but to truly unite the organization and build a unified force, leadership must extend beyond the inspiring individual. Indeed, though persuasion and communication are important and can do much to create change, ultimately such tactics are limited by the frequency and intensity with which leaders have direct contact with their employees. The leader's task will therefore be to create leaders at all levels. Only through the talents, drive, and commitment of others can leaders succeed in creating long-term competitive advantage and a bright future for their organizations.

Together, these workforce trends will demand that leaders of the future be all of the following:

- Sensitive to issues of diversity

- Interpersonally competent

- Skillful communicators and motivators

- Community builders

- Capable of building well-aligned organizational architectures

- Developers of leaders

How well are we currently developing these workplace competencies in our future leaders? We find a mixed scorecard. For example, interpersonal skills and motivation have long been a part of educational programs, and more recently, we see more offerings of diversity training. The other competencies are largely absent from development initiatives and so continue to be left to chance. But even in the case of interpersonal skills, our current educational approaches appear to have limited impact. For example, we train interpersonal skills such as active listening and feedback or build awareness of individual differences through programs that rely on assessment tools or experiential exercises. But generally, these are one-time experiences in traditional classroom settings. Rarely if ever are programs able to go deeper to uncover the fundamental reasons why a manager has difficulty listening, poor relations with superiors, or chemistry problems with other employees. As a result, when managers return to the office they often appear to have forgotten the very lessons that seemed so apparent in the classroom. In large part, this is because interpersonal ability stems mainly from one's character. A few days of training is therefore wholly insufficient to . produce noticeable behavioral changes. At best, classrooms can provide awareness of the problem and its impact on others. Because of this, coaching must play a greater role in supplementing educational programs. Its absence is a principal reason why interpersonal skills training, we believe, is not as effective as it could be.

Education in diversity issues, though growing in popularity, must begin with information on the common challenges that a particular group faces in the workplace, on demographic trends, and on management approaches that engender negative reactions and that have positive effects. In the ideal case, educational experiences would include classroom simulations and exercises that trigger common diversity issues so that participants could see firsthand the very situations and behaviors that require sensitivity. Field projects that assign managers to understand or work with unfamiliar ethnic groups are another vehicle for learning about diversity. The mix of participants and educators themselves is another means of real-time learning. Though participants certainly should not be selected for programs based on demographic characteristics, religious beliefs, or ethnic background, once they are selected according to performance indicators (for example, demonstrated competencies and leadership potential), programs can use the natural variation and diversity among participants to explore diversity issues and teach awareness. In this way, developing leaders can come into contact with diversity issues firsthand—learning directly from the experiences of their peers and feeling the challenges of diversity themselves.

Community-building competencies are more difficult to develop. Realistically, future leaders may need to spend time with individuals in their company who are already skilled in building a community spirit. From watching and participating, they may be able to pick up the abilities and attitudes necessary to build their own workplace communities. As well, selecting and encouraging those who are already talented in these competencies is another option.

Action learning experiences, simulations, and extensive case study experiences can be effective in teaching leaders how to build integrated architectures within their organizations. The aim is to develop future leaders who can think with great breadth across one's work unit or organization to see how the various systems and functions are interlocked. In addition, this competence relies on individuals breaking free of historical company paradigms concerning the rationale behind existing reward, performance measurement, and reporting relationship systems. They must be able to see that these systems are not "givens" but rather may have to change in order to drive new directions within their organizations.

Finally, teaching leaders how to develop leaders below them is clearly a competence that has been largely overlooked. We can begin by teaching our leaders how to be effective coaches and teachers. In some ways, programs like those at PepsiCo, where practicing leaders teach future leaders, are models of what may be possible. But remember the amount of legwork that PepsiCo designer Paul Russell put into getting his executive-instructors up to speed in order to make such programs successful. Leaders who teach must have opportunities to reflect on and then synthesize their guiding philosophies and experiences into teachable materials that are compelling to company managers. In many cases, they must learn the essentials of how to teach.

Leveraging What We Know About Adult Learning to Develop Future Leaders

Robert House, a Wharton Business School professor who has studied leadership for more than twenty-five years, recently noted how rare it is for well-established research findings to make their way into the practitioner's tool kit: "Despite some three thousand empirical studies of leadership conducted by academic researchers, this literature has gone largely unnoticed or ignored by policy makers, the press, and practicing managers. In 1988 and again in 1993 *Time* magazine published cover articles addressing the need for leadership in the U.S. political system. Not a single reference was made to any academic studies conducted by leadership scholars" (House, 1995, p. 413).

This same disconnect is also found in the application of adult learning principles to the field of leadership development. Action learning programs represent perhaps one of the few training designs that utilize learning principles to develop complex leadership skills. As we noted in Chapter Eight, however, most action learning programs continue to be implemented with little understanding of the design elements that are needed to ensure learning actually takes place. Leadership programs of the future will have to do a better job of leveraging adult learning principles if they hope to accelerate and enhance strategic thinking and other critical and complex capabilities.

For example, we know from the adult learning literature that novelty plays an important role in developing deeper, more complex conceptual skills (Cleaves, 1987; Ericsson and Smith, 1991). Principles and concepts illustrated through diverse experiences and across diverse contexts allow learners to form a deeper, more tacit understanding of complex relations. Novelty is an especially effective learning tool to the extent that learners are conscious of the novelty and recognize it as relevant and meaningful to the learning process and what they are trying to accomplish. Adult learning theory also tells us that conceptual development requires drawing creative connections among various events (Clark, 1992). For example, strategic thinking capabilities require that individuals be able to link seemingly unrelated but actually similar events to new problems. This requires that learners form an understanding of how numerous variables relate to and interact with one another in a variety of situations. Developing such an understanding entails observing hundreds, perhaps thousands, of different factors in many novel combinations. Thus, in learning how to enter new markets, leaders might—over years of experience—observe how different types of customers respond to different product characteristics. They might observe how the timing of product introductions influences purchasing behavior. And they might observe how certain regulatory issues affect costs. Each new experience provides new insight that progressively builds into a deeper, more intuitive understanding of the dynamics of market entry.

Though adult learning theory may tell us how to facilitate learning—for example, by providing meaningful and novel experience—the challenge becomes one of translating abstract learning principles into a meaningful leadership development experience that accelerates the learning process in a relatively short time. Accumulating and synthesizing novel events may enhance a leader's ability to think strategically, but traditional development programs (such as formal training) are limited in the novelty they can provide. More progressive approaches such as action learning also tend to be somewhat limited because they typically involve participants in a one-time event and thus provide little variety. And succession planning and job rotation can take years to provide the range of experiences necessary to develop conceptual understanding. In short, the majority of approaches used today fail to provide the range of necessary experiences or else require years to do so.

To conquer this seemingly insurmountable challenge, educational programs of the future will have to do three things differently. First, they will have to define and bound each training experience more definitively. If the company views better customer service as a key strategic issue, then the firm's leadership development programs should focus to some extent on developing their leaders' understanding of how they can improve service quality for their customers. Only by carefully focusing and bounding the content provided by each program will leadership development efforts have the time and variety of related experiences needed to build conceptual understanding.

Second, leadership development programs will have to rely on new technologies to enhance the learning process. In particular, computer-assisted technologies are likely to play an increasingly important role in developing complex skills. Fortunately, a variety of information technologies are now available to support this complicated endeavor. Such technologies include exploratory microworlds, management "flight simulators," collaborative work environments, and other computer-based simulations of business processes (Senge, 1994). With advances in computing power, these technologies are now better equipped to handle high volumes of data and are more capable of simulating complex processes. No longer do they simply deliver information; they also build strategic thinking skills. They have also become more affordable (Lewis, 1997).

Computer simulations like the "Sim" games developed by the Maxis Corporation and its spin-off Thinking Tools hold particular promise for accelerating the development of certain leadership skills. These sophisticated applications take complex technological, political, ecological, and industrial systems and interactively simulate their operations on a desktop computer. These simulations can provide a safe, inexpensive way for leaders to experiment with various strategies and thereby learn about different approaches to business problems. For example, Telesim—a telecommunications market simulation developed for NYNEX and Pacific Telesis—presents developing leaders with the simulated challenge of restructuring a telecommunications company to meet a rapidly changing marketplace (Perkins, 1994). In Telesim, leaders must deal with challenges in three environments: the internal company, the physical landscape, and the larger market, or "marketscape." In the internal environment, leaders get experience grappling with office politics, interpersonal communication, and people management. In the physical environment, leaders figure out how to utilize representations of the company's sales and service regions illustrated through graphic depictions of their urban, suburban, and rural wire and fiber optic networks. Finally, and perhaps most important, leaders must learn to analyze and react to the hypothetical firm's marketscape. In this environment, leaders encounter a variety of market challenges that require them to formulate strategies for developing new technologies, capturing markets, and orchestrating strategic alliances. They are also placed in situations that require them to make decisions about possible mergers or spin-offs.

Using another Thinking Tools product, SimRefinery, Chevron has also leveraged sophisticated simulations to develop the strategic skills of its leaders. In SimRefinery, managers experiment with various grades of oil and other petroleum products using different pricing models and production processes. Developing managers must make trade-offs in both the production and revenue of their products. The overall objective of the simulation is to achieve not only smooth refinery operations, but also optimal profitability (Perkins, 1994). As with Telesim, SimRefinery allows up-and-coming leaders to experiment with a variety of strategic approaches to a wide range of problems. Moreover, it allows them to try out different strategic options in a safe environment and in a relatively short time. By playing with the simulation, leaders can see the long-term results of moves such as changing prices, adding workers, borrowing money, and switching production processes. Some simulations can also allow managers to experiment with various marketing strategies, such as segmentation strategies or promotional schemes. Computer-based simulations can enhance learning because leaders work on highly relevant issues, experiment with a range of strategic options, and get direct and immediate feedback on results. Unlike in the real world, where managers may wait years to see the outcomes of their strategic decisions, simulations allow leaders to see the long-term impact of their efforts quickly.

Simulations can also help leaders develop better communication and negotiation skills, thereby improving collaboration across an entire firm. For example, Sound Disk-tributors, a videotape distribution company, has used a management simulation tool to improve the cross-functional systems thinking of its managers. Prior to adopting the simulation, managers had little understanding of how actions in one part of the organization affected operations in other parts. Sales managers would often fail to tell the purchasing department about plans for special customer promotions, subsequently causing sudden runs on inventory and excessive back orders. By experimenting with the simulation, however, managers were able to observe the systemwide impact of their individual decisions. The simulation process helped managers learn who they needed to communicate with and gave them a bigger picture of the business as a whole and an appreciation for the architecture of their organization (Henricks, 1998).

Of course, simulations also have certain drawbacks and limitations. Any simulation is a model or approximation of an actual system, and thus is only as good as the assumptions on which it is based. Moreover, most programs do not allow learners to look beneath the surface of the simulation to understand how and why the system performs as it does. Such a "black-box" approach prevents learners from directly inspecting the simulation, and thus limits their understanding of the actual system being represented (Lewis, 1997). More sophisticated microworld approaches enhance the learning process by giving learners greater opportunity to critique and adjust the simulation's parameters. This more transparent approach improves learning by providing the opportunity not only to try out different scenarios but to critique the simulation itself and engage in hypothesis testing. Learners change and experiment with the underlying simulation and then observe results, once again speeding the development of complex conceptual skills. Both microworlds and simulations can be particularly powerful learning devices, especially when they incorporate actual data from an organization's real business processes (Lewis, 1997).

Finally, as the business world becomes more socially and technologically complex, truly successful firms will leverage the capabilities of strategic partners to access the full range of expertise needed to keep their leaders on the cutting edge. Recognizing that leadership development will continue to be critical but not central to their primary mission, organizations will look to their suppliers and partners for more than tangible resources, one-time solutions, and limited services. They will search for collaborators who can help them build more sustainable capabilities. Partners who can help a firm's leadership develop greater insight into an industry or market, a better understanding of how to think and act strategically, or specific skills, models, and approaches to improving organizational performance will become particularly valuable.

We are already beginning to see firms that creatively structure their strategic relations not only to improve business results but to enhance and accelerate their leadership development opportunities. A whole range of possibilities exists. In some cases, firms may simply form a long-term relationship with a trusted facilitator or group of facilitators. As described in Chapter Six, facilitators can help leaders develop important teaming and process skills and can help in structuring group decision efforts. In other cases—especially for small firms and those dependent on a few large clients—firms may participate in training that is offered and encouraged by their primary customer. Such training typically focuses on quality improvement methods, communication techniques, teaming, and other practices that can improve firms' ability to work together. For example, Ford and Motorola encourage managers from many of their supplier organizations to take courses alongside their own managers. Junior leaders participating in these courses develop a broader understanding of the extended enterprise, a deeper appreciation of particular analytic techniques and methodologies, and a greater sensitivity to the needs and demands of their customers.

Organizations have also begun to leverage their relations with management consulting firms as a way of developing their leadership talent. For many years, management consultants simply sailed into and out of their client firms using a "strike-force" approach. Hired by the CEO or other senior executive, they would draw on their industry expertise, apply their strategic analysis capabilities, and use their number-crunching skills to solve difficult, often politically nettlesome problems. They might interact with managers in scoping a problem, collecting data, or recommending solutions, but in most cases they performed their analyses and crafted their strategies separate from the client's staff. The consultant's role was that of objective outsider or external expert, not tutor or guide. As such, consultants typically figured out an organization's problems, recommended some well-reasoned solutions, then left. Not surprisingly, their solutions were often poorly implemented—if they were implemented at all—because the strike force approach failed to engage the management structure sufficiently to build the understanding and buy-in required to effect significant change.

Some firms continue to rely on the strike force approach; however, client organizations are increasingly looking for more sustainable solutions from their consulting partners. As a result, the more astute management consulting firms have begun to act as facilitators, coaches, and teachers in addition to their traditional role as expert analyst. Working with teams of client-managers, conducting offsite strategy reviews, and sharing models and methodologies will become an increasingly important part of the management consultant's role. Working with client teams, consultants can enhance the learning process by pushing developing managers to think and act more analytically. They can help leaders develop important analytic skills by providing them with new analytic frameworks to use in structuring problems. They can also draw on their experience with other firms to help leaders identify invalid assumptions and consider alternative strategies that have been used successfully to solve problems in other contexts. Most important, they can do all of these things while focusing on the organization's most pressing business needs and working toward immediate solutions. Unlike university programs or those offered by other outside providers, management consultants can potentially provide development experiences that simultaneously improve the organization's bottom line.

Of course, simply hiring a group of consultants and pairing them with developing managers does not in any way guarantee that learning will occur. In fact, as we observed in several of our action learning programs, consultants can often be extremely poor teachers. To the extent they see their role as providing solutions rather than building capabilities, consultants may be unwilling or unable to instill within their clients an understanding of their strategies and tactics. Moreover, effective learning may require a different forum than that provided in a typical consulting engagement. Learning requires time for reflection. It also may require concerted interaction and support across multiple levels of management and across different parts of the organization. A typical consulting engagement tends to be rapidly paced and to involve only a small number of managers. Sometimes these managers may come from a single function or division and may be removed from their immediate jobs and responsibilities. As we noted in several previous chapters, the trans-

fer of new learning is often seriously limited when the learner ultimately returns to a job where others have not been exposed to the
same concepts.

Recognizing that organizations are increasingly looking to
develop their leadership capabilities while simultaneously addressing immediate business needs, some consulting firms have begun to
experiment with new approaches to delivering value to their clients.
Booz·Allen & Hamilton, for example, has developed a Strategic
Leadership Center designed specifically to build the leadership capabilities its clients often need to carry out large-scale change. The
center rests on the premise that an organization requires superior
leadership at all levels to achieve significant change and reach its
full potential. To improve an organization's leadership capacity, the
center brings top management leadership teams together with skilled
experts and facilitators to work on leadership issues specific to their
organization and its challenges. Consistent with a consulting model,
there is a heavy emphasis placed on diagnosis, action, and results.
However, the center also draws on academic research and experts to
design programs that are truly developmental, ensuring that executives are engaged, challenged, and learning from their experiences.
The center represents an important blend and evolutionary step
beyond traditional consulting, which focuses on problem solving and
process improvement separate from leadership development, and
business schools and leadership institutes, which focus on building
individual skills and knowledge separate from practical application
and an organizational context. In the future, we expect that more
firms will begin to offer services consistent with this hybrid model,
as organizations continue to leverage the capabilities of their strategic partners in pursuit of developmental opportunities.

Concluding Thoughts

If we think about leadership as a form of expertise, we can begin to
appreciate the long gestation period required for it to truly flower
in any one individual. Readers will remember the ten-year rule of

thumb we described earlier as the threshold time for individuals in many fields to attain the status of expert. This, however, can only be achieved through extensive experience and training during those ten years. Now consider how organizations currently approach the problem of leadership development: with a one-week training program, 360-degree feedback surveys, and opportunistic job placements. As readers may now appreciate, what we need is a radical change in our perspective of what it takes to truly create new generations of leaders. It clearly takes enormous persistence and commitment. It is by no means an easy task. It requires a fundamental understanding that leadership development is a neverending process, and that it must involve all levels of an organization. When we wrote *Learning to Lead* (Conger, 1992), one of our interviewees, Peter Thigpen, then senior vice president of operations at Levi Strauss, captured the challenge: "One gets a great sense of the starts and stops of these processes, of their difficulty, of their magnitude, of the down days, of the persistence required. In a way, I think the biggest risk we face is that we will lose patience" (pp. 213–214). His words still ring true. The danger we see is that executives and managers will continue to believe that a single program or initiative is all that it takes to begin the leadership development process. In reality, an organization needs the mind-set of the military, where leadership development becomes an integral part of a manager's daily life and essential to the organization's future success. As a result, it is seen as a long-term investment requiring continual training, guidance, mentoring, rewarding, and the provision of a continuous stream of developmental opportunities over one's career. Simultaneously, organizations must be attuned to the fact that their leadership needs are changing in response to a shifting world. They must be prepared to reinvent the very content and focus of what they are developing on a regular basis.

We believe that the leadership development field is today at a critical juncture. We have learned a great deal over the last decade about designing more sophisticated interventions to educate our future leaders. Yet in other ways, we have simply progressed from the Bronze Age of leadership development to the Iron Age. We have advanced, but we have yet to truly enter the Information Age. Our designs and initiatives still have a long ways to go to reliably produce leaders who can cope with and, more importantly, shape the future. The risk is that tough times or competing demands will lead companies to believe that other needs are more important and that leadership development should be tabled until difficulties subside. The worst case would be that organizations return to older notions that the cream will naturally rise to the top (so who needs education and career planning). The challenge facing the corporate world, then, is to see our current efforts as still in the entrepreneurial phase of the product life cycle of leadership development, not as in its mature phase. We must continue to experiment and innovate in our development approaches and to confidently and steadily invest in one of the few forces—leadership—that can guarantee a bright future no matter how difficult the challenges ahead.

References

American Management Association. *Blueprints for Service Quality: The Federal Express Approach*. (2nd ed.). New York: American Management Association, 1994.

American Society for Training and Development. "Leadership Development 1994 Survey Results." In *National HRD Executive Survey*. Alexandria, Va.: American Society for Training and Development, 1994.

Army Leadership. FM 22–100 Initial Draft, Apr. 1997, p. iii.

Baldwin, T. T., and Ford, J. K. "Transfer of Training: A Review and Directions for Future Research." *Personnel Psychology*, 1988, *41*, 63–101.

Bandura, A. "Self-Efficacy: Toward a Unifying Theory of Behavioral Change." *Psychological Review*, 1977, 84(2), 191–215.

Bartlett, C. A., and Ghoshal, S. "Rebuilding Behavioral Context: Turn Process Reengineering into People Rejuvenation." *Sloan Management Review*, Fall 1995, pp. 11–23.

Bass, B. M. *Leadership and Performance Beyond Expectations*. New York: Free Press, 1985.

Bennis, W. G., and Nanus, B. *Leaders: The Strategies for Taking Charge*. New York: HarperCollins, 1985.

Boehm, V. R. "Using Assessment Centers for Management Development—Five Applications." *Journal of Management Development*, 1985, 4(4), 40–51.

Bongiorno, L. "Corporate America's New Lesson Plan." *Business Week*, Oct. 25, 1993, p. R4.

Boyatzis, R. *The Competent Manager*. New York: Wiley, 1982.

Boyatzis, R. "Beyond Competence: The Choice to be a Leader." Paper presented at the Academy of Management Meetings, San Francisco, 1990.

Briggs, G. E., and Naylor, J. C. "The Relative Efficiency of Several Training Methods as a Function of Transfer Task Complexity." *Journal of Experimental Psychology*, 1962, *64*, 505–512.

Brown, J. S., and Duguid, P. "Organizational Learning and Communities-of-Practice: Toward a Unified View of Working, Learning, and Innovation." *Organizational Science*, 1991, *2*(1), 40–57.

Burke, M. J., and Day, R. R. "A Cumulative Study of the Effectiveness of Managerial Training." *Journal of Applied Psychology*, 1986, *71*(2), 232–245.

Burnside, R. M., and Guthrie, V. A. *Training for Action: A New Approach to Executive Development*. Greensboro, N.C.: Center for Creative Leadership, 1992.

The Carnegie Foundation for the Advancement of Teaching. *The Learning Industry: Education for Adult Workers*. Princeton, N.J.: University Press, 1990.

Clark, R. "How the Cognitive Sciences are Shaping the Profession." In H. D. Stolovitch and E. J. Keeps (eds.), *Handbook of Human Performance Technology*: San Francisco: Jossey-Bass, 1992, pp. 688–700.

Cleaves, D. A. "Cognitive Biases and Corrective Techniques: Proposals for Improving Elicitation Procedures for Knowledge-Based Systems." *International Journal of Man-Machine Studies*, 1987, *27*(2), 155–166.

Conger, J. A. *The Charismatic Leader*. San Francisco: Jossey-Bass, 1989.

Conger, J. A. *Learning to Lead*. San Francisco: Jossey-Bass, 1992.

Conger, J. A. "The Brave New World of Leadership Training." *Organizational Dynamics*, 1993, *21*(3), 46–58.

Conger, J. A. "Personal Growth Training: Snake-Oil or Pathway to Leadership." *Organizational Dynamics*, 1993, *3*(3), 19–30.

Conger, J. A. *Winning 'Em Over: A New Model for Management in the Age of Persuasion*. New York: Simon & Schuster, 1998.

Conger, J. A., and Xin, K. "Adult Learning Theory: Its Implications for Executive Education." Lexington, Mass.: International Consortium for Executive Development Research, 1996.

Conger, J. A., and Xin, K. "Executive Education: Survey of International Trends." Lexington, Mass.: International Consortium for Executive Development Research, 1997.

Dalton, M. A., and Hollenbeck, G. P. "How to Design an Effective System for Developing Managers and Executives." Greensboro, N.C.: Center for Creative Leadership, 1996.

Davis, H. L., and Hogarth, R. M. "Rethinking Management Education: A View from Chicago." In *Selected Papers from the Graduate School of Business at the University of Chicago*, 1992.

Dewar, J. A., Builder, C. H., Hix, W. M., and Levin, M. H. *Assumption Based Planning: A Tool for Very Uncertain Times*. RAND MR-114-A. Santa Monica, Calif.: RAND, 1993.

Dotlich, D. L., and Noel, J. L. *Action Learning*. San Francisco: Jossey-Bass, 1998.

Downham, T. A., Noel, J. L., and Prendergast, A. E. "Executive Development." *Human Resource Management*, 1992, *31*(1–2), 95–107.

Edelstein, B. C., and Armstrong, D. J. "A Model for Executive Development." *Human Resource Planning*, 1993, *16*(4), 51–64.

Ellis, J., and Williams, D. R. *Philips NV: Operation Centurion, Creating and Sustaining Fundamental Change*. Wellesley, Mass.: European Case Clearing House, Babson College, 1996.

Ericsson, K. A., and Charness, N. "Expert Performance." *American Psychologist*, 1994, *49*(8), 725–747.

Ericsson, K. A., Krampe, R. T., and Tesch-Romer, C. "The Role of Deliberate Practices in the Acquisition of Expert Performance." *Psychological Review*, 1993, *100*(3), 363–406.

Ericsson, K. A., and Smith, J. *Towards a General Theory of Expertise*. Cambridge: Cambridge University Press, 1991.

Facteau, J. D., and others. "The Influence of General Perceptions of the Training Environment on Pretraining Motivation and Perceived Training Transfer." *Journal of Management*, 1995, *21*(1), 1–25.

Fiedler, F. "Research on Leadership Selection and Training: One View of the Future." *Administrative Science Quarterly*, 1996, *41*, 243.

Freedman, N. "Transformation in Major Companies: The Philips Experience." *Long Range Planning Journal*, Autumn 1996.

Fulmer, R. M., and Vicere, A. A. *Executive Education and Leadership Development: The State of the Practice*. University Park, Pa.: Penn State Institute for the Study of Organizational Effectiveness, 1995.

Goldstein, I. L. *Training in Organizations: Needs Assessment, Development, and Evaluation*. Belmont, Calif.: Brooks/Cole, 1986.

Grove, A. S. *Only the Paranoid Survive*. New York: Currency-Doubleday, 1996.

Hall, D. T., and Otazo, K. L. "Executive Coaching Study: A Progress Report." Boston: Human Resource Policy Institute, Boston University School of Management, 1995.

Henricks, M. "Dress Rehearsal." *Entrepreneur Magazine*, Apr. 1998.

Hollenbeck, G. P., and McCall, M. W. "Leadership Development: Contemporary Practice." In A. I. Kraut and A. K. Korman (eds.), *Evolving Practices for Human Resources Management: Responses to a Changing World of Work*. San Francisco: Jossey-Bass, 1999.

House, R. J. "Leadership in the Twenty-First Century: A Speculative Inquiry." In Ann Howard (ed.), *The Changing Nature of Work*. San Francisco: Jossey-Bass, 1995.

Huczynski, A. A., and Lewis, J. W. "An Empirical Study into the Learning Transfer Process in Management Training." *Journal of Management Studies*, 1980, pp. 227–240.

Kanter, R. M., Stein, B. A., and Jick, T. D. *The Challenge of Organizational Change*. New York: Free Press, 1992.

Kaye, B., and Jacobson, B. "Reframing Mentoring." *Training & Development*, Aug. 1996, pp. 44–47.

Kilburg, R. R. "Toward a Conceptual Understanding and Definition of Executive Coaching." *Consulting Psychology Journal*, 1996, 48(2), 134–144.

Kotter, J. P. *A Force for Change*. New York: Free Press, 1990.

Kotter, J. P. *Leading Change*. Boston: Harvard Business School Press, 1996.

Kouzes, J. M., and Posner, B. Z. *The Leadership Challenge*. San Francisco: Jossey-Bass, 1987.

Lane, M., Blakely, S., Gerald, L., and Martinec, C. "Management Development Training in the 1990s: Present Trends and Future Directions." *Executive Development*, 1992, 5(2), 17–19.

Lewis, M. "Technologies for Training: Insights for NCO Leadership Development." In *Future Leader Development of Army Noncommissioned Officers: Workshop Results*, RAND CF-138–A, Santa Monica, Calif., 1997.

Loevinger, J. *Ego Development*. San Francisco: Jossey-Bass, 1980.

MacDonald, S. "Learning to Change." *Organization Science*, 1995, 6(5), 557–568.

Maltby, L. "The Projected Economic Impact of the Model Employment Termination Act." *Annals of the American Academy of Political and Social Science*, Nov. 1994, pp. 103–118.

McCall Jr., M. *High Flyers*. Boston: Harvard Business Press, 1998.

McCall Jr., M., Lombardo, M., and Morrison, A. *The Lessons of Experience: How Successful Executives Develop on the Job*. Lexington, Mass.: Lexington Books, 1988.

McCauley, C. D. *Developmental Experiences in Managerial Work: A Literature Review*. Technical Report no. 26. Greensboro, N.C.: Center for Creative Leadership, 1986.

McCauley, C. D., Moxley, R. S., and Van Velsor, E. *Handbook of Leadership Development*. San Francisco: Jossey-Bass, 1998.

Mohr, D. C. "Negative Outcome in Psychotherapy: A Critical Review." *Clinical Psychology: Science and Practice*, 1995, 2(1), 1–27.

Mumford, A. "How Managers Can Become Developers." *Personnel Management*, June 1993, pp. 42–45.

Mumford, A. "Authors and Authorities in Action Learning." *Management Bib-
    liographies & Reviews*, 1994, *20*(6/7), 2–69.

Naylor, J. C., and Briggs, G. E. "The Effect of Task Complexity and Task Orga-
    nization on the Relative Efficiency of Part and Whole Training Methods."
    Journal of Experimental Psychology, 1963, *65*, 217–224.

Noe, R. A. "Trainees' Attributes and Attitudes: Neglected Influences on Train-
    ing Effectiveness." *Academy of Management Review*, 1986, *11*(4), 736–749.

Noel, J. L., and Charan, R. "Leadership Development at GE's Crotonville."
    Human Resource Management, 1988, *27*(4), 433–447.

Noel, J. L., and Charan, R. "GE Brings Global Thinking to Light." *Training &
    Development*, July 1992, pp. 29–33.

O'Reilly, C., and Pfeffer, J. *Southwest Airlines*. Palo Alto, Calif.: Stanford Uni-
    versity Graduate School of Business, 1995.

Pascale, R. T. "The Paradox of Corporate Culture: Reconciling Ourselves to
    Socialization." *California Management Review*, 1985, *27*(2), 26–41.

Perkins, M. "The Information Highway." *Red Herring Magazine*, July 1994.

Ready, D. *Champions of Change*. Lexington, Mass.: International Consortium for
    Executive Development Research, 1994, pp. 26–28.

Revans, R. W. *Action Learning*. London: Blond & Briggs, 1980.

Saari, L. M., Johnson, T. R., McLaughlin, S. D., and Zimmerle, D. M. "A Survey
    of Management Training and Education Practices in U.S. Companies."
    Personnel Psychology, 1988, *41*, 731–743.

Schaffer, G. "Competency-Based Managerial and Leadership Development."
    Boston: Proceedings of the National Conference on Using Competency
    Tools & Applications to Drive Organizational Performance, Nov. 1994.

Schein, E. H. *Organizational Culture and Leadership*. San Francisco: Jossey-Bass, 1992.

Schmitt, N., Ford, J. K., and Stults, D. M. "Changes in Self-perceived Ability
    as a Function of Performance in an Assessment Center." *Journal of Occu-
    pational Psychology*, 1986, *59*, 327–335.

Senge and others. *The Fifth Discipline Fieldbook: Strategies and Tools for Building a
    Learning Organization*. New York: Doubleday, 1994.

Sims, H. P., and Manz, C. C. "Modeling Influences on Employee Behavior." *Per-
    sonnel Journal*, Jan. 1982, pp. 45–51.

Spreitzer, G. M., and Quinn, R. E. "Empowering Middle Managers to Be Trans-
    formational Leaders." *Journal of Applied Behavioral Science*, 1996, *32*(3),
    237–261.

Tichy, N. M., and Devanna, M. A. *The Transformational Leader*. New York:
    Wiley, 1986.

Tichy, N. M., and DeRose, C. "The Pepsi Challenge: Building a Leader-Driven
    Organization." *Training and Development*, May 1996, pp. 58–66.

Tichy, N. M., and Sherman, S. *Control Your Destiny or Someone Else Will.* New York: Doubleday Currency, 1993.

U.S. Department of the Army. *ODCSOPS Staff Guide: America's Army Leader Development Support System—Process, Procedures, and Products,* 1994.

U.S. Department of the Army. *Officer Ranks Personnel.* 14, Sept. 17, 1990.

U.S. Department of the Army. *Army Leadership.* FM 22–100, 1997.

U.S. Department of the Army. *Army Leadership.* FM 22–100 Initial Draft, Apr. 1997, p. iii.

U.S. Department of Defense. *Military Manpower Training Report FY 1997.* U.S. Department of Defense, June 1996.

U.S. Department of Labor. *Commission on the Future of Worker-Management Relations: Fact-Finding Report,* 1994.

VanLehn, K. "Cognitive Skills Acquisition." *Annual Review of Psychology,* 1996, *47,* 513–539.

VanMaanen, J., and Schein, E. "Toward a Theory of Organizational Socialization." *Research in Organizational Behavior,* 1979, *1,* 209–264.

Verlander, E. G. "Executive Education for Managing Complex Organizational Learning." *Human Resources Planning,* 1992, *15*(2), 1–18.

Vicere, A., and Fulmer, R. M. *Leadership by Design.* Boston: Harvard Business School, 1997.

Waldman, D. A., Atwater, L.E., and Antonioni, D. "Has 360 Degree Feedback Gone Amok?" *Academy of Management Executive,* 1998, *12*(2), 86–94.

Wallace, M. "Can Action Learning Live Up to Its Reputation?" *Management Education and Development,* 1990, *21*(2), 89–103.

Westley, F. "Vision Worlds: Strategic Visions as Social Interaction." *Advances in Strategic Management,* 1992, *8,* 271–305.

Wexley, K. N., and Thorton, C. L. "Effect of Verbal Feedback of Test Results upon Learning." *Journal of Educational Research,* 1972, *66,* 119–121.

Winkler, J. D., and others. *Future Leader Development of Army Noncommissioned Officers.* RAND CF–138–A, Santa Monica, Calif., 1998.

Woodruffe, C. *Assessment Centres: Identifying and Developing Competence.* London: Institute of Personnel Management, 1993a.

Woodruffe, C. "What is Meant by a Competency?" *Leadership & Organizational Development Journal,* 1993b, *14*(1), 29–36.

Young, D., and Dixon, N. *Helping Leaders Take Effective Action: A Program Evaluation.* Greensboro, N.C.: Center for Creative Leadership, 1996.

Yukl, G. *Leadership in Organizations.* (3rd ed.) Englewood Cliffs, N.J.: Prentice Hall, 1994.

Index